Understanding Grief

Understanding Grief is a comprehensive and accessible 'one stop' introduction to all the major models of grief. In addition to the individual perspective, bereavement is discussed in relation to social, cultural, and religious factors and influences. Richard Gross also examines the impact of different types of bereavement, such as the death of a child, parent, spouse/partner, and sibling, and discusses the impact of traumatic death in relation to complicated grief. The text also covers pet loss, death anxiety, and post-traumatic growth.

This innovative book combines personal accounts of grief with clinical accounts of patients provided by psychiatrists and psychologists, and research involving large numbers of bereaved individuals.

Understanding Grief will be invaluable to all those working with bereaved clients, including bereavement counsellors, counselling and clinical psychologists, healthcare professionals, social workers, and the interested layperson. It is also suitable for people training to work with bereaved individuals.

Richard Gross is a leading author of psychology texts. Since 2006 he has been working as a bereavement volunteer and trainer with Cruse Bereavement Care.

Understanding Grief

An introduction

Richard Gross

Routledge
Taylor & Francis Group

LONDON AND NEW YORK

First published 2016
by Routledge
2 Park Square, Milton Park, Abingdon, Oxon, OX14 4RN

And by Routledge
711 Third Avenue, New York, NY 10017

Routledge is an imprint of the Taylor & Francis Group, an informa business

British Library Cataloguing-in-Publication Data
A catalogue record for this book is available from the British Library

Library of Congress Cataloging-in-Publication Data
Gross, Richard (Psychologist)
    Understanding grief : an introduction / Richard Gross. — First Edition.
        pages cm
    Includes bibliographical references and index.
    1. Grief.   2. Bereavement—Psychological aspects.   3. Loss (Psychology)   I. Title.
    BF575.G7G775 2015
    155.9'3—dc23
    2015015407

ISBN: 978-1-138-83978-6 (hbk)
ISBN: 978-1-138-83979-3 (pbk)
ISBN: 978-1-315-72793-6 (ebk)

Typeset in Times
by Apex CoVantage, LLC

Contents

Preface

The idea for this book first appeared while I was running the Foundation Course ('ABC' Course) for Cruse Bereavement Care supporters. Not surprisingly, there is great emphasis on all aspects of grief, including major theories and models, both 'classical' and more recent. Both for trainees who might already be qualified Counsellors (or still in training), as well as those coming into the counselling world for the first time, these theories and models constitutes a substantial amount of material that needs to be assimilated in a short period of time and from a variety of sources.

While the Course provides an extensive list of books and articles to supplement the course materials, for most trainees this represents a luxury that their busy lives doesn't allow them to indulge in. It was against this background that the idea of a book that could offer a 'one-stop' journey into the academic study of grief came about: the result is *Understanding Grief: An Introduction*.

The title acknowledges that 'one-stop' does not imply 'the only resource you will (ever) need'; rather, the book is intended as an anchor, a synthesis of the major ideas relating to grief, ranging from personal accounts to major research studies. Perhaps 'first-stop' is more accurate than 'one-stop', a point of reference to help those working with bereaved individuals, as well as the general reader (including bereaved individuals). From this base, the interested reader should be equipped to engage in further reading: we all have to start somewhere! (I like the analogy of an introductory text as a *map* for finding your way round some unfamiliar territory!)

As well as major theories and models, *Understanding Grief: An Introduction* considers the nature of grief (how it is experienced), both from an individual and a socio-cultural perspective, the impact of kinship on grief (how our relationship to the deceased affects our response to his/her death), and the debate regarding how 'normal' (or uncomplicated) grief can be distinguished from complicated (or pathological) grief (including risk factors). The book also considers the wider implications of bereavement, including fear of our own death and how personal growth can emerge from what, for most people, is the most terrible event imaginable, namely, the death of a loved one.

Richard Gross
January 2015

Dedication

To Lily and Gerald, in loving memory

Acknowledgements

I'd like to thank Joanne Forshaw at Routledge for commissioning this text. Both she and Kirsten Buchanan have guided me through what has been quite a different publishing journey from what I've been used to for many years. Kirsten, especially, has made this relatively pain-free and I want to thank her for her support and assistance. I should probably also thank Russell George who put me in touch with Joanne in the first place.

Chapter 1

The nature and experience of grief

The chapter will address the following questions:

- What is meant by 'bereavement'?
- What is the relationship between 'bereavement' and 'loss'?
- Are there different kinds of loss?
- Are there different kinds of bereavement?
- Are there different kinds of grief?
- What is the difference between intuitive, instrumental, and blended grieving?
- What is meant by 'disenfranchised' grief?
- What is the relationship between 'grieving' and 'mourning'?
- Are there different meanings to the term 'mourning'?
- What is meant by 'grief work'?
- What is grief like?
- How has grief been studied?
- What are the most common stages or phases of grief?
- How valid is this account of grief?
- Is grief an inevitable response to natural and/or traumatic bereavement?

Bereavement, grief, and loss

There are many euphemisms for 'death' – words that serve to soften the impact and meaning of the awful reality that is death. One of the most common (at least in English-speaking countries) is 'loss' ('I'm sorry for your loss'; 'I lost my husband five years ago now').

'Loss' is also used much more broadly than just denoting death. Everyday life is full of losses, both trivial and substantial, tangible and intangible, literal and metaphorical. When you see your keys disappear down the drain in the road, this is a literal, tangible loss; losing a bet, this is more metaphorical and not quite so tangible. When for example, you lose the ability to speak (as a result of a stroke), you're being *deprived* of something that you've always taken for granted as a means of operating in the world. Related to that (*primary*) loss, there may be one or more *secondary* losses (such as independence, self-esteem, even livelihood). Often, the secondary losses may reflect the *meaning* that the primary loss has for the individual; for example, for a singer, loss of his/her voice is critical and likely to be devastating, while a footballer losing his/her voice would still be able to play the game (just more quietly!).

While 'grief' is commonly associated with death, it is also used in everyday communication in a much broader context (as when a parent pleads with his/her teenage son or daughter to 'stop giving me grief'). Also, it isn't just death of a loved one (i.e. *bereavement*) that causes grief: other major losses can produce essentially the same response (see below), as when a pet dies (e.g. Carmack and Packman, 2011: see Chapter 8).

The loss of keys illustrates what Doka and Martin (2010) call *physical* loss; bereavement involves both physical loss (the deceased person is no longer physically, literally, 'there') and *relational* loss, being deprived of the relationship with someone with whom one had an emotional tie (i.e. an *attachment*). Again, relational loss occurs when we get divorced, or separate from any partner (sexual or otherwise). If we think of bereavement as involving both a primary, physical loss, and (potentially multiple) secondary (including relational) losses, then it might be helpful to consider the impact of those secondary losses as what produces grief.

Put another way, to be able to understand (and, in turn, to support) someone's grief, the primary loss ('the deceased') needs to be 'broken down' into the secondary losses; these may include the physical contact with another body (and the attendant warmth, smells, and other bodily sensations), the sense of security that s/he provided, and social status (e.g. husband or wife). Secondary losses may include what Rando (1993) calls *symbolic* loss (such as loss of one's dreams, hopes, or faith).

So, grief is about much more than bereavement: it denotes a response to any significant loss, be it primary/secondary, tangible/intangible, physical/relational etc. In the rest of this book, the loss that we are mainly concerned with is bereavement and grief will be taken as a response to this particular form of loss.

Varieties of bereavement

Of course, 'bereavement' covers a wide range of (potential) losses-through-death. By far the most discussed – and researched – example is *spousal bereavement*, that is, death of a husband or wife. Much has also been written about death of parents and children (including adult children); death of a child can refer to pre-natal death (including miscarriage and termination/abortion), stillbirth, neonatal death, and death of an older baby, child, or teenager. Rather less attention has been given to death of siblings, grandchildren, and friends. (See Chapter 6.)

Varieties of grief

While grief is commonly regarded as a natural (i.e. evolved, universal) reaction to bereavement, involving both psychological and bodily experiences, individuals within a cultural group, as well as different cultural groups, describe these experiences differently; indeed, the experiences themselves may actually be different (see Chapter 5).

While it is commonly agreed that the *intensity* of grief, as well as the *form* that it can take, will vary between individuals, much more controversial is the distinction between 'normal' and *complicated grief* (CG). Part of the controversy reflects a much more general debate that has raged within psychiatry for much of its history, namely, whether psychological disorders represent a more intense/extreme form of 'normal' experiences and behaviour (the *dimensional approach*) or whether they represent a distinct 'syndrome' (the *categorical approach*). Since 2013, American psychiatrists have formally recognised complicated grief (CG) (in particular, *prolonged grief disorder/PGD*) as a distinct mental disorder (see Chapter 7).

Another important (and less controversial) distinction is that between grief that is recognised by others as 'legitimate' and 'reasonable' and that which is not (i.e. *disenfranchised* grief). Disenfranchised grief refers to a situation where a loss is not openly acknowledged, socially sanctioned, or publicly shared (Doka, 1989a, 2002). These include types of losses (e.g. divorce, prenatal deaths, pet loss), relationships (e.g. lovers, friends, ex-spouses), grievers (e.g. the very old, very young, people with learning disabilities), and circumstances of the death (e.g. AIDS, suicide).

Many individuals have to conceal their grief from others in order to conceal the relationship whose loss has triggered it; for example, individuals having a secret love affair, love between homosexual men or women, or love for someone 'from afar' (where the deceased may not even know s/he is loved or may not even know the person at all). In all these cases, the bereaved individual would be seen as 'having no right' to grieve as far as others ('society') is concerned.

Another distinction is that between *intuitive* and *instrumental grieving* (Doka and Martin, 2010). These represent two distinct *patterns* (or *styles*) of grief and differ according to (i) the cognitive and affective components of internal experience of loss, and (ii) the individual's outward expression of that experience. The differences between these two patterns/styles are summarised in Table 1.1.

In both cases, what the griever is experiencing can only be *inferred* from his/her behaviour – it can never be directly observed: in particular, the desire for social

Table 1.1 Major differences between intuitive and instrumental grieving patterns/styles (based on Doka and Martin, 2010)

Intuitive

1 Converts *more* energy into the *affective* domain and *less* into the *cognitive*.
2 Grief consists primarily of profoundly painful feelings (including shock and disbelief, overwhelming sorrow, and sense of loss of control).
3 Intuitive grievers tend to spontaneously express their painful feelings through crying and want to share their inner experiences with others.

Instrumental

1 Converts most energy into the *cognitive* domain.
2 Painful feelings are tempered; grief is more of an intellectual experience.
3 Instrumental grievers may channel energy into activity.

support, the need to discuss feelings, and the intensity and scope of activities are how grievers express their grief and, hence, reveal their intuitive or instrumental tendencies.

However, rather than any individual being an intuitive or instrumental griever, almost everyone uses *both* patterns; few people display a 'pure' or 'ideal' pattern. Most grievers are a *blend* of both patterns, although any one individual may display one to a greater degree than the other. According to Doka and Martin (2010) the overall responses of 'blended grievers' are more likely to correlate with the phases or stages of grief as identified, for example, by Parkes (e.g. 1986) and Bowlby (1980) (see below). Early on, for instance, the griever may need to suppress feelings in order to plan and arrange the funeral; later, s/he may give full vent to feelings, seeking help and support. Later still, cognitive-driven action may take precedence over affective expression when the griever has to return to work, resume parenting roles, and so on. In reality, there are *three* primary patterns: intuitive, instrumental, and blended. Finally, women are more likely to be intuitive grievers, and men, instrumental grievers. However, while gender *influences* grieving style, it does *not determine* it (Doka and Martin, 2010).

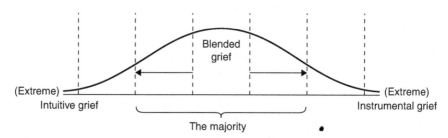

Figure 1.1 The normal curve of intuitive and instrumental grief (Based on Doka & Martin, 2010)

Box 1.1   Intuitive grief and bereavement support

At the core of bereavement support and counselling is the assumption that clients need to acknowledge and express their grief. While this may be facilitated in a variety of ways, the primary means of expression – and the major tool that supporters use to enable the client to express – is *language*. As Shakespeare put it:

> Give sorrow words; the grief, that does not speak,
> Whispers the o'er-fraught heart, and bids it break.
> (*Macbeth*, 4.3, lines 209–210)

Shakespeare could have been describing the intuitive griever, or, at least, had him/her in mind. Putting feelings and thoughts into words (or externalising them in some other way, as in art or music) is what intuitive grievers are likely to be better able to do: they confront their feelings in a direct way, rather than (re-) channelling them through other activities as instrumental grievers tend to do.

Again, intuitive grievers want and need to discuss their feelings: talking about his/her experience is 'tantamount to having the experience' (Doka and Martin, 2010, p. 60).

> This retelling the story and re-enacting the pain is a necessary part of grieving and an integral part of the intuitive pattern of grieving. It also represents the intuitive griever's going "with" the grief experience.
>
> (Doka and Martin, 2010, p. 60)

Grief, grief work, and mourning

The terms 'grief' (a noun) and 'mourning' (a noun, adjective, and verb) are often used interchangeably; 'grieving' is *grammatically* equivalent to 'mourning' (i.e. they can be used as a noun, adjective, or verb). But how are they related in terms of their *meaning*?

We defined 'grief' earlier as a universal reaction to bereavement, involving both psychological and bodily experiences; 'grief work' is often used to refer to the process by which the bereaved individual comes to terms with his/her bereavement. Doka and Martin (2010) define grief work as a process, both short- and long-term, of *adapting* to the bereavement. It includes the shorter-term process of *acute grief*, in which the griever deals with the immediate aftermath of the loss. According to Doka and Martin (2010):

> The energy of grief, generated by the tension between wishes to retain the past and the reality of the present, is felt at many levels – physical, emotional, cognitive, and spiritual – and expressed in a wide range of observable behaviours
>
> (p. 25)

All these grief responses represent initial, fragmentary attempts to adapt to the immediate aftermath of loss. (These responses are described in more detail below.)

While acute grief can last for many months or longer (for a discussion of complicated grief, see Chapter 7), there is a longer-term process that involves living the rest of one's life without the deceased. Derived from Freud's (1917) *Mourning and Melancholia*, this longer-term process is commonly referred to as 'mourning'; this describes the bereaved person's attempts to redefine their relationship to the deceased, their sense of self, and the external world. 'Successful' mourning, according to Freud, involves the severing of the emotional tie to the deceased and investing emotional energy in new relationships. The means by which this is achieved is commonly referred to as 'grief work' (rather than 'mourning work') and is central to a number of well-known and influential theories/models of grief, including stage or phase models (see below and Chapter 3).

However, 'mourning' is also used in a very different sense, namely to denote 'the culturally patterned expressions or rituals that accompany loss and allow others to recognise that one has become bereaved' (Doka, 1989b, p. 127) (see Chapter 4); examples include funerals, wearing black clothes or armbands, and covering mirrors in Jewish homes (see Chapter 5). As Doka and Martin (2010) observe, distinguishing mourning in this social sense from grief helps to illustrate what we described earlier as disenfranchised grief: the (private) grief of, say, the mistress of a man who has died, will not be displayed publicly or socially by attending the funeral as a 'chief mourner'. Conversely, many who do attend as funeral may not be grieving; they may be there to support others who are grieving, out of respect (rather than love) for the deceased, or they may even be there to *be seen to be grieving*. Julian Barnes, in his account of grief for his wife (*Levels of Life*, 2013), uses the term 'doing grief' at funerals, an empty, insincere pretence at (true) grief. To some degree, culture (including religion) dictates how one *should* behave at funerals, so that it is sometimes difficult to infer what degree of grief the mourners are (privately) experiencing (see Chapter 5).

What is grief like?

Studies of grief

There are four main sources of information about the nature of grief:

- Personal accounts by bereaved individuals; these are commonly well-known authors (such as C.S. Lewis, Dannie Abse, and Julian Barnes) but also include first-time authors, driven to describing their grief in print both as a way of dealing with their pain and as a form of dedication to their loved one. A recent example of the latter is Anne-Marie Cockburn's *5,742Days* (2013), the title denoting the duration of her 15-year-old daughter's life. These accounts tell us what grief is like in the sense of how it is *experienced* by grievers, be they husbands, mothers, (adult) children, and so on; arguably, these first-hand accounts capture the true nature of grief more accurately than the other methods described below.
- The reference to Freud's *Mourning and Melancholia* (1917/1953) above represents a more detached, less personal account, but one which reflects a

particular theoretical bias, namely *psychoanalytic theory* (sometimes 'psy-choanalysis'). While important in his own right, it's Freud's influence on later theorists (and researchers – see below), including Bowlby, Parkes, Worden, and Kübler-Ross, that makes him such a key figure in the clinical study of grief. Interestingly, one of Freud's most famous – and influential – case studies involved loss: Bertha Pappenheim (known as Anna O.), who was actually treated by Freud's then colleague, Joseph Breuer, displayed symptoms of 'hysterical neurosis' in response to the progressive illness and death of her father (Breuer and Freud, 1895/1955).

•   Most of our understanding of grief comes from research studies with large numbers of bereaved people (as opposed to individuals). These empirical studies are often conducted by psychiatrists, such as Parkes, in order to understand the circumstances under which bereavement can lead to psychiatric disorders and to set up programmes of prevention or treatment (see Box 1.2). Two of the studies described in Box 1.2 were also aimed at determining what is meant by 'normal' or 'typical' grief (see Chapter 7).

Box 1.2   Major studies of bereavement conducted by Parkes and colleagues

Bethlem Study (Parkes, 1965 a and b): This investigated reactions among people seeking psychiatric help following bereavement. Interviews were conducted with 21 bereaved patients (4 male, 17 female) at the Bethlem Royal and Maudsley Hospitals (in London) on average 72 weeks following bereavement (range 4–367 weeks).

The London Study (Parkes, 1970, 1972): This was an attempt to find out how an unselected group of widows under 65 would cope within the first year of bereavement. They were interviewed at the end of the 1st, 3rd, 6th, 9th, and 13th months (allowing for the 'anniversary reaction').

In both studies, bereaved people were asked to describe, in their own words, their bereavement and how they'd reacted to it. Some notes were taken during the interviews and assessments made immediately afterwards.

Harvard Study (The Harvard Bereavement Project) (Glick et al., 1974; Parkes & Weiss, 1983): This involved 68 unselected widows and widowers (aged 45 and below) at Harvard Medical School in Boston. They were interviewed 14 months after bereavement and compared with a control (i.e. *comparison*) group of 68 married men and women of the same age, gender, social class background, and family size.

(Continued)

Box 1.2 Continued

Love and Loss Study (Parkes, 2006): The Retrospective Attachment Questionnaire (RAQ) was administered to 278 psychiatric outpatients at the Royal London Hospital. It was aimed at testing the hypothesis that love and loss are intertwined, that childhood attachment patterns, separations from parents and relationships in later life all influence how we cope with stress and loss and predict the kinds of problem which cause people to seek help following bereavement in adult life (see Chapter 2). Parkes hoped to explain any patterns that were found, to understand the chains of causation, and to clarify the reasons why some people come through the pain of bereavement and emerge stronger and wiser than before, while others suffer lasting damage to their physical and/or mental health. A control group of 78 young women who had not sought any psychiatric help was used, 35 of whom had suffered bereavement in the previous five years. The RAQ comprises five sections: (i) *parenting* (the person's view of their parents, including adoptive/foster parents); (ii) *childhood vulnerability* (their view of themselves as children); (iii) *events and circumstances of adult life* (including adult relationships and bereavements); (iv) *coping* (with stress); and (v) *current symptoms and emotions* (at the time the form was completed).

Other influential empirical studies

Coconut Grove fire study (Lindemann, 1944)

This was the earliest well-known empirical study of grief, involving 101 people, comprising (i) psychoneurotic patients who'd lost a relative during the course of their treatment; (ii) relatives of patients who had died; (iii) relatives of people killed in World War II; (iv) bereaved victims and close relatives of the nearly 500 people killed at a Boston nightclub (the Coconut Grove), following a Harvard-Yale football match in 1942.

Lindemann interviewed each patient, allowing feelings to emerge freely. The interviews were recorded and analysed in terms of 'symptoms' as well as changes in mental state during the course of the interview. While this pioneering study had a strong influence on later grief research, it has been criticised on methodological grounds. One criticism is that Lindemann relied heavily on the reports of the Coconut Grove sub-sample, which consisted of only 13 people. Also, the psychiatric in-patients were hardly comparable to bereaved people living in the community (Archer, 1999).

Marris (1958)

This was the first study of bereavement among *community samples*. Marris, a British psychologist, interviewed 72 young or middle-aged women whose husbands had died during the previous two years. This was a more representative sample than Lindemann's and was more concerned with the social context of widowhood.

Hobson (1964)

In another British study, Hobson interviewed 40 widows (aged 25–28) from a small Midlands town; they'd all been bereaved over six months previously. Like Marris, Hobson interviewed the widows only once (Archer, 1999).

Gorer (1965)

Like Lindemann, Gorer was interested in the clinical manifestations of grief, especially when it was incomplete or arrested (see Chapter 7). He identified two types of what would now be described as complicated grief, namely *mummification* (where the bereaved kept everything as it was before the death) and *despair* (emotional flatness and social isolation).

Yale Bereavement Study (Prigerson et al., 1995a, 1995b)

This looked at the psychiatric complications of bereavement using the Index of Complicated Grief (ICG). This widely used instrument has been replaced by the simpler, but equally reliable and valid, Prolonged Grief index (PG-13)

The studies described above are among the most commonly cited studies of grief and will be referred to at various points throughout the book. There are many others besides these (see Archer, 1999; Parkes and Prigerson, 2010).

- The fourth major source of our understanding regarding the nature of grief are *anthropological* or *ethnographic studies*. These are concerned with identifying patterns of grief across different cultures and so are essential for testing the claim that grief is a universal reaction to bereavement (see above). As Archer (1999) points out, ethnographic sources, while extremely informative, have traditionally focused on rituals and beliefs surrounding death – rather than the psychological aspects of grief. In particular, rituals and beliefs regarding the afterlife (for which life is a preparation) distinguish traditional cultures from (modern) Western cultures. A commonly-made distinction is drawn between *individualistic* and *collectivist* societies/cultures (Triandis, 1995), corresponding to Western, capitalist, and non-Western, traditional societies, respectively. (These are discussed in detail in Chapter 5.)

However, Bowlby (1980) describes some relevant studies in relation to 'normal' grieving, and, in relation to *complicated grief*, studies have been conducted which make direct comparisons between Western and non-Western cultures possible (Rosenblatt, 2013a: see Chapters 5 and 7).

Stage or phase accounts of grief

- It's probably true to say that part of the 'common sense' understanding of grief is the belief that the bereaved progress through a fixed series of stages. These beliefs regarding the natural 'course' of grief reflects the theoretical accounts proposed by psychiatrists and others working in the area of death and dying, which have found their way into popular cultural understanding.

    While different accounts vary in the details of particular stages, the two most commonly cited are those of Bowlby (1980) and Kübler-Ross (1969).

Box 1.3   Bowlby's (1980) (and Bowlby and Parkes, 1970) four phases of mourning

Observations of how individuals respond to the loss of a close relative show that over the course of weeks and months their responses usually move through a succession of phases. Adult grief is an extension of a general distress response to separation commonly observed in young children, and so can be regarded as a form of *separation anxiety* in response to the disruption of an attachment bond (see Chapter 2)

1. *Phase of numbing:* Numbness and disbelief, which can last from a few hours up to a week, may be punctuated by outbursts of extremely intense distress and/or anger.
2. *Phase of yearning and searching* for the deceased can last for months and sometimes years.
3. *Phase of disorganisation and despair:* Feelings of depression and apathy occur when old patterns have been discarded.
4. *Phase of greater or lesser degree of reorganisation:* This represents recovery from grief and acceptance of what has taken place.

The relationship with the deceased continues to fill a central role in a bereaved person's emotional life, although this generally changes form over the months and years. This continuing relationship explains the yearning and searching, as well as the anger, characteristic of phase 2, and the despair and subsequent acceptance of loss as irreversible that occur when phases 3 and 4 are passed through successfully.

Bowlby bases phases 1 and 2 largely on findings from the London study, and phases 3 and 4 largely on the Harvard study (and others, including Gorer) (see Box 1.2).

- Kübler-Ross's (1969) stage account was based on her pioneering work with more than 200 terminally ill patients. She was interested in how they prepared for their imminent deaths (*anticipatory grief*), and so her stages describe the *process of dying*. However, the stages were later applied (by other researchers) to *grief for others*; her account remains very influential in nursing and counselling with both dying patients and the bereaved (Wortman and Silver, 1987, 1992).

Box 1.4   Kübler-Ross's (1969) stages of dying

- *Denial and isolation* (*'No, not me, it cannot be true'.*): This prevents the patient from being overwhelmed by the initial shock and is used by most patients not only at this early stage of their illness but also later on. Denial acts as a buffer, allowing the patient time to develop other coping mechanisms. It can also bring about isolation. The patient may fear rejection and abandonment in suffering and feels that nobody understands what their suffering is like. Searching for a second opinion was a very common initial response, representing a desperate attempt to change the unpredictable world they had just been catapulted into, back into the world they knew and understood (March and Doherty, 1999).
- *Anger* (*'Why me? It's not fair!'*): This may be directed at doctors, nurses, relatives, other healthy people who will go on living, or God. This can be the most difficult stage for family and staff to deal with: they may react personally to the patient's anger and respond with anger of their own, which only increases the patient's hostile behaviour (Parkinson, 1992).
- *Bargaining* (*'Please God, let me . . .'*): This is an attempt to postpone death by 'doing a deal' with God (or fate, or the hospital), much as a child might bargain with its parents to get its own way. So, the bargaining has to include a prize for 'good behaviour' and sets a self-imposed 'deadline', such as a son or daughter's wedding or the birth of a grandchild: the patient promises not to ask for more time if this postponement is granted.
- *Depression* (*'How can I leave all this behind?'*): This is likely to arise when the patient realises that no bargain can be struck and that death is inevitable. S/he grieves for all the losses that death represents. This is *preparatory depression*, a form of preparatory grief that helps the patient to finally separate from the world. *Reactive depression* involves expressions of fear and anxiety, and a sense of great loss (see the discussion of *secondary loss* at the beginning of the chapter).
- *Acceptance* (*'Leave me be, I'm ready to die'*): Almost devoid of feelings, the patient seems to have given up the struggle for life, sleeps more, and withdraws from other people, as if preparing for 'the long journey'.

Another, less well-known stage/phase account is Rando's (1993) six 'Rs' mourning processes (see Table 1.2).

Table 1.2 Rando's (1993) six 'Rs' mourning processes

Avoidance phase

1. **R**ecognising the loss (e.g. acknowledging and understanding the death).

Confrontation phase

2. **R**eacting to the separation (which includes experiencing the pain, expressing the psychological reactions to the loss, and identifying and mourning *secondary losses*).
3. **R**ecollecting and re-experiencing the deceased and the relationship (including cognitive and affective dimensions).
4. **R**elinquishing the bold attachments to the deceased and the old assumptive world.

Accommodation phase

5. **R**eadjusting to move adaptively into the new world without forgetting the old.
6. **R**einvesting in new relationships.

An evaluation of stage/phase accounts of grief

- One of the problems with stage accounts is that they imply that individuals *should* pass through this fixed series of stages, implying, in turn, that this is the 'correct' and universal way to experience and respond to loss. This is a mere *assumption* held by researchers, other professionals, and 'the general population' about how people should respond to bereavement (Wortman and Silver, 1987, 1992).
- But perhaps the belief that these stage accounts of grief stipulate a fixed order that applies to everyone rigidly is itself a myth. Bowlby (1980) himself, before describing the stages, says that:

Admittedly these phases are not clear cut, and one individual may oscillate for a time back and forth between any two of them. Yet an overall sequence can be discerned.

(Bowlby, 1980, p. 85)

Similarly, Kübler-Ross's stages can last for different periods of time and can replace each other or coexist (Parkinson, 1992).

- As Archer (1999) points out, both Kübler-Ross's and Bowlby's accounts were proposed before prolonged, detailed follow-up studies of bereaved people had been conducted. Parkes's London study, the Yale study (Prigerson et al., 1995a, 1995b) and others (such as Schuchter and Zisook, 1993) have shown that, with the possible exception of shock and disbelief, the process of change over time is much more of a mixture of reactions which wax and wane in relation to external events and may be delayed, prolonged, or exaggerated according to the individual's mental state and circumstances (Archer, 1999).

- Consistent with this view is C. S. Lewis's (1961) description of his personal account of grief for his wife:

For in grief, nothing 'stays put.' One keeps on emerging from a phase, but it always recurs. Round and round. Everything repeats. Am I going in circles, or dare I hope I am on a spiral?

(Lewis, 1961, p. 49)

Again, grief is like a 'long valley, a winding valley,' one in which you are likely to encounter 'the same sort of country you thought you had left behind miles ago.'

(p. 50–51)

- A different type of criticism, specifically of Kübler-Ross's account, is made by Parkes (2013); he observes that her claim to have discovered the 'stages of grief' fails to acknowledge that they were originally described by Robertson and Bowlby (1952) in their studies of children separated from their mothers and applied to adult bereavement by Bowlby and Parkes (1970). She clearly knew about Bowlby and Parkes's work but makes no reference to it in the 1969 book.
- Some researchers prefer to talk about the *components* of grief. Ramsay and de Groot (1977), for example, identify nine such components, some of which occur early and others late in the grieving process. These are *shock, disorganisation, denial, depression, guilt, anxiety, aggression, resolution*, and *reintegration*.
- A different approach to analysing grief in terms of component responses is to identify specific examples of *physical* (somatic or bodily), *affective* (or emotional), *cognitive, spiritual*, and *behavioural* reactions (see Table 1.3).

Table 1.3 Specific examples of physical, affective, cognitive, spiritual, and behavioural grief reactions (based on Doka and Martin, 2010)

Physical/somatic: headaches; muscular aches; nausea; tiredness and exhaustion; menstrual irregularities; loss of appetite; pain; insomnia; tenseness; sensitivity to noise.
C.S. Lewis (1961) describes the sheer physical/bodily nature of grief. The opening paragraph reads:
No one ever told me that grief felt so much like fear. I am not afraid, but the sensation is like being afraid. The same fluttering in the stomach, the same restlessness, the yawning. I keep on swallowing. (p. 5)
Other terms he uses are 'being mildly drunk, or concussed'.

(Continued)

Table 1.3 Continued

Edward Hirsch (2014), in *Gabriel*, a poem written for his dead son, describes mourning as like carrying a bag of cement up a mountain during the night.

Affective/emotional: sadness; anger; guilt; jealousy; fear and anxiety; shame; relief; emancipation; powerless/hopelessness; pining; emotional pain.

Julian Barnes (in *Levels of Life*, 2013) refers to a friend whose husband died almost instantly of a stroke in his mid-50s, who described her anger not at him, but at the fact that that he *didn't know* that he was going to die, didn't have time to prepare, to say farewells to her and their children. Barnes describes this as a form of being angry with the universe for its indifference: life merely carries on until it ends.

Cognitive: obsessive thoughts; inability to concentrate; fantasising; apathy; dreams; disorientation and confusion; continued thoughts about the loss; rehearsing and reviewing the circumstances of the loss; a sense of the deceased's presence (hallucinations); attempts to rationalise or understand the loss.

C.S. Lewis describes the effort needed to carry out even the most routine, mundane tasks. According to Julian Barnes, grief 'reconfigures' space and time. It also destroys all patterns – and even the belief that any pattern exists. But we can't survive without such belief, so we have to pretend to find/re-erect a pattern.

Spiritual: searching for meaning in loss; asking about the meaning and purpose of life without the deceased; changes in spiritual feelings or beliefs.

Julian Barnes questioned not so much his belief in God (does He exist?) but what sort of God He is (not there when you most need Him). (See Chapter 8.)

Behavioural: crying; illness-related behaviours (e.g. observable symptoms, expressions of illness); outward expression of emotion; observable changes in spiritual behaviours/ expressions; searching behaviours; avoiding or seeking reminders of the deceased; obsessive activity; activities that provide some sense of continued connection to the loss (e.g. visiting the cemetery); physical activities (e.g. exercise, sport, gardening); social withdrawal; absentmindedness; accidents; increases in the use of alcohol, smoking, and other substances.

- However, any purely descriptive account of grief as a series of components might (unintentionally) imply a set of independent reactions. At least the stage approach provides a *holistic* view, i.e. it recognises that these various components must be organised into some *whole* (Archer, 1999). Similarly, stages provide a *framework* for understanding the experiences of the bereaved (and dying individuals). According to Parkes and Prigerson (2010), numbness, commonly the first response, gives way to pining, which is often followed by a period of disorganisation and despair; in the long run, this too declines as acceptance grows. Many people use the term 'recovery' to describe this time, although we are all, to some degree, permanently changed by our losses. However, each of these 'states' of grief has its own characteristics and there are considerable individual differences both in terms of their duration and form. Also, people can move back and forth through the states, sometimes years after it was first (or last) encountered. For all these reasons, 'phases' (or 'stages') of grief tend not to be used any longer: the framework they provide is too rigid.

- While there is a tendency for the symptoms that distinguish these phases/stages to *peak* in the order described (Maciejewski et al., 2007), one phase doesn't have to end before the next can begin, and there's considerable *overlap* between them (Parkes and Prigerson, 2010).
- Perhaps the greatest value of phase/stage accounts has been to draw attention to the fact that grief is a process that people pass through and that, in doing so, most tend to move from a state of relative disorientation and distress to one of growing understanding and acceptance of the loss (Prigerson and Maciejewski, 2008).
- However, stage accounts (which are purely *descriptive*) fail to identify the *functions* of grief; this is dealt with, to varying degrees, by the theories/models that are discussed in Chapter 3.

Some other assumptions about grief

The notion of fixed stages/phases can be added to a list of four 'myths of coping with loss' proposed by Wortman and Silver (1989), namely that:

(a) every bereaved person necessarily shows distress and depression;
(b) the absence of these indicates pathological grieving;
(c) recovery always occurs given time;
(d) 'grief work' is necessary for recovery.

Clearly, (b), (c), and (d) assume that (a) is true (and can be described as the 'universalist assumption': see below). (b) is discussed in Chapter 7 and (d) in Chapter 3.

While Stroebe et al. (1994) argued strongly that such beliefs are *not* widely held by researchers, they found them to be widely endorsed in a study of Dutch GPs, clergymen, and social workers.

Regarding (a), Wortman and Boerner (2011) report on their follow-up of a group of bereaved people, mostly widows and widowers, for up to five years. They found that between 26 and 65 per cent displayed *no* significant symptoms of either distress (yearning for the deceased, feeling that life had lost its meaning, feeling anxious about the future, or experiencing shock at the loss) or depression (feelings of sadness, being self-critical, having suicidal thoughts, lacking energy, or disturbed sleep and eating patterns) during this period. Only 9 to 41 per cent had any such symptoms. (The variability in the results is partly due to how the symptoms were measured; also the depression of some of the bereaved may have been chronic rather than a response to the death: Arkowitz and Lilienfeld, 2011.)

Very much influenced by Wortman and Silver's (1989) 'Myths of coping with loss' argument, Bonanno began testing their claims during the 1990s and into the 2000s. As he reports in his ground-breaking *The Other Side of Sadness*, one of the most consistent findings is that bereavement is *not* a one-dimensional experience;

It's not the same for everyone and there do not appear to be specific stages that everyone must go through. Rather, bereaved people show different patterns or trajectories of grief reactions across time . . .

(Bonanno, 2009, p. 6)

These trajectories are described in Box 1.5.

Box 1.5   The three most common patterns or trajectories of grief (Bonnano, 2009)

Chronic grief: The pain of loss simply overwhelms the bereaved person, who finds it almost impossible to return to his/her normal daily routine. This kind of struggle can continue for years.

Recovery: This is a gradual process; the bereaved person suffers acutely but then slowly picks up the pieces and begins putting his/her life back together.

Resilience: As frightening as the pain of loss can be, for most of us grief is not overwhelming or unending. Some of us cope so effectively, in fact, that we hardly seem to miss a beat in our everyday lives. We may be shocked, even wounded, by a bereavement, but we still manage to regain our equilibrium and move on. While we may experience anguish or sadness, there is much more involved.

Above all, it [bereavement] is a human experience. It is something we are wired for, and it is certainly not meant to overwhelm us. Rather, our reactions to grief seem designed to help us accept and accommodate losses relatively quickly so that we can continue to live productive lives (Bonanno, 2009, p. 7–8)

In one of Bonnano's studies (Bonnano et al., 2002), 1,500 married individuals (aged 65 and over) were followed up over several years; during that time, 205 lost a spouse, after which the study continued to track them for 18 months. Surprisingly, 46 per cent of the bereaved spouses experienced no significant depression, either before or after the death; nor did they display serious distress, although some did feel sad for a short time. Eight per cent of the participants were depressed *before* losing his/her spouse – and stayed that way. For about 10 per cent – individuals who had reported being very unhappy in their marriage – the death actually brought relief from pre-existing depression.

In 27 per cent of cases, the spouse's death *did* precipitate depression. Of these individuals, a substantial proportion (about 11 per cent of the total) began to improve after six months and were symptom-free within 18 months. The rest of that sub-group did *not* recover. However, more than 70 per cent of the 1,500 spouses neither developed depression nor became more depressed as a result of their bereavement. (However, there were 5 per cent who had *low* depression scores at 6 months but *higher* scores at 18 months.) At least when the deceased is an elderly partner, most people are resilient and do not become seriously depressed or distressed. Bonnano's research is important for the light it throws on the roots of resilience. It also confirms the common observation that in elderly people, especially among those whose partner suffered a long illness, high levels of depression often *precede* bereavement, which may sometimes come as a relief (Parkes and Prigerson, 2010).

Bonnano's research hasn't been confined to the death of a loved one; he has also investigated how people react to war (such as Sarajevo in the Bosnian civil war), terror (such as the September 11 terrorist attack on the World Trade Center in 2001), disease (Hong Kong residents who'd lived through the SARS epidemic), natural disasters (such as Hurricane Katrina in 2005), and sexual abuse. In all these different situations, Bonnano has found that most people adapt surprisingly well to whatever the world throws at them: life returns to a measure of normality in a matter of months. Typically, in the immediate aftermath of the event, a third to two-thirds of those surveyed experienced few, if any, symptoms of trauma (such as sleeping difficulties, hypervigilance, or flashbacks: see Chapter 7); within six months, fewer than 10 per cent reported such symptoms.

Bonnano used the term 'coping ugly' to help explain this ability to success-fully manage such (potentially) traumatic experiences. Some people engaged in *self-enhancing bias*, inflated perceptions of who they were and how they acted. For example, they avoided asking themselves the troubling question, 'Could I have done something different to have prevented this from happening?' Others *repressed* negative thoughts and emotions or just convinced themselves that they could cope with whatever life threw at them. Still others laughed and smiled their way through, behaviour that many psychologists would consider an unhealthy form of denial.

Bonnano argues that melancholy helps us with healing following a major loss, but unrelenting grief – like clinical depression – is overwhelming. So, for most people, instead of getting stuck in an inconsolable psychological state, the brain's alarm system (the fight-or-flight syndrome, which involves various brain structures and the release of various hormones, including *cortisol*, the 'stress hor-mone') is toned down. If emotions become extreme, a kind of internal sensor (a 'resilience-stat') returns us to a more balanced state.

When he began his research (in the 1990s), the prevailing wisdom stressed the importance of 'grief work' (one of Wortman and Silver's 'myths' – see above). As a psychologist, he used a range of methods to test these assumptions, includ-ing both interviews (as in the study of elderly bereaved spouses described above) and more observational and experimental approaches. For example, Bonnano and Keltner (1997) analysed videotapes of facial expressions of people who had recently lost loved ones. While the videos revealed sadness and anger, there were no visible signs of permanent sorrow; significantly, there were also expressions of happiness: facial expressions commonly changed from dejection to laughter and back again.

So, for Bonnano, there's more to grief than simply getting over it and moving on. Bereavement is a powerful experience, even for the most resilient among us: it forces us to ask questions about the world and our place in it that might never otherwise have occurred to us. (Some of these questions are discussed in Chapter 8.)

Summary and conclusions

- Bereavement is a particular form of loss, involving the death of a loved one. Loved ones may be a spouse, sibling, child, and child deaths can occur both pre- and post-natally.
- Losses come in many different forms, including primary and secondary, physical and relational, tangible/intangible, and symbolic.
- Grief, as a natural reaction to bereavement, can vary in both intensity and the form it takes. Controversially, some psychiatrists claim that complicated grief (in particular, prolonged grief disorder (PGD)) represents a distinct mental disorder.
- Disenfranchised grief highlights the role of social factors in individuals' experience and expression of grief.
- Three major kinds of grieving are intuitive, instrumental, and blended. While women are more likely to display intuitive, and men instrumental grieving, bereavement support is based on the assumption that bereaved people need to acknowledge and express their grief.
- 'Grief work' (what Freud called 'mourning') is defined as the process by which bereaved people come to terms with their bereavement. Grief work is central to several theories/models of grief, including stage/phase models.
- 'Mourning' is also used to denote the culturally defined ways of publicly expressing one's grief, as in rituals and customs related to the funeral.
- Grief has been studied in various ways, including (i) personal accounts by bereaved individuals; (ii) research studies involving large numbers of bereaved people, such as Parkes's Bethlem, London, and Love and Loss studies, the Harvard Bereavement Project, Lindemann's Coconut Grove fire study, and the Yale Bereavement study.
- The common sense understanding of grief reflects *stage/phase models* of grief, such as those of Bowlby, Bowlby and Parkes, and Kübler-Ross. Others include Rando's six 'Rs' mourning processes.
- These stage/phase accounts have been heavily criticised, in particular for creating the impression of a *fixed* sequence which every bereaved individual *should* go through. Some researchers prefer to talk about the *components* of grief.

- The *experience* of grief has been described in terms of physical, affective/emotional, cognitive, spiritual, and behavioural grief reactions. While these might imply that grief comprises a set of independent reactions, the stage/phase approach provides a *holistic* view and a framework for understanding the bereaved individual's experience.
- Not only may grief work not be necessary for 'recovery' from grief, but significant numbers of bereaved people show no overt signs of distress or depression.
- Grief is a highly individualised response to bereavement, and Bonnano describes three patterns or *trajectories*: chronic grief, recovery, and resilience. Resilience has also been observed in relation to a range of traumatic events and experiences.

Chapter 2

Attachment, loss, and grief

The chapter will address the following questions:

- What is the relationship between love and loss?
- What is meant by 'attachment'?
- What are the main features of Bowlby's evolutionary theory of attachment?
- What were the main influences on Bowlby's ideas?
- How is young children's distress response to separation related to adult grief?
- Is grief unique to human beings?
- How has attachment in young children been studied?
- How do young children differ in their attachment styles?
- How are these attachment styles related to the type of parenting they receive?
- How are childhood attachment styles related to adult attachment styles?
- How have attachment styles been studied in the context of adult romantic relationships?
- How are adult attachment styles assessed?
- How do adult attachment styles affect grief reactions to loss of a partner?
- What are the three phases of Shaver and Fraley's model of attachment?

Love and attachment

According to Parkes (2006):

> For most people, love is the most profound source of pleasure in our lives while the loss of those whom we love is the most profound sense of pain. Hence, love and loss are two sides of the same coin. We cannot have one without risking the other.
>
> (p. 1)

This applies as much to children as it does to adults, but when discussing children the term 'attachment' is more likely to be used than 'love'. Despite a great deal of scientific (social psychological) research having been concerned with the objective study of 'love' (arguably, one of the most subjective of all human emotions), most researchers now use the term 'attachment' for all bonds of love and then qualify this by specifying 'parent-child', 'child-parent', 'adult-adult' etc. While this helps to put things on a more scientific (objective) footing, the very neutrality of 'attachment' may create the false impression that love is cognitive and instrumental when, in fact, it is experienced as a complex set of feelings and emotions (Parkes, 2006). In *Love and Loss* (2006), Parkes reports the findings of a major research project whose aim was, essentially, to try to answer the following question: Are the problems which cause bereaved adults to seek psychiatric help attributable, in some degree, to the particular kinds of attachment, the patterns of loving, which they made to their parents in childhood?

Before examining Parkes's findings, and those of other researchers who have asked a similar question, we need to consider the nature of attachment, the important differences between individuals in their attachments to parents, and the continuity between childhood and adult attachment styles. We shall then be in a better position to appreciate Parkes's findings identifying 'the intervening links in the chain of causation between patterns of love and patterns of grief' (2006, p. 9). What emerges from his research, he says, is a new understanding of the 'anatomy of love'.

Bowlby's evolutionary theory of attachment

As we noted in Chapter 1, Bowlby regarded adult grief as a form of *separation anxiety*, first observed in young children when separated from an attachment figure (in particular, the mother-figure). While his ideas regarding loss and grief were developed over several decades, they were expressed most completely in the third volume of his landmark trilogy (*Attachment and Loss*), *Loss: Sadness and Depression* (1980) (Shaver and Fraley, 2008).

Two of Bowlby's aims in that book were:

(i) To show that seemingly irrational or 'immature' grief reactions (such as disbelief, anger, searching, and sensing the continued presence of a lost attachment figure) are understandable when viewed from an *ethological* or *evolutionary* perspective. Bowlby, a trained psychoanalyst, was very much influenced by the work of ethologists (zoologists who study animal behaviour in its natural environment/habitat), in particular, Lorenz, famous for his study of imprinting in goslings (1935). In turn, ethologists base their research on Darwin's evolutionary theory, and Bowlby's attachment theory is commonly described as an evolutionary theory.

(ii) To show that how an individual responds to loss stems partly from how his/her attachment system became organised during childhood. Bowlby claimed that people whose attachment systems are such that they chronically anticipate rejection and loss (i.e. high attachment *anxiety*) or defensively suppress attachment-related feelings (i.e. high attachment *avoidance*) are likely to suffer from psychological and physical distress following bereavement.

Bowlby (1969, 1973) argued that because new-born human infants are entirely help-less, they're *genetically programmed* to behave towards their mothers in ways that ensure their survival: these *species-specific* behaviours are described in Box 2.1.

Box 2.1 Species-specific behaviours used by infants to shape and control their caregivers' behaviour

Sucking: While sucking is important for nourishment, not all sucking is nutritive. *Non-nutritive sucking* seems to be an innate tendency which inhibits a new-born's distress. In Western societies, babies are often given 'dummies' (or 'pacifiers') to calm them when they're upset.

Cuddling: Human infants adjust their postures to mould themselves to the contours of the parent's body. The reflexive response that encourages front-to-front contact with the mother plays an important part in reinforcing the caregiver's behaviour.

Looking: When parents don't respond to an infant's eye contact, the infant usually shows signs of distress; an infant's looking behaviour, therefore, acts as an invitation to its mother to respond. If she fails to do so, the infant becomes upset and avoids further visual contact. By contrast, mutual gazing is rewarding for an infant.

Smiling: This seems to be an innate behaviour, since babies can produce smiles shortly after birth. Although the first 'social smile' doesn't usually occur before six weeks, adults view the smiling infant as a 'real person', which they find very rewarding.

Crying: Young infants usually cry only when hungry, cold, or in pain, and crying is most effectively ended by picking up and cuddling them.

In addition to the behaviours described in Box 2.1, infants possess a *motivational* system (the attachment system) designed by natural selection to regulate and maintain proximity to their caregivers. One of the functions of this system is to provide the infant with a sense of security, which enables it to explore its environment and play; ultimately, the function of attachment is *detachment* (i.e. the ability to be independent of the caregiver: Rutter, 1981).

The mother also inherits a genetic blueprint which programmes her to respond to the baby; there is a critical period during which the *synchrony of action* between mother and infant produces an attachment. (Strictly speaking, it's only the child who's *attached* to the mother, while she is *bonded* to her baby.) The child's attachment to its mother helps to regulate how far away from her the child will move, and the amount of fear it will show towards strangers.

Generally, attachment behaviours are more evident when the child is distressed, unwell, afraid, or in unfamiliar surroundings. In Bowlby's (1951) view, mothering is useless for all children if delayed until after two-and-a-half to three years, and for most children if delayed until after 12 months.

When an attachment figure is judged to be sufficiently available and responsive, an infant is thought to experience 'felt security' (Sroufe and Waters, 1977). In contrast, when the attachment figure is judged to be inaccessible or unresponsive, the infant experiences anxiety and desperately tries to re-establish contact by calling, searching, approaching, and clinging. Similarly, if the infant/child is separated from the attachment figure (for whatever reason), s/he will typically display *distress*. One example of short-term deprivation (days or weeks, rather than months or years) is that of a child going into a nursery while its mother goes into hospital. Another is that of the child itself going into hospital. Bowlby showed that when young children go into hospital, they display distress, which typically involves three components or stages.

Box 2.2   The components or stages of distress

Protest: The initial, immediate reaction takes the form of crying, screaming, kicking, and generally struggling to escape, or clinging to the mother to prevent her from leaving. This is an outward and direct expression of the child's anger, fear, bitterness, and bewilderment.

Despair: The struggling and protest eventually give way to calmer behaviour. The child may appear apathetic, but internally still feels all the anger and fear previously displayed, keeping these feelings 'locked up' and wanting nothing to do with other people. The child may no longer anticipate the mother's return, and barely reacts to others' offers of comfort, preferring to comfort itself by rocking, thumb-sucking, and so on.

Detachment: If the separation continues, the child begins to respond to people again, but tends to treat everyone alike and rather superficially. If reunited with the mother at this stage, the child may well have to 'relearn' its relationship with her and may even 'reject' her (as she 'rejected' her child). The detachment is more apparent than real: rather than a simple weakening of the attachment bond, this third stage represents a *defensive* suppression of attachment behaviours.

According to Bowlby (1969), the protest reactions are biologically functional: in the *environment of evolutionary adaptiveness* (the environment in which it is believed human beings (*Homo sapiens*) evolved, thought to be the African savannah: Rose, 2000), they would have kept infants close to their protective caregivers; this, in turn, would have increased their chances of survival in a hostile and unpredictable world. This natural anxiety and yearning for an attachment figure motivate continued searching and calling until either success is achieved or the infant gives up trying. Viewed in this light, many of the apparently puzzling reactions to separation and loss (such as continuing to yearn and search even when a lost caregiver is objectively – and permanently – unavailable (i.e. dead)) seem more reasonable and, in many situations, adaptive (Shaver and Fraley, 2008) (see Chapter 1).

The same tendency to search and reunite with the attachment figure expresses itself strongly when an adult loses a loved spouse (e.g. Parkes, 2006; Parkes and Weiss, 1983). This may sometimes manifest as the wish to die oneself in order to be reunited with the beloved wife or husband (Collins, in Gilbert, 2006); unfortunately, this natural impulse sometimes leads to suicide (see Chapter 7). Feelings of loneliness stem specifically from the absence of the attachment figure and cannot be fully overcome by the presence of others. However, many bereaved individuals do derive comfort from the company of close, supportive friends or family; they may be seen as members of a hierarchy of attachment figures (Bowlby, 1969). At the same time, such support networks often cannot fill the emotional gap left by the deceased spouse: Bowlby believed that attachment bonds are *person-specific*, involving shared experiences and memories that are unique to a history (often of several decades) of interactions with that particular person.

Originally, Bowlby used 'detachment' for the final phase of adult mourning; importantly, he changed it to 'reorganisation' (see Box 1.3). The change reflects Bowlby's belief that many mourners do not, and do not wish to, 'detach' defensively from their lost attachment figure; instead, they rearrange their representations of self and the lost loved one so that a *continuing bond* and adjustment to life without the deceased are both possible. (This belief in continuing bonds represents a reaction against the 'classical' view of successful, healthy mourning, largely attributable to Freud, according to which the attachment to the deceased must be broken. This is discussed in detail in Chapter 3.)

As we might expect, given the impact of ethology and evolutionary theory on Bowlby's theory, there is considerable evidence that grief responses are not unique to human beings (Archer, 1999). This is discussed further in Box 2.3.

Box 2.3 Grief among non-human animals and early humans

- Lorenz (1963) describes the response of a greylag goose to the loss of its mate as 'roughly identical with those accompanying human grief'.
- Harlow's work with rhesus monkeys in the 1950s and 1960s, in which he separated babies from their mothers, revealed a pattern of response very similar to that of young human children. (Harlow's work was another major influence on the development of Bowlby's theory.)

- King (2013) describes a large amount of recent research that points to the conclusions that cetaceans (such as dolphins), elephants, great apes, and a wide range of other species (from farm animals to domestic pets) grieve when a relative or close companion dies.
- Jane Goodall describes a young chimpanzee's decline and death from grief only weeks after the death of his mother, and Cynthia Moss reported that elephants attend to dying comrades and stroke the bones of deceased relatives.
- Grief in non-humans usually requires two major conditions to be met: (i) two (or more) animals choose to spend time together beyond survival-oriented behaviours (such as foraging or mating); (ii) when one animal dies, the survivor changes its normal behavioural routine (perhaps reducing the amount of time devoted to eating or sleeping, adopting a body posture or facial expression indicative of depression or agitation, or generally failing to thrive) (King, 2013).
- In the evolution of *Homo sapiens*, grief increasingly became expressed through symbolically rich rituals, such as decorating corpses in red ochre (starting about 100,000 years ago).
- At a site in Russia called Sunghir, two children from 24,000 years ago were found buried along with elaborate grave goods (including mammoth tusks, animal figures carved from ivory, and thousands of ivory beads). The examples of animal grief described above strengthen an emotion-based interpretation of the archaeological evidence: our ancestors of many thousands of years ago mourned for their lost children (King, 2013).

Individual variations in attachment

A pioneering study of individual differences in children's attachment to their mothers was conducted by Ainsworth (1967) in Uganda. Ainsworth replicated her Ugandan study in Baltimore, USA (Ainsworth et al., 1971, 1978), which Van Ijzendoorn and Schuengel (1999) describe as the most important study in the history of attachment research. Like the earlier study, both interviews and naturalistic observation were used, but the latter now played a much greater role.

Also like the Uganda study, the Baltimore study was *longitudinal*: 26 mother–infant pairs were visited at home every three to four weeks, each visit lasting three to four hours, for the first year of the baby's life. In order to make sense of the enormous amount of data collected for each pair (72 hours' worth), there needed to be an *external criterion* measure (some standard against which to compare the observations). The criterion chosen was the *Strange Situation Test* (SST) (see Table 2.1).

Table 2.1 The eight episodes of the Strange Situation Test(SST)

Episode	Persons present	Duration	Brief description
1	Mother, baby, observer	30 seconds	Observer introduces mother and baby to experimental room, then leaves
2	Mother, baby	3 minutes	Mother is non-participant while baby explores; if necessary, play is stimulated after two minutes
3	Stranger, mother, baby	3 minutes	Stranger enters. First minute: stranger silent. Second minute: stranger converses with mother. Third minute: stranger approaches baby. After three minutes, mother leaves unobtrusively
4	Stranger, baby	3 minutes or less*	First separation episode. Stranger's behaviour is geared to the baby's
5	Mother, baby	3 minutes or more**	First reunion episode. Stranger leaves. Mother greets and/or comforts baby, then tries to settle baby again in play. Mother then leaves, saying 'bye-bye'
6	Baby	3 minutes or less*	Second separation episode
7	Stranger, baby	3 minutes or less*	Continuation of second separation. Stranger enters and gears her behaviour to baby's
8	Mother, baby	3 minutes	Second reunion episode. Mother enters, greets baby, then picks up baby. Meanwhile, stranger leaves unobtrusively

*Episode is ended early if baby is unduly distressed.
** Episode is prolonged if more time is required for baby to become reinvolved in play.
(Based on Ainsworth et al., 1978; Krebs and Blackman, 1988)

The SST had been devised earlier by Ainsworth and Wittig (1969), who wanted to study how the baby's tendencies towards attachment and exploration interact under conditions of low and high *stress*. They believed that the balance between these two systems could be observed more easily in an unfamiliar environment. In the Baltimore study, the SST was modified to enable infant and maternal behaviour patterns to be classified.

Group data confirmed that babies explored the playroom and toys more vigorously in the mothers' presence than after the stranger entered or while the mother was absent. However, Ainsworth was particularly fascinated by the unexpected variety of infants' reactions to the mothers' return (*reunion behaviours*: see Table 2.2). This provides a clearer picture of the state of attachment than even the response to separation itself (Marrone, 1998).

According to Main (1991; Main and Hesse, 1990), many babies don't fit neatly into Ainsworth et al.'s three attachment types. She identifies a fourth type, namely *insecure–disorganised* (type D). This describes a baby whose behaviour appears to lack observable goals, intentions, or exploration. There are contradictory behaviours (either sequential or simultaneous), misdirected, incomplete and interrupted

Table 2.2 Behaviour associated with three types of attachment in one-year-olds using the SST

Category	Name	Sample (%)
Type A	*Anxious–avoidant*	15

Typical behaviour: Baby largely ignores mother, because of *indifference* towards her. Play is little affected by whether she's present or absent. No or few signs of distress when mother leaves, and actively ignores or avoids her on her return. Distress is caused by being alone, rather than being left by the mother. Can be comforted as easily by the stranger as by the mother. In fact, *both adults are treated in a very similar way.* This behaviour can be viewed as a small, short-term version of failure to become anxious, angry, or bereft in the face of loss (Shaver and Fraley, 2008).

Type B	*Securely attached*	70

Typical behaviour: Baby plays happily while the mother is present, whether the stranger is present or not. Mother is largely 'ignored', because she can be trusted to be there if needed. Clearly distressed when the mother leaves, and play is considerably reduced. Seeks immediate contact with mother on her return, quickly calms down in her arms, and resumes play. The distress is caused by the mother's absence, not by being alone. Although the stranger can provide some comfort, *she and the mother are treated very differently.*

Type C	*Anxious–resistant*	15

Typical behaviour: Baby is fussy and wary while the mother is present. Cries a lot more than types A and B, and has difficulty using mother as a safe base. Very distressed when she leaves, seeks contact with her on her return, but simultaneously shows anger and resists contact (may approach her and reach out to be picked up, then struggles to get down again). This demonstrates the baby's *ambivalence* towards her. Doesn't readily return to play. *Actively resists stranger's efforts to make contact.* The refusal to calm down once the mother returns is a miniature version of grief: becoming extremely distressed by separation and then finding it impossible to 'resolve' this upset when it no longer seems necessary (Shaver and Fraley, 2008).

movements, stereotyped behaviour (such as rocking backwards and forwards or repeatedly hitting themselves), freezing/stilling, and apparent fear of the parent (Rutter et al., 2009). Compared with the other categories, these children show increased levels of cortisol (the stress hormone) as measured in their saliva 20–30 minutes after the SST (Spangler and Grossmann, 1993; Hertsgaard et al., 1995).

Relationship between child's attachment style and pattern of parenting

Secure (Ainsworth's Category B)

The parents of securely attached children display 'good enough' sensitivity and responsiveness to their needs for security and a safe base from which to explore the world. Although some of the mothers of Category B children may have experienced problems with their own parents, they are aware how their past has influenced the present and can describe and accept their parents in a realistic and credible way; i.e. they have overcome any attachment problems of their own. Their marriages are also more likely to be conflict-free compared with the parents of insecurely attached children (Simpson and Rholes, 1994).

Anxious-avoidant (Category A)

The mothers of these children do not show feelings, cannot tolerate closeness, and/or punish the child's attachment behaviour. As shown in Table 2.2, anxious-avoidant children are described as 'indifferent' towards their mothers; however, they do become physiologically aroused (as indicated by a rapid heart rate) both during the period of separation and for a long time after the mother has returned. This indifference, therefore, is more apparent than real (Sroufe and Waters (1977). Belsky et al. (1984) found that many mothers of avoidant children are responsive to their child at low levels of stress but become less responsive if the stress level rises. As Parkes (2006) observes, this reversal of the usual pattern seems to defeat the purpose of care, namely, to provide protection and security when it's most needed and to encourage autonomy when it's not.

Anxious-ambivalent (Category C)

These children have mothers who tend to be over-anxious, insensitive to their infants, and discourage exploration. As shown in Table 2.2, these children's distress, which is very evident during the periods of separation, continues after reunion for much longer than that of the securely attached infants (Parkes, 2006).

Disorganised/disorientated (Category D)

Main and Hesse (1990) found that most of the mothers of these children had suffered major losses or other traumas shortly before or after the child's birth and had reacted by becoming severely depressed. Fully 56 per cent of mothers who had lost a parent by death before age 18 went on to have children classified as Type D. Her grief is 'unresolved', and her depression makes her measurably less sensitive and responsive to her baby's needs. Such mothers are often helpless, frightened of their own children, and lacking confidence in their ability to care for and control them. They may see their infants as more powerful than themselves; consequently, their behaviour is both 'frightened' and 'frightening': what should be the child's 'haven of safety' is a source of fear.

Type D has been linked to infant maltreatment or hostile caregiving (Carlson et al., 1989); alcoholism (el-Guebaly et al., 1993) and drug abuse (Rodning et al., 1991); maternal history of loss through separation, divorce, or death (Lyons-Ruth et al., 1991); maternal depression (Radke-Yarrow et al., 1995); and being raised in institutions (Rutter et al., 2009).

Continuity between early and later attachment patterns

Later childhood attachment patterns

These patterns, having become established during the first two years of life, remain remarkably stable (assuming that the family's living conditions don't change) and predict the quality of relationships to other people during later childhood (Parkes, 2006); this applies in both the short term (six months: Waters, 1978) and the long term (up to five years: Main et al., 1985). This is commonly interpreted as reflecting a fixed attribute of the child, such as temperament.

However, Vaughn et al. (1980) showed that attachment type *may* change depending on variations in the family's circumstances. Children of single parents living in poverty were studied at 12 and 18 months. Significantly, 38 percent were classified differently on the two occasions, reflecting changes in the families' circumstances, particularly changes in accommodation and the mothers' degree of stress. This suggests that attachment types aren't necessarily permanent characteristics. In general, the longer the gap between assessments, the more likely it is that children will be found to have changed classification status (Schaffer, 2004).

Also, patterns of attachment to mothers and fathers are *independent*, so the same child might be securely attached to its mother, but insecurely attached to its father (Main and Weston, 1981). This shows that attachment patterns derived from the SST reflect qualities of distinct relationships, rather than characteristics of the child (such as temperament, e.g. van Ijzendoorn and De Wolff, 1997).

The effects of early attachments on later adult relationships

Although until recently attachment was studied almost exclusively within parent–child relationships, Bowlby (1979, 129) maintained that 'attachment behaviour is held to characterise human beings from the cradle to the grave'. But clearly, the patterns of attachment and their consequences become much more complicated by the time we reach adulthood (Parkes, 2006).

According to Hazan and Shaver (1987), attachment theory, as developed by Bowlby and Ainsworth in particular, offers a valuable perspective on adult romantic love, helping to explain both positive emotions (caring, intimacy, and trust) and negative emotions (fear of intimacy, jealousy, and emotional 'ups and downs'). Hazan and Shaver were the first to apply Ainsworth et al.'s three basic attachment styles to adult–adult sexual/romantic relationships, asking how adults' attachment patterns (in their adult relationships) are related to their childhood attachments to their parents.

Box 2.4   Romantic love conceptualised as an attachment process (Hazan and Shaver, 1987)

- Ainsworth et al.'s three attachment styles were 'translated' in a way that would make them suitable for the study of adult attachments. As part of a 'love quiz' in a local newspaper, respondents were asked to indicate which of three descriptions best applied to their feelings about romantic relationships.
- They were also asked to complete a simple adjective checklist describing their childhood relationships with their parents (their recollections of the kind of parenting they received). This was then correlated with their chosen attachment style.
- 56 per cent of respondents were classified as securely attached, 24 per cent as anxious-avoidant, and 20 per cent as anxious-ambivalent.

Hazan and Shaver's findings closely mirror Ainsworth et al.'s findings with 12- to 18-month-olds. Although these results provided encouraging support for an attachment perspective on romantic love, Hazan and Shaver warned against drawing any firm conclusions about the continuity between early childhood and adult experience. It would be excessively pessimistic, at least from the point of view of the insecurely attached person, if continuity were the rule, rather than the exception. The correlations suggest that as we go further into adulthood, continuity with our childhood experiences *decreases*. The average person participates in several important friendships and love relationships, which provide opportunities for revising our *mental models* (or what Bowlby, 1973, called *internal working models*/IWMs) of self and others (see below).

Intergenerational continuity

Another way of looking at the continuity between early and later attachment patterns is to ask how *parents'* attachment styles are related to their *children's* attachment styles: Do people parent their children as they themselves were parented? This is the issue of *intergenerational continuity* (or *intergenerational transfer* of attachment patterns: Meins, 2003).

A commonly used measure of how parents are/were attached to their own parents is the *adult attachment interview* (AAI). Apart from the SST, the AAI is probably the most widely used and best-developed measure of attachment (Goldberg, 2000); according to Parkes (2006), it is commonly regarded as the most reliable measure, in adult life, of the lasting influence of childhood attachments. It is based on the assumption that what's crucial for predicting parenting behaviour isn't so much the objective facts about our early attachments, but rather how we *construe* these facts, that is, the nature of our IWMs: it's less about accuracy of recall and more about how memories are reported in adult life.

Box 2.5   The adult attachment interview (AAI) (Main and Weston, 1981; Main et al., 1985) and associated attachment styles

The AAI is a structured interview, comprising 15 questions designed to tap an individual's experience of attachment relationships in childhood, and how s/he considers those experiences to have influenced later development and present functioning. More specifically, for each parent, the person is asked to choose five adjectives which best describe that relationship during childhood. The person then has to illustrate each of these choices by drawing on childhood memories.

Later, the person is asked how they reacted when upset, to which parent they felt closest and why, whether they ever felt rejected or threatened, why parents may have acted as they did, how these relationships may have changed, and how these earlier experiences (including major loss up to the present time) may have affected their adult functioning and personality.

Each interview (which lasts about 90 minutes) is classified as a whole, giving an overall 'state of mind' regarding attachment. Four attachment styles are possible:

Autonomous/secure (F): These individuals discuss childhood experiences openly, coherently and consistently, acknowledging both positive and negative events and emotions. This is the most common style among parents of *securely attached* infants; 50 to 60 per cent of adults fall into this category.

Insecure-dismissing (D): These individuals seem cut off from the emotional nature of their childhood, denying especially their negative experiences and dismissing their significance. They appear cooperative, but contradictions make them seem dishonest. This is the most common style among parents of *anxious–avoidant* infants and describes 25 to 30 per cent of adults.

Insecure preoccupied/entangled (E): Such people are overinvolved with what they recollect, appearing so overwhelmed that they become incoherent, confused, even angry. They're still actively trying to please their parents. This is the most common style among parents of *anxious–resistant* infants; 10 to 15 per cent of adults fall into this category.

Unresolved/disorganised (U): This style describes mainly those who've experienced a trauma (which may include physical or sexual abuse), or the early death of an attachment figure, and who haven't come to terms with it or worked through the grieving process. This is the most common style among parents of *disorganised* infants.

Table 2.3 Mother's prenatal AAI classification and children's Strange Situation Test classification of the mother (based on Fonagy et al., 1991)

Classification of the children	Dismissing	Autonomous	Preoccupied
Anxious–avoidant	15	8	7
Secure	5	45	5
Anxious–resistant	2	6	3

So, the AAI may predict how the mother's child will be attached to her as determined by the SST (Heard and Lake, 1997; Main, 1995). However, it's possible that these findings are affected by the mother's selective recall: how she remembers her childhood might be influenced by her current experiences with her own child. Fonagy et al. (1991) tried to rule out this possibility by giving the AAI to 96 women *before* the birth of their children (i.e. during pregnancy), then classifying the children (using the SST) when they were 12 and 18 months old. As Table 2.3 shows, Main et al.'s (1985) results (see Box 2.5) were largely replicated (with the exception of the preoccupied mothers). The correlation was especially strong for the autonomous mother–secure child pairing.

These results have been replicated in later studies by Fonagy and his colleagues, for both infant–mother attachment (Fonagy et al., 1994; Steele *et al.*, 1995) and father–infant attachment (Steele et al., 1996). Overall, mothers' perceptions of their own childhood attachments predicted their children's attachments to them 75 per cent of the time. Benoit and Parker (1994) found that the AAI categories of grandmothers correctly predicted 75 per cent of their daughters' AAI categories; in turn, these predicted 77 per cent of the SST categories of their grandchildren

While acknowledging the need to explain the 25 per cent 'failure' rate (Clarke and Clarke, 2000), how can we explain this evidence for intergenerational continuity?

Inner working models

According to Bowlby (1973), expectations about the availability and responsiveness of attachment figures are built into our *inner working models* (IWMs) of attachment. These reflect memories and beliefs stemming from our early experiences of caregiving, which are carried forward into new relationships, both during childhood and beyond. They play an active role in guiding perceptions and behaviour.

Bowlby (1973) argued that, at least under normal circumstances, our IWMs are resistant to change. Children tend to identify with their parents, unwittingly, and so when they become parents themselves, they adopt the same patterns of

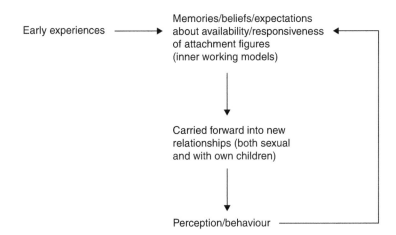

Early experiences ⟶ Memories/beliefs/expectations about availability/responsiveness of attachment figures (inner working models)

Carried forward into new relationships (both sexual and with own children)

Perception/behaviour

Figure 2.1 How inner working models link early caregiving experiences and later relationships.
Reproduced by permission of Hodder Education.

behaviour towards their own children as they themselves experienced as children. In this way, patterns of interaction are transmitted, more or less unchanged, from one generation to another.

However, IWMs usually can be updated or modified, as new interactions develop. While for young children such change must be based on actual physical events, such direct interaction isn't necessary in older children and adults. Main et al. (1985), for example, found that some adults, who reported being insecure in their relationships with their own parents, managed to produce children who were securely attached, at both twelve months and six years. They had mentally worked through their unpleasant experiences with their parents, and their IWMs were now more typical of secure types (Hazan and Shaver, 1987).

Van Ijzendoorn and Bakermans-Kranenburg (1996) reviewed 33 studies involving the AAI. Similar proportions of mothers, fathers, and older adolescents fell into the four attachment categories, but people from lower socio-economic groups were slightly more likely to be classified as dismissing. The largest difference is for people having treatment for mental disorder, who are very unlikely to score as autonomous. Some mothers who had very negative early experiences seemed to have come to terms with them, explaining them in rational terms (such as marital stress, overwork). They were more likely to have secure infants, perhaps because they'd successfully updated their own IWMs. In fact, Bowlby (1988) recognised that attachment behaviour and IWMs cannot be regarded as fixed in infancy and unchanging throughout life.

Also, the AAI does not predict the bonds which adults will form with other adults. However, 'dismissing' adults are less likely to support their romantic partner (Hazan and Shaver, 1987), score lower on expressiveness, kindness, and awareness of others (Collins and Read, 1990), and are less likely to offer their partner reassurance and support in an anxiety-provoking situation (Simpson et al., 1992). 'Preoccupied' adults are more emotional and self-critical (Mikulincer et al., 1993), they idealise their romantic partners and depend too much on them (Feeney and Noller, 1990).

In a review of the research, Feeney (2008) concludes that individuals with high anxiety about relationships report greater relationship conflict, suggesting that much of this conflict is driven by basic insecurities over issues of love, loss, and abandonment. They also adopt coercive and distrusting ways of dealing with conflict, which are likely to produce the very outcomes they fear.

However, like the AAI (and SST) categories, patterns of romantic attachment – and the underlying IWMs – *can* (and do) change, such as when a stable, satisfying relationship challenges pre-existing expectations. IWMs both shape experiences in intimate relationships (hence acting as a source of continuity/stability) and are influenced by relational events (and hence are subject to change) (Feeney, 2008).

An evolutionary theory of love: love as attachment

An *evolutionary* account of love focuses on the functions that love evolved to meet. Compared with other primates, humans are dependent on their parents for an exceptionally long period of time. As length of childhood (and related brain size) increased steadily over the last million years or so of *Homo* evolution, so there were strong selection pressures toward the development of (relatively) *monogamous pair-bonding*. In other words:

> Love is . . . an evolutionary device to persuade couples to stay together for long enough to give their children a good shot at making it to adulthood . . .
>
> (Fletcher, 2002, p. 89)

In our hunter-gatherer ancestral environment, two parents were better than one. Attachment bonds between procreative partners would have greatly enhanced the survival of their offspring (Zeifman and Hazan, 2000).

Bowlby (1969) identified three basic behavioural systems that bond male–female pairs together: *attachment, caregiving*, and *sex*. Shaver et al. (1996) have proposed a theory of adult romantic love in terms of these three systems. So, when we say 'I love you', we can mean any or all of the following.

- *Love as attachment*: 'I am emotionally dependent on you for happiness, safety and security; I feel anxious and lonely when you're gone, relieved and stronger when you're near. I want to be comforted, supported emotionally, and taken care of by you . . .'
- *Love as caregiving*: 'I get great pleasure from supporting, caring for and taking care of you; from facilitating your progress, health, growth, and happiness . . .'

- *Love as sexual attraction*: 'I am sexually attracted to you and can't get you out of my mind. You excite me, "turn me on", make me feel alive . . . I want to see you, devour you, touch you, merge with you, lose myself in you, "get off on you" . . .'

Grief and attachment theory

The Harvard Study (Parkes and Weiss, 1983) was one of the earliest attempts to identify the factors that determine how people will fare following bereavement (see Chapter 1); subsequent studies have confirmed and expanded these findings. Four types of risk factors that have been identified are:

- the personal vulnerability of the bereaved person
- the kinship to the deceased person (see Chapter 6)
- the events and circumstances leading up to and including the death (see Chapter 7)
- the social supports and other circumstances obtaining after the death (see Chapters 4 and 5).

The first of these is most relevant to attachment theory.

The Harvard study showed that a powerful determinant of problematic reactions to bereavement was the attachment to the deceased. Two types of attachment were found to produce two distinct types of problematic grief:

1   a *dependent* relationship predicted *chronic grief* (i.e. intense from the outset and continues for an undue length of time);
2   an *ambivalent* relationship predicted *conflicted grief* (which is often delayed, reaching a peak some time later, and complicated by feelings of anger and/or guilt)

Waskowic and Chartier (2003) administered the Relationship Scale Questionnaire (RSQ) (Bartholomew and Horowitz, 1991) to 65 widows and 11 widowers at varying times following their bereavement. Secure attachment to the deceased was associated with less anger, social isolation, guilt, death anxiety, somatic symptoms, despair, depersonalisation and rumination, and greater 'interchange' with and reminiscence about the deceased compared with the insecurely attached.

The attachment patterns originally identified by Ainsworth et al. represent ways of *coping* and may influence subsequent coping strategies. Anxious-ambivalent (or dependent) attachments are ways of coping with parents who pay attention to, and reward, emotional demands. Anxious-avoidant attachments are ways of coping with parents who discourage emotional demands; disorganised attachments may reflect situations of helplessness in which high levels of anxiety and depression are likely to occur (Parkes, 2006).

While secure attachments teach the developing child to trust itself and others, and are generally regarded as the most desirable pattern, they may also limit the child's ability to cope, later in life, with untrustworthy people and with situations they cannot control. According to Parkes (2006), ultimately, it is the fit between a particular situation and a particular worldview that determines who will cope well and who will cope badly.

The love and loss study (Parkes, 2006)

The basic design and aims of this study are described in Box 1.2. To remind ourselves here, it was aimed at testing the hypothesis that love and loss are inter-twined, that childhood attachment patterns, separations from parents and relation-ships in later life all influence how we cope with stress and loss and predict the kinds of problems which cause people to seek help following bereavement in adult life. The account of the major findings that follows is based on Parkes's *Love and Loss* (2006).

Some overall findings

The findings confirmed Parkes's clinical impression, obtained over many years, that people who grow up in *secure* family environments with their parents experi-ence less intense distress after bereavement in adult life than those from insecure relationships. Evidence from both the psychiatric and non-psychiatric (control) samples suggested that this reflects a more positive view of self and others with harmonious marriages, and a greater willingness to turn to others for support at times of stress. This supports Bowlby's claim that the main function of a loving family is to provide a secure base from which children can discover their own potential and can learn that other people can be trusted to provide support and guidance when necessary. As they get older, children from such a family achieve a good degree of autonomy.

However, the study also found that the incidence of *insecure* attachment was very similar in both the psychiatric and control samples; this suggests *either* that insecure attachments played little part in causing the psychiatric problems *or* that insecurity of attachment can have mixed effects, some of which reduce the ten-dency to seek psychiatric help following bereavement, while others increase it. The insecurely attached who do well are unlikely to have been found in a sample of psychiatric patients but may well have been present in the control group. More generally, insecure attachments sometimes remain useful ways of coping with the less-than-perfect world of adult life.

Anxious-resistant/ambivalent attachments

As expected, people who experienced anxious-resistant/ambivalent attachments in childhood, and those who make dependent attachments in adult life, were both likely to suffer severe and lasting grief and loneliness following bereave-ment. What it did *not* show was that one led to the other: rather, people who develop these sorts of childhood attachments tend to have very conflict-ridden relationships in adulthood and this contributes to the lasting grief and loneliness post-bereavement. Their tendency to cling remains a problem and has important implications for those who attempt to help this group of people.

Anxious-avoidant attachments

The study identified anxious-avoidant attachment as a strategy developed in childhood as a means of coping with parents who cannot tolerate the expression of attachment needs. In time, these strategies become associated with, and can reasonably be assumed to produce, similar strategies in adulthood; they reflect attitudes and assumptions that may complicate love relationships and give cause for deep regrets.

While this pattern sometimes caused people to seek psychiatric help, it was found to be equally common among those who did not seek such help; it may enable some people to develop a type of independence and assertiveness which can be to their advantage if society values these characteristics. Major bereavements leave most of us needing the love and support of others, but those with an anxious-avoidant attachment style find it difficult to accept or seek them. It is usually safer and more rewarding to get close to the people you love than it is to maintain an unnecessarily 'safe' distance.

Disorganised attachments

These have elements of the two other insecure attachment patterns and can be seen as reflecting lack of trust in both self and others. Without effective ways of coping, people feel helpless and tend to turn in on themselves in the face of stress. Love relationships, though difficult, provide what little security these people can achieve; when these relationships are ended through bereavement, they more than others were likely to become very anxious and to panic. They may also become depressed and/or rely on alcohol to calm them down. The combination of helplessness, fear, shame, depression, and the disinhibiting effects of alcohol increase the risk that they will both punish themselves and solve their problems by suicide. It is essential for the disorganised person and for those who care for them to discover that their underlying self-doubts and distrust of others are not justified: they reflect a view of the world that is now obsolete.

Other evidence relating to attachment style differences and adjustment to loss

Shaver and Fraley (2008) cite evidence relating to how individuals with different attachment styles/patterns adjust differently to the loss of a close relationship partner. This evidence generally supports the hypothesis that attachment security contributes to emotional adjustment following a loss.

For example, van Doorn et al. (1998) interviewed adults while they were caring for their terminally ill spouses and found that attachment security in romantic relationships in general, and specific attachment security in the marriage, were both associated with less intense grief following the spouse's death. Similarly, Fraley and Bonnano (2004) found that people classified as securely attached four months after the death of a spouse reported relatively low levels of bereavement-related anxiety, grief, depression, and posttraumatic stress 4 and 18 months after the loss.

There is also evidence relating to *anxiously attached* individuals' complicated grief reactions (e.g. Field and Sundin, 2001; Fraley and Bonnano, 2004). Field and Sundin (2001) found that anxious attachment, assessed 10 months after the death of a spouse, predicted higher levels of psychological distress 14, 25, and 60 months after the loss. Research studies have generally found *no* association between *avoidant attachment* and depression, grief, or distress (e.g. Field and Sundin, 2001; Fraley and Bonnano, 2004). However, Wayment and Vierthaler (2002) did find that avoidance was associated with somatic symptoms (see Chapter 1), implying that avoidant defences might block conscious access to anxiety and depression without blocking more subtle and less conscious bodily reactions (Shaver and Fraley, 2008). These findings are consistent with those of other studies, such as that of Bonanno and Field (2001). Also, Fraley and Bonnano (2004) found that the combination of avoidance and attachment anxiety (see below) was associated with the highest levels of anxiety, depression, grief, trauma-related symptoms, and alcohol consumption following the death of a spouse.

There is also evidence concerning attachment style differences in continuing attachment to, and detachment from, a lost partner. The issue of *Continuing Bonds* is discussed in Chapter 3.

A three-phase model of adult attachment

A large body of research aimed at testing Bowlby's attachment theory indicates that individual differences in attachment style can be assessed using self-report measures of a person's location along two independent ('orthogonal') dimensions: *attachment-related anxiety* and *attachment-related avoidance* (Shaver and Fraley, 2008).

- A person's position on the avoidance dimension indicates the extent to which s/he distrusts relationship partners and strives to maintain independence and emotional distance from others.
- A person's position on the anxiety dimension indicates the extent to which s/he is dependent and often worries that a partner will not be available and supportive when needed.
- People who score *low* on *both* dimensions are described as *securely attached*.
- People who score *high* on *both* dimensions are described as *fearfully avoidant* (Bartholomew and Horowitz, 1991).

Fraley and Shaver (2000) and Mikulincer and Shaver (2007) proposed a three-phase model of attachment system activation and dynamics in adulthood.

Phase I

Following Bowlby (1969), these researchers assumed that relatively continuous monitoring of internal and external events (e.g. thoughts, worries, external stressors) leads to activation of the attachment system (AS) when a potential threat is detected. Once this has occurred, if the answer to the question 'Is an attachment figure available and likely to be responsive to my needs?' is 'yes', then the individual will experience a sense of security. At the same time, *security-related affect regulation strategies* (SRARSs) are facilitated.

SRARSs consist of optimistic beliefs about distress management, trust in others' good will, a sense of self-efficacy about coping with threats (i.e. the belief that one is capable of coping with them), genuinely constructive coping strategies, effective support-seeking, and successful problem-solving. They are aimed at alleviating distress, maintaining comfortable and supportive relationships, and increasing effective adjustment. There is considerable evidence demonstrating SRARSs in people judged to be securely attached (Mikulincer and Shaver, 2007).

Phase 2

Perceived unavailability or unresponsiveness of an attachment figure arouses feelings of insecurity, which forces a decision about seeking or not seeking proximity to an attachment figure. When proximity seeking is expected (or at least hoped) to be successful, the individual makes energetic, insistent attempts to attain proximity, protection, and support (*hyperactivating strategies*): they involve strong activation of the AS until an attachment figure is perceived as available and responsive, and include

(i)   approaching, begging, crying, clinging;
(ii) being hypervigilant concerning a partner's intentions, motives, and behaviour; and
(iii) intense distress and protest if a partner seems insensitive or unresponsive.

Phase 3

If proximity seeking is seen as unlikely to achieve safety or comfort, and perhaps even likely to elicit anger or punishment (and thereby increasing distress), then *deactivating strategies* are likely to be used: their primary goal is to keep the AS shut down. This involves denying or de-emphasising attachment needs, avoiding emotional involvement in and dependence on close relationship partners, suppressing attachment-related thoughts, and remaining autonomous (what Bowlby, 1973, called 'compulsive self-reliance').

Reorganisation of attachment working models following bereavement involves some degree of *both* hyperactivating and deactivating strategies; this is consistent with Stroebe and Schut's (1999) *Dual-Process Model* (DPM) of grief that is discussed in detail in Chapter 3. Hyperactivation forces the bereaved person to experience the pain of loss, to reactivate memories of the deceased at the same time as realisations that s/he is no longer 'here', and to yearn for the deceased's proximity and love; all this allows the mourner to explore the meaning of the loss and to find ways of reorganising symbolic bonds with the lost loved one. If this is tolerable and manageable (i.e. not overwhelming or disorganising), the bereaved person is able to incorporate the past into the present without splitting off important segments of personal history and identity. (This corresponds to the *loss orientation* of the DPM.)

Deactivating strategies can also contribute to post-loss reorganisation by enabling detachment from thoughts of the deceased loved one and inhibiting or suppressing painful thoughts and memories. While using a certain degree of 'avoidance' and denial, the bereaved person can manage the funeral, sort out (and 'get rid of') the deceased's partner's possessions (importantly, clothes), begin to explore and create a new life, return to work and daily activities, and recognise that the lost relationship continues to have meaning while life presents new opportunities. (This corresponds to the *restoration orientation* of the DPM.)

Without some degree of hyperactivation, a bereaved person could not experience and take account of all aspects of his/her new situation and find constructive ways of remembering the deceased loved one. Equally, without some degree of deactivation, the bereaved person might continue to pine, feel hopeless, and be unable to cope with new demands (i.e. s/he might suffer from chronic grief). The two processes need to act in dynamic balance – what the DPM refers to as *oscillation* between the loss and restoration orientations.

Shaver and Fraley (2008) note that there has been no longitudinal (follow-up) study on hyperactivation-deactivation oscillation and their implications for mental health and adjustment. Most of the research has focused on attachment style differences in coping with loss. However, Schut et al. (1997) found that men who habitually avoided confronting their grief benefited from counselling that encouraged them to deal with neglected aspects of their loss. Also, women who habitually dwelled on the emotional meaning and deep personal implications of the loss benefited from counselling that focused on learning how to deal with changed everyday activities. (See Chapter 3.)

Summary and conclusions

- Love and loss are two sides of a coin.
- Researchers tend to use 'attachment' when describing both a child's love for its parents and adult romantic partners' mutual love.
- Bowlby's attachment theory was influenced by ethologists, in particular Lorenz's study of imprinting in goslings, and Harlow's studies of separated rhesus monkey infants.
- Newborn human infants are genetically programmed to behave towards the mother in ways that ensure their survival, namely, sucking, cuddling, looking,

smiling, and crying. They also possess a motivational system (the *attachment system*) that helps provide them with a sense of security.

- Mothers are also programmed to respond to these infant species-specific behaviours.
- These attachment behaviours are most evident when the child is distressed, such as when separated from the attachment figure. Distress comprises protest, despair, and detachment.
- Protest helped infants close to their caregivers in the *environment of evolutionary adaptiveness*.
- Infants' distress response is mirrored in adult grief reactions, especially when the deceased is a spouse. But Bowlby replaced 'detachment' with 'reorganisation' in his stage/phase account of adult grief: he recognised that a *continuing bond* with the deceased is possible alongside adjustment to life without him/her.
- Research evidence suggests that many non-human species (including dolphins, elephants, great apes) display grief. In the evolution of *Homo sapiens*, grief increasingly became expressed through symbolic rituals.
- Based on her Uganda study, Ainsworth used the *Strange Situation Test* (SST) to study attachment among one-year-olds. This yielded three major *attachment styles: secure, anxious-avoidant*, and *anxious-resistant/ambivalent*. Main later identified a fourth category, *insecure – disorganised*. These infant attachment styles are related to the degree of maternal sensitivity and responsiveness to the infant's needs for security and a safe base.
- The child's attachment styles may change if family circumstances change, and they reflect qualities of distinct relationships with different attachment figures.
- Hazan and Shaver were the first to apply Ainsworth's attachment styles to adult romantic relationships, finding similar distributions as with infants.
- The *adult attachment interview* (AAI) is the most commonly used measure of adult attachment to their own parents and is based on how we *construe* our childhood experiences. The resulting styles are autonomous/secure, insecure/dismissing, insecure preoccupied/entangled, and unresolved/disorganised. These are correlated with – and predict – their child's attachment style towards themselves.
- At the core of attachment styles are the individual's *inner working models* (IWMs). These act both as a source of continuity/stability and are subject to change.
- Love evolved to ensure that couples stayed together long enough to raise their children to adulthood. Bowlby identified attachment, caregiving, and sex as three behavioural systems that help maintain male-female pair-bonds.
- Several studies have shown that the nature of the attachment to the deceased is a major determinant of problematic responses to bereavement. For example, a *dependent* relationship predicts *chronic grief*, while an *anxious-resistant/ambivalent* attachment predicts *conflicted grief*.

- The evidence largely supports the hypothesis that attachment security contributes to emotional adjustment following a bereavement.
- According to the three-phase model, reorganisation of attachment IWMs following bereavement involves some degree of both *hyperactivating* and *deactivating* strategies; these correspond to the Dual-Process Model's *loss orientation* and *restoration orientation*, respectively.

Chapter 3

Theories and models of grief

The chapter will address the following questions:

- Do bereaved people inevitably go through the stages of grief as described by Bowlby, Bowlby and Parkes, and Kübler-Ross?
- What are the major features of Freud's account of grief in *Mourning and Melancholia*?
- How did Freud's theory contribute to the concept of 'grief work'? And what is meant by the term?
- What are the main features of Lindemann's account of acute grief?
- What criticism have been made of the grief work hypothesis (GWH)?
- What are the main features of Worden's Four Tasks of Mourning?
- What are the main features of Rando's Six 'Rs' Processes of Mourning?
- What are the main features of Parkes's psychosocial transition theory (PTT)?
- What are the major features of Stroebe and Schut's Dual-Process Model (DPM) of coping with bereavement?
- How does the DPM address the limitations of the GWH and how does it relate to other theories/models (such as attachment theory)?
- How does the DPM help to explain complicated grief?
- How are Rubin's Two-Track Model (TTM) and the DPM related?
- What are the major features of Klass et al.'s Continuing Bonds (CB) approach and how does it relate to other theories/models?

In Chapter 1, we considered two stage (or phase) accounts of grief, namely, those of Bowlby (1980; Bowlby and Parkes, 1970) and Kübler-Ross (1969). We noted that these accounts have become familiar to the layperson, who is likely to understand them as *prescriptions* for grieving, that is a statement of the course of healthy grieving. In technical terms, they provide *normative* accounts of the grieving process (strictly, in Kübler-Ross's case, of the process of dying), that is, they describe how people typically grieve *and* how we *should* grieve.

However, we also noted that Bowlby himself stated quite clearly that his stages are *not* meant to describe a *linear* sequence; in other words, not everyone goes through these stages in the order described, and people may move back and forth for a time between any two of them. However, he did believe that 'a sequence can be discerned'. This suggests that there is a certain 'logic' to the sequence, which is perhaps what the layperson can relate to his/her own and others' experience.

Interestingly, Kübler-Ross has also acknowledged that there is no inevitability or necessity about her stages:

> The stages have evolved since their introduction, and they have been very misunderstood over the past three decades They are responses to loss that many people have, but there is not a typical response to loss, as there is no typical loss. Our grief is as individual as our lives.
>
> The five stages are tools to help us frame and identify what we may be feeling. But they are not stops on some linear timeline in grief. Not everyone goes through all of them or goes in a prescribed order.
>
> (Kübler-Ross and Kessler, 2005, p. 7)

While these stage accounts are sometimes referred to as 'theories', 'theory' usually implies an attempt to *explain* the phenomenon in question; however, these stage accounts are primarily *descriptive*: they tell us what grief is *like* but not what its *function* or *purpose* may be. True theories (or models) of grief go beyond description and propose what grief is *for*. (Theories are much more complex – and broader – explanations than models, as illustrated by attachment theory (see Chapter 2); this goes far beyond an account of grief, while the extremely influential *Dual-Process Model* (Stroebe and Schut, 1999, 2010) is concerned exclusively with grief.)

Freud's grief theory: mourning as detachment

Sigmund Freud was one of the first to formally address the nature of grief – and its function – in *Mourning and Melancholia* (1917). By 'melancholia' Freud meant what we would now call clinical (major) depression, a deviant, complicated, and unhealthy form of mourning (or grieving). Normal (or uncomplicated) mourning involves a healthy, non-pathological response to the loss of a loved person (or object – physical or symbolic). Because the bereaved person has invested a great deal of psychic or psychological energy (*libido*) in the person or object, its loss inevitably involves pain.

For Freud, mourning represents the work involved in uncoupling or achieving detachment (or emancipation) from the lost person/object; this reflects both a desire to hold onto the lost object *and* a growing recognition that it is no longer available. This work is complex and can take considerable time and effort. The goal is to withdraw libido from the lost object, thereby freeing the ego (the conscious, decision-making part of the personality) for new and healthy attachments. This is the *work* of grief – or *grief work*. In *Totem and Taboo* (1912–1913/1961, p. 65), Freud wrote: 'Mourning has a quite precise psychical task to perform: its function is to detach the survivor's memories and hopes from the dead'.

Grief work

As with the notion of stages of grief (see above), the notion that one 'has to do one's grief work' is well-known in popular as well as scientific literature on bereavement (Stroebe and Schut, 1999). However, Stroebe and Schut also point out that many modern researchers have questioned the 'wisdom' of this widely-held belief. For example, they quote Wortman and Silver, who state that:

> Those who show the most evidence of working through the loss are those who ultimately have the most difficulty in resolving what has happened.
> (Wortman and Silver, 1987, p. 207)

The concept of grief work refers to the cognitive processes of confronting the reality of a loss through death, of going over events that occurred before and at the time of death, and of focusing on memories and working toward detachment from (or relocating) the deceased. The bereaved person needs to bring the reality of the loss into awareness as much as possible; suppressing this reality is pathological (Stroebe, 1992). From this definition, the *grief work hypothesis* (GWH) can be derived, i.e. the notion that one has to confront the experience of bereavement in order to come to terms with loss and avoid detrimental health consequences (Stroebe, 1992).

Both Bowlby (1980: see Chapters 1 and 2) and Lindemann (1944) incorporated the concept of grief work into their own explanations of the grieving process. Lindemann's account is summarised in Box 3.1. Also, the Task Model (Worden, 1982, 1991, 2002, 2009) provides guidelines to understanding what needs to be done for successful outcomes to occur following bereavement (see below).

Box 3.1 Lindemann and acute grief

- Lindemann (1944) described typical characteristics of acute grief, including somatic distress, preoccupation with the image of the deceased, guilt, hostility, and alterations in usual behaviour patterns.
- Many bereaved individuals also adopt traits that were possessed by the deceased, displaying them in their behaviour.
- In keeping with Freud's account, Lindemann saw grief work as involving efforts to emancipate oneself from bondage to the deceased, readjust to an environment in which the deceased is missing, and form new relationships.
- Individuals who try to avoid the intense distress involved in the experience of grief may only inhibit and complicate their grief work.
- Delaying or distorting grief reactions lead to morbid or unhealthy forms of grief.

Lindemann described difficulties in post-loss adjustment, and proposed that short-term interventions of 8–10 sessions could be sufficient during the initial acute grief period (which lasts for four to six weeks) (Rubin et al., 2012).

According to Bowlby, working through grief is important for the purpose of rearranging representations of the lost person and the self. Although this enables 'detachment' (the term he used in describing young children's separation distress: 1973) or 'reorganisation' (the last of his four phases of adult grief: 1980), or the breaking of affectional bonds (Bowlby, 1979), at the same time it also strengthens the continuation of the bond (a relocation of the deceased so that adjustment to his/her physical absence can gradually be made).

An evaluation of the GWH

As Stroebe and Schut (1999) say, it's not surprising that the notion of grief work has been such an influence both theoretically and in the applied field, even to the extent that it has become a 'blueprint' for coping with grief. It seems intuitively true that we must 'give sorrow words' (Shakespeare; see Chapter 1 for full discussion of quote); expressing grief (in any form, but especially in words – spoken or written) is essential. It is difficult to deny that the GWH has dominated much of our thinking about bereavement.

Rosenblatt (1983) analysed 19th-century descriptions of how people dealt with grief in order to evaluate contemporary scientific research on coping, and, in particular, to assess the validity of the GWH. Although the emotional experience appeared to be similar in both centuries, people in the 19th century did not struggle to detach themselves, their memories, and hopes, from the deceased.

As we noted in the quote above, Wortman and Silver (1987) argued that working through was not only *not* associated with recovery, but even detrimental to it. Worden (1991) helped to redefine the principles of grief intervention by reformulating the grieving process in terms of distinct *tasks* that the bereaved have to undertake (see below).

Stroebe (1992) identified four major shortcomings associated with the GWH:

- the lack of clarity in the definition of grief work (e.g. the confounding of negative associated *rumination* and more positively associated aspects of working through);
- the poor quality of operationalisations in empirical studies (i.e. how grief work has been defined in a way that allows it to be measured) (e.g. yearning and pining);
- the absence of sound evidence in support of grief work (some studies failed to confirm that confronting grief predicts adaptation); this was later confirmed by Stroebe et al. (2005);
- lack of apparent application across cultures (i.e. it isn't a *universal* feature of human grief: see Chapter 5). Not only are the types of confrontation specified by the GWH not universal, but non-confrontation is *not* systematically linked with mal-adaptation (Stroebe and Schut, 2010).

Having stated that grief work was a fundamental notion underlying the development of stage/phase models, Stroebe and Schut (2010) claim that the process itself, as these models describe it, seems rather *passive*: the person appears to be 'put through' the stages, neglecting the active, effortful struggle which is so much part of grieving.

They also don't allow for any respite: grief is arduous and exhausting, and a 'break' can be recuperative. Also, the GWH focuses exclusively on the *primary loss* (see Chapter 1), namely, the deceased person, thus neglecting the many *secondary losses* which, collectively (if not individually) can demand as much, if not greater, adjustment.

Worden: The tasks of mourning

Worden (1982, 1991, 2002, 2009) recommended that we think of mourning as an active process involving four tasks (see Box 3.2). Although the tasks don't necessarily follow a specific order, the names of the tasks *imply* a sequence. For example, you cannot handle the emotional impact of a loss until you have first come to terms with the fact that the loss has happened. Since mourning is a *process* rather than a state, the tasks require effort ('grief work'). Also, Worden argues that it is possible for someone to finish *some* of the tasks; this would make his/her bereavement (i.e. grief work) *incomplete*.

Box 3.2 Worden's Tasks of Mourning

Task 1: To accept the reality of the loss (Worden, 1982, p. 11): This involves overcoming disbelief and denial of death by acknowledging and accepting the reality of the death. The searching behaviour as described extensively by Bowlby and Parkes is directly related to this task. Denial can occur on several levels and take various forms, but it most often involves either the details of the loss, the meaning of the loss, or the irreversibility of the loss. One example of denial is *mummification* (Gorer, 1965), in which the bereaved person keeps the deceased's possessions in a mummified condition ready for use when s/he returns. This often takes the form of keeping the loved one's room exactly as it was before the death – especially if a young child or teenager is involved.

Task 2: To experience the pain of grief (Worden, 1982, p. 13; 'To process the pain of grief' (Worden, 2009)) Productive mourning acknowledges that it is appropriate to experience pain during bereavement, provided the pain that is experienced doesn't overwhelm the bereaved individual. The pain is both literal

(Continued)

Box 3.2 Continued

(i.e. physical) and emotional, and spiritual (see Chapter 1). It is necessary to acknowledge and work through this pain or it will manifest itself through some symptom or other form of aberrant behaviour. Not everyone experiences the same intensity of pain or feels it in the same way, but it is impossible to lose someone we have been deeply attached to without experiencing some degree of pain.

Task 3: To adjust to an environment in which the deceased is missing (Worden, 1982, p. 14; 'To adjust to a world without the deceased (Worden, 2009)): In pursuing this task, bereaved individuals engage in a voyage of discovery to determine the significance of the now-severed relationship, to identify each of the various roles the deceased played in the relationship, to adjust to the fact that the deceased is no longer available to fill those roles, and often to develop new skills to fulfil the deceased's former roles (Corr and Corr, 2013). The bereaved person is usually not aware of all the roles played by the deceased until after his/her death.

Task 4: To withdraw emotional energy and reinvest in another relationship (Worden, 1982, p. 15; 'To emotionally relocate the deceased and move on with life' (Worden, 1991, p. 16; 2002, p. 35); 'To find an enduring connection with the deceased in the midst of embarking on a new life' (Worden, 2009, p. 50)): The main point is to encourage bereaved people to modify or restructure their relationship with the deceased in ways that remain satisfying but that also reflect the changed circumstances of life following a bereavement. This task requires bereaved individuals to re-think their personal identity, restructure their relationship with the deceased in the light of the loss, avoid becoming neurotically burdened by the past in ways that diminish future quality of life, and remain open to new attachments and other relationships (Corr and Corr, 2013).

Worden believes that many people – especially bereaved spouses – find this task the most difficult of the four tasks. They think that if they withdraw their emotional attachment, they are somehow dishonouring the memory of the deceased. They may get stuck at this point in their grieving.

According to Corr and Corr (2013), Worden's tasks reflect an interpretation of mourning as, in principle, a proactive way of striving to manage one's loss and grief, a means of enabling the bereaved person to regain some degree of control over his/her life.

Rando's six 'Rs' processes of mourning

In Chapter 1, we described Rando's (1993) six 'Rs': (i) **R**ecognising the loss; (ii) **R**eacting to the separation; (iii) **R**ecollecting and re-experiencing the deceased and the relationship; (iv) **R**elinquishing the bold attachments to the deceased and the old assumptive world; (v) **R**eadjusting to move adaptively into the new world without forgetting the old; and (vi) **R**einvesting in new relationships.

Bereaved people need to acknowledge and gain insight into their losses, experience and express their reactions to those losses, connect with and restructure their former attachments, and find ways to move forward in new modes of living. Rando also drew attention to the many secondary losses that are always associated with the primary loss (see Chapter 1). Reference to the assumptive world (in (iv) above) relates to Parkes's *psychosocial transition theory* which we discuss below.

Rando maintained that these six 'R' processes must be undertaken for healthy mourning; they are interrelated and tend to build upon one another, although a number of them may occur simultaneously. While the list of 'Rs' is intended to describe a 'typical' order, the sequence is *not* invariant:

> Mourners may move back and forth among the processes, with such movement illustrating the nonlinear and fluctuating course of mourning.
>
> (Rando, 1993, p. 44)

Parkes's psychosocial transition theory: Grief as adapting to change

According to Parkes:

> Grief is essentially an emotion that draws us toward something or someone that is missing. It arises from awareness of a discrepancy between the world that is and the world that 'should be'.
>
> (Parkes, 1993, p. 92)

The world that should be is an internal construct, which means that each person's experience of grief is individual and unique.

Psychosocial transitions

Studies of the life events that commonly precede the onset of mental illness suggest that the most dangerous life-change events are those that:

- require people to undertake a major revision of their assumptions about the world (their *assumptive world*: Parkes, 1971);
- are lasting in their implications rather than transient; and
- take place over a relatively short period of time, such that there is little opportunity for preparation.

These criteria are the defining features of *psychosocial transitions* (PTs). The internal world that must change as a result of a PT is the assumptive world:

everything we assume to be true based on our previous experience, every-thing we take for granted about the world, which includes ourselves and other people.

> The death of a spouse invalidates assumptions that penetrate many aspects of life, from the moment of rising to going to sleep in an empty bed. Habits of action and thought must be revised if the survivor is to live as a widow.
>
> (Parkes, 1993, p. 94)

Like all habits, these habits of action and thought have become *automatic*; this makes change very difficult. Parkes gives the examples of the leg amputee who 'forgets' that s/he no longer has two legs and collapses onto the floor when getting out of bed. Grief following bereavement is aggravated if the deceased is the person one would normally turn to in times of trouble: faced with the worst imaginable situation, we may repeatedly find ourselves turning toward a person who is not there. [I have often observed bereaved people wanting to share their grief with the deceased more than anyone else!]

These examples help to explain why PTs are so painful and take so much time and energy. The familiar world suddenly seems to have become unfamiliar and we lose confidence in our own internal world. In many ways, every PT is a 'job of work' that must be done if we are to adapt to the requirements of the real world. However, the mind that is carrying out the revision is also the object that is being revised:

> A person is literally lost in his or her own grief, and the more disorganised one's thinking the more difficult it is to step aside from the disorganisation and to see clearly what is lost and what remains.
>
> (Parkes, 1993, p. 95)

Since we rely on having an accurate assumptive world to keep us safe, people who have lost confidence in their model of the world feel very unsafe; anxiety and fear cloud our judgement and impair concentration and memory.

Almost by definition, PTs involve a large number of simultaneous dysfunc-tions in several areas of functioning (what we've previously called *secondary losses*). Thus, the loss of a spouse may produce any or all of the following losses: sexual partner, protection from danger, reassurance of worth, job, com-panionship, income, recreational partner, status, expectations, self-confidence, home, and parent for one's children. On the 'gains' side, it may also produce relief from responsibilities, entitlement to care and sympathy of others, and an increase and freedom to realise potentialities that have been inhibited. (See Figure 3.1.)

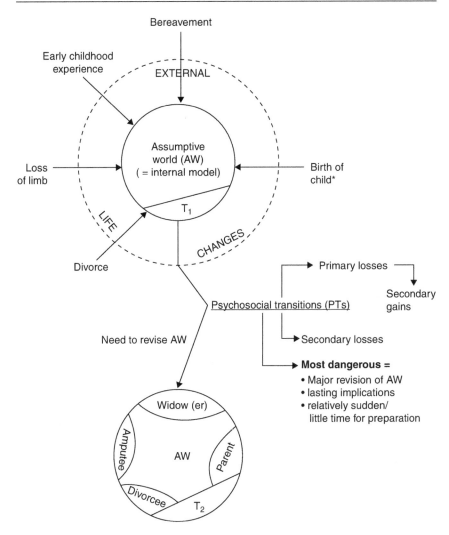

* Even happy/positive events can have negative consequences,
   requiring a revision of one's assumptive world

Figure 3.1 Psychosocial transition theory based on (Parkes, 1993)

Psychosocial transition theory and trauma

According to Parkes (2006):

> Much of the work of relearning which follows a major loss and which, in
> the past, has been termed 'grief work', is better seen as part of the work of

transition. The issues involved are particularly clear and relevant following traumatic life events.

(p. 32)

Most studies of the psychological consequences of bereavement have shown that deaths that are (i) sudden; (ii) unexpected; and (iii) untimely are more likely to create problems than those that have been anticipated and prepared for. Other factors that contribute to bereavement risk (i.e. complicated grief) include witnessing violence or mutilation, deaths for which someone is to blame (including murders and suicides), and those in which no intact body is recovered. These are all examples of *traumatic losses* (see Chapter 7).

The Harvard study (Parkes and Weiss, 1983: see Chapter 1) found that unexpected and untimely bereavements in young widows and widowers were associated, in the short term, with greater disbelief and avoidance of confrontation with the loss. Over time, there was a persisting sense of the presence of the deceased spouse, a feeling of continued obligation to them and social withdrawal along with constant anxiety, depression, loneliness, and, often, self-reproach. All of these were less common in those who had anticipated their loss.

Horowitz (1986) suggests that numbing, disbelief, and failure to integrate a traumatic death into the bereaved person's assumptive world are defences against overwhelming feelings of helplessness and insecurity which threaten to erupt (see Chapter 2). Despite these attempts at avoidance, traumatised individuals commonly experience intense anxiety, hypervigilance, and startle reactions, which can be triggered by any reminder of the loss. The 'Impact of Events' scale (Horowitz et al., 1979) was designed to measure these twin aspects of avoidance and intrusive recall. This relates to the more general research into 'traumatic stress' and, more specifically, post-traumatic stress disorder (PTSD) (Parkes, 2006: see Chapter 7).

Parkes (2006) asks if attachment theory and psycho-social transition theory can be integrated.

If attachment theory explains the urge to cry and to search for someone who is lost and psycho-social transition theory explains the need to rethink and replan one's life in the face of a major change, how are these two alternatives worked out in the moment-to-moment life of bereaved people?

(Parkes, 2006, p. 34)

The answer, he states, is to be found in Stroebe and Schut's *Dual-Process Model*, to which we now turn.

Dual-Process Model: Oscillation between loss and restoration

Stroebe and Schut's (1999, 2010) Dual-Process Model (DPM) of Coping with Bereavement grew out of the growing concern among bereavement theorists, during the 1990s in particular, about the adequacy of the GWH as an explanation of effective coping. In addition to the criticisms that we considered above, Stroebe and Schut (1999) identify two further concerns: (i) whether the observed phenomena of grieving are adequately represented in the GWH; and (ii) its lack of general application.

Limitations of the GWH

Inadequate representation of bereavement-related phenomena

The GWH focuses on the need to *confront* the primary loss, while paying little attention to both the tendency to *avoid* this and all the associated secondary losses (or *stressors*, as Stroebe and Schut call them). Also, while the GWH presents grief work as a purely internal, *intrapersonal* process (i.e. going on within the head of the bereaved person), Stroebe and Schut argue that the dynamic process of coming to terms with a death does *not* take place in isolation. The bereaved person is surrounded by others, some of whom are themselves grieving; hence, grieving takes place at both the intrapersonal and *interpersonal* levels. They give the example of discrepancy between how a bereaved mother and father express their distress: this can be interpreted in terms of greater or lesser grieving by each partner and may affect their relationship, well-being, and how they cope together and apart.

They also argue that a grief work framework creates a biased focus on health outcome factors (what they call a 'medical model' focus); this runs the risk of presenting grief as essentially involving psychological and medical *problems* (something needs 'curing', 'fixing', or 'overcoming') and so neglects well-being and adjustment as outcome variables. There is the implicit assumption that, following the death of a loved one, one must return to a positive state of mind and well-being as quickly as possible. In turn, this implies that human suffering is bad and that the human condition should only, ideally, involve positive states and emotions, a far from universal view (see Chapter 5).

Alternatives to this medical approach include 'positive growth' outcomes (Tedeschi and Calhoun, 1995: see Chapter 8), creation of a durable narrative about the deceased and reconstruction of the meaning of the deceased in ongoing life (Walter, 1997: see discussion of Continuing Bonds and Meaning Reconstruction below, and emergence of different roles and identities such as reassignment of the roles of the deceased to other family members).

Lack of universal application

Stroebe and Schut (1999) also question the GWH's relevance to (i) *gender* and (ii) *cultural patterns*.

Regarding (i), Stroebe (1998) noted that the GWH does not take sufficient account of preferred masculine ways of going about grieving; these are typically less overtly expressive of distress and depression compared with female responses.

In Chapter 1, we referred to typical male and female styles of grieving as *instrumental* and *intuitive*, respectively (Doka and Martin, 2010); as these researchers argue, while gender *influences* grieving style, it does not *determine* it (otherwise there'd be no exceptions to the gender 'rule').

Also, the GWH was based on the study of largely female samples; this implies that the GWH is a 'female model of grieving' and so begs the question as to whether or not it is valid to apply it to male grievers.

Regarding (ii), Stroebe and Schut (1999) claim that the GWH is *culture-bound*, at least with respect to the overt level of grief. Different views regarding acceptable or 'healthy' ways of coping can be found in non-Western cultures (Stroebe and Schut, 1998; Stroebe and Stroebe, 1987). Some cultures show little or no evidence of 'working through' patterns: this apparently would be considered detrimental to the health of the bereaved and those around them (e.g. among the Muslim community in Bali: Wikan, 1990). (Cultural differences are discussed in greater detail in Chapter 5.)

Rationale for development of the DPM

The DPM was intended to provide a model of *coping* with loss, as opposed to a generic model aimed at explaining the broad range of phenomena and manifestations associated with bereavement. It was also aimed at better understanding individual differences in how people come to terms with this most stressful of life events:

> Coping refers to processes, strategies, or styles of managing (reducing, mastering, tolerating) the situation in which bereavement places the individual. Coping is assumed to impact on adaptation to bereavement.
>
> (Stroebe and Schut, 2010, p. 274)

The DPM makes a fundamental distinction between coping as a *process* and the *consequences* of bereavement (an *outcome variable*).

The main components of the DPM

Stroebe and Schut refer to the DPM as a taxonomy for describing how people come to terms with the loss of a loved one. While originally developed as relevant to the death of a partner, it is potentially applicable to other types of bereavement.

The DPM owes much to *Cognitive Stress Theory* (CST) (Lazarus and Folkman, 1984; Folkman, 2001), especially its definition of a number of factors related to coping: *stressors* (the nature of the events that cause stress); *appraisal processes* (how potential stressors are assessed); *coping processes* (ways of dealing with the threat posed by stressors); and *outcome variables* (such as mental and physical health measures).

A fundamental contrast with earlier models is that the DPM distinguishes between two categories of stressors associated with bereavement, namely, those that are *loss-oriented* versus *restoration-oriented* (see Box 3.3).

Box 3.3   Loss-orientation *versus* restoration-orientation

- *Loss-orientation* refers to the bereaved person's concentration on, appraisal of, and processing of some aspect of the loss experience itself (i.e. the *primary* stressor) and, as such, incorporates grief work. It involves a painful yearning for, even searching for, the lost person, a phenomenon that lies at the heart of grieving. Other features include rumination about the life shared with the deceased, and the circumstances and events surrounding the death. A range of emotional reactions are involved, from pleasurable reminiscing to painful longing, from happiness that the deceased is no longer suffering to despair that one is left alone.

- *Restoration-orientation* refers to the focus on *secondary* stressors that are also consequences of the bereavement, reflecting a struggle to reorient oneself in a changed world without the deceased person. Rethinking and replanning one's life in the face of bereavement can also be regarded as an essential feature of grieving (see Parkes's *psychosocial transition theory* above). The focus is on *what* needs to be dealt with (e.g. social isolation) and *how* it is dealt with (e.g. by joining social organisations), rather than the *result* of this process (e.g. restored well-being and social integration). As with the loss orientation, a wide range of emotions can be involved, from relief and pride at mastering a new skill or taking the courage to go out alone, to fear and anxiety that one will not succeed or despair at the loneliness of being with others and yet being 'single'.

Oscillation

Both orientations are sources of stress and can be associated with outcomes such as distress and anxiety; both are also involved in the coping process, as in being attended to (confronted versus avoided) in varying degrees (according to individual and cultural differences). The process of attending to or avoiding these two types of stressors is dynamic and fluctuating, and it also changes over time.

In the DPM, this dynamic coping process is called *oscillation*. The principle underlying oscillation is that at times the bereaved person will confront aspects of loss, and at other times avoid them; the same applies to restoration tasks. Also, there will sometimes be 'time out', when the person is not grieving at all.

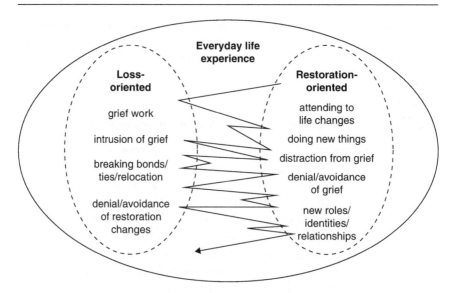

Figure 3.2 A Dual-Process Model of coping with bereavement

Stroebe, M. and Schut, H., (1999) A Dual-Process Model of coping with bereavement: Rationale and description, *Death Studies, 23*, 3. Taylor & Francis reprinted by permission of the publisher (Taylor & Francis Ltd, http://www.tandfonline.com/).

Therefore, coping with bereavement is a complex regulatory process of confrontation and avoidance, and oscillation between the two types of stressors is necessary for adaptive coping. (See Figure 3.2.)

The original version of the DPM (Stroebe and Schut, 1999) was extended (Stroebe and Schut, 2001) to include further analysis of types of cognitive processing. *Oscillation between positive and negative affect(re)appraisal* is now seen as integral to the coping process, and to be a component of both loss- and restoration-oriented coping. Persistent negative affect (related to grief work) increases grief, while positive reappraisals enhance the coping process. However, if positive states are maintained to the exclusion of negative ones, grieving is neglected.

Clearly, the DPM is not a stage or phase account of grief; rather, it sees grief as waxing and waning, an ongoing flexibility, over time. Early on in bereavement, the loss orientation dominates; later, attention turns increasingly to secondary losses and restoration. For example, early on there's generally relatively little attention given to forming a new identity and far more to going over the circumstances of the death; over time, a gradual reversal in attention to these different concerns is likely to occur. Also, over time, the total amount of time spent on coping with loss and restoration tasks will decrease (Stroebe and Schut, 2008, 2010).

Evaluation of the DPM

As Corr and Corr (2013) make clear, 'restoration' is *not* about trying to make real once again the bereaved person's former world of lived experiences (which no longer exists) or the old assumptive world (which has also been shattered or at least rudely shaken by the loss). Rather, it has to do with effort to adapt to the new world in which bereaved individuals find themselves. What is restored, therefore, is not a past mode of living, but the ability to live productively in the present and future.

Unlike the models that preceded it, the DPM was originally formulated to address, specifically, coping with loss of a spouse; more recently, it has come to be applied to *all* types of bereavement, including loss of a child (Wijngaards et al., 2008), and to bereavement specifically among the elderly (Hansson and Stroebe, 2007). Stroebe et al. (2002) have also suggested an application of the DPM to *homesickness*, which can be thought of as a 'mini-grief' experience (Stroebe and Schut, 2010).

DPM and Worden's Task Model

Worden (2009) argued that there is little difference between his Task Model and the DPM, claiming that the tasks are almost identical to the DPM's stressors. As we saw above (see Box 3.2), Worden has changed the names of his tasks in successive editions of his book (between 1982 and 2009) and are now more explicitly inclusive of restoration stressors. While the two accounts have grown more similar over the years, Stroebe and Schut (2010) believe that their explicit distinction between loss- and restoration-stressors is unique, reflecting the reality of bereaved people's experience, and useful for both clinical application and research.

DPM and complicated grief

Stroebe and Schut (1999, 2010) argue that the model provides a framework for understanding complicated or pathological forms of grief (such as *chronic, absent* or inhibited (cf. Lindemann, 1944: see Box 3.1; Parkes, 1996; Parkes and Weiss, 1983). In earlier models, these forms of grief were not nearly so differentiated or explicit, with chronic grievers focusing on loss, absent grievers on restoration-oriented activities; those who suffer a complicated form of traumatic bereavement might be expected to have trouble alternating smoothly between the two orientations, and manifesting extreme symptoms of intrusion and avoidance. However, in both loss-oriented (e.g. chronic) and restoration-oriented (e.g. absent) types of complicated grief, *reactions are extreme*, focusing excessively on one orientation and avoiding the other. Stroebe and Schut (2010) point out that these patterns are *very different* from the confrontation-avoidance oscillation that the DPM sees as characteristic of 'normal' coping with bereavement. As they put it:

In general, there are substantial individual differences in the extent to which (normally) bereaved persons focus on loss- or restoration-orientation: only in extreme cases of confrontation with one, and avoidance of the other are complications in grieving and poor adaptation likely to occur.

(Stroebe and Schut, 2010, p. 282)

Such pathological forms of grieving can be regarded as disturbances of oscillation (Stroebe and Schut, 1999).

DPM, complicated grief, and attachment theory

The relationship between complicated grief and patterns of attachment have recently been discussed within the context of DPM (e.g. Mikulincer and Shaver. 2008; Parkes, 2006; Stroebe et al., 2005). For example, the DPM predicts that the extent to which bereaved individuals will engage in either loss-oriented or restoration-oriented processes depends on various factors, in particular their attachment styles (see Chapter 2):

*   *Securely-attached* individuals are expected to be able to access their attachment-related emotional memories without difficulty and to be able to discuss them coherently, thus presenting normal grief reactions. They would be expected to display healthy oscillation between loss- and restoration-related activities.
*   *Anxious-avoidant* individuals would suppress and avoid attachment-related emotions and present absent or inhibited grief reactions, behaving as if nothing had happened and focusing on restoration-related activities. The bond with the deceased would be too loose (Zech and Arnold, 2011). (It has also been pointed out by several writers – e.g. Zech and Arnold, 2011 – that absent grief doesn't always or necessarily indicate pathological processes: it might actually indicate that the attachment with the deceased wasn't sufficiently strong to produce grief, or that s/he is no longer grieving.)
*   *Anxious-ambivalent* individuals are expected to be highly emotional, clinging to ties with the deceased; they would focus on the loss-orientation to the exclusion of restoration-related activities (i.e. chronic grief). The bond with the deceased would be too strong (Zech and Arnold, 2011).
*   *Disorganised* individuals would be unable to think and talk coherently about attachment-related memories and would show *traumatic grief* reactions (Stroebe et al., 2005).

Borrowing from the trauma literature, it is possible to regard anxiously-attached individuals as *hyperaroused* (i.e. experiencing emotional 'overwhelm', panic, impulsivity, and anger) and avoidantly-attached individuals as *hypoaroused* (i.e. numb, disconnected, and shut down) (Ogden et al., 2006). This would subsequently impact on bereavement outcomes, specifically, the ability to meet the challenges in an integrated way (i.e. oscillating between loss- and restoration-orientations).

Consistent with the DPM, Stroebe et al. (2005) have proposed that anxious-avoidant and anxious-ambivalent bereaved individuals should be guided to oscillate between loss- and restoration-oriented strategies. Indeed, anxiously attached people could benefit from loosening their ties to the deceased, whereas avoidant individuals could benefit from doing more loss-oriented tasks (such as going over memories of the deceased).

In a review of the efficacy of the therapeutic relationship, it has been suggested that anxiously-attached people may require more supportive and containing interventions that help them to control overwhelming emotions; avoidantly-attached individuals may require interventions that facilitate emotional expression and connection (Meyer and Pilkonis, 2002). This suggests that oscillations in coping need to be reinstated and that interventions that complement or counterbalance clients' natural ineffective coping strategies will be necessary if they are to be helped (Zach and Arnold, 2011).

In an examination of the therapeutic implications of attachment theory, Bowlby (1988) proposed that therapeutic change would require the revision of the client's insecure inner working models into more secure models. The therapist should work to become a safe haven and secure base from which clients could then explore their inner world, including painful memories and emotions, destructive defences, and maladaptive behaviours. Thus, the therapist-client relationship should be structured so that the therapist is consistent, reliable, and emotionally available. In the case of grief therapy with insecurely-attached bereaved clients, the quality of the therapeutic relationship may be crucial.

DPM and gender differences

Stroebe and Schut (1999) say that the DPM accommodates male and female differences in ways of grieving better than earlier models. Stroebe et al. (2001) explored gender differences in coping with bereavement in relation to health outcomes. Women appear to be more loss-oriented, feeling and expressing their distress (i.e. they focus more on the *primary* loss), while men are more restoration-oriented, actively engaging with the problems and practical issues associated with loss (the *secondary* losses) (Wijngaards et al., 2008). These tendencies may generally work well, unless one or other orientation is adhered to the exclusion of the other – i.e. there's a lack of oscillation (Stroebe and Schut, 2010).

In terms of Doka and Martin's (2010) distinction between *intuitive* and *instrumental* grief (see Chapter 1), women are more likely to be intuitive grievers; this fits very neatly with the DPM's description of them as more loss-oriented. Similarly, men are more likely to be instrumental grievers, consistent with their tendency to be more restoration-oriented (see Figure 3.3). Stroebe and Schut (2010) give the example of a heterosexual couple who lose a child: the more loss-oriented mother may perceive the more restoration-oriented father to be 'grieving less than I am', rather than simply grieving *differently*. Making the attribution that she does could impact negatively on the couple's adjustment to the child's death. Wijngaards et al. (2008) used the DPM framework to examine the relationship between a bereaved parent's own and their partner's way of coping with the death of their child: men whose wives were, like themselves, high in restoration-oriented coping, displayed positive adjustment. This demonstrated the role of *interpersonal factors* in coping and adjustment.

DPM and cultural differences

According to Stroebe and Schut (2010), cultural differences in the norms governing the manifestations and expressions of grief can be understood in terms of loss- versus restoration-oriented coping. For example, Wikan (e.g. 1988) reported that the Muslim community on the island of Bali would be described as restoration-oriented, showing little or no overt signs of grief and continuing daily life as though nothing untoward had happened. By contrast, Muslim people in Egypt express their grief openly, gathering together to reminisce and share anguish over their loss. Other vivid examples of such cultural differences compatible with the DPM can be found in Rosenblatt (2008a: see Chapter 5).

The Two-Track Model: Biopsychosocial functioning and continuing relationship with the deceased

The Two-Track Model (TTM) of Bereavement was originally proposed by Rubin in the late 1970s and early 1980s (e.g. Rubin, 1981). It combined the insights of Freudian-inspired grief work theories and the more empirically-oriented approach associated with stress, trauma, and life change. The aim was to create a scaffolding that would capture more fully the complexity of the response to interpersonal loss across the life cycle.

According to the TTM, the bereavement response should always be understood as occurring along two main axes, each of which is *multidimensional* (Rubin et al., 2012):

- **Track I: Biopsychosocial functioning:** This relates to how people function naturally and how this functioning is affected by the cataclysmic life experience that loss may entail.
- **Track II: Relationship to the deceased:** This is concerned with how the bereaved maintain and change their relationships to the deceased; they may not always appreciate the extent, or be aware, of the nature of this relationship and their investment in it, or of their consequences. Nonetheless, this is critical for appreciating what the human bereavement response involves across the life cycle.

The implications of the TTM are relevant for theory, research, clinical work, and counselling intervention. One can always ask to what extent the bereaved person's response along each of the tracks is addressed and understood at any point in the life cycle and at any time following the loss. The major components of each track are listed in Table 3.1.

Track I addresses functioning and assesses the individual's adaptive and disrupted life functioning. The two basic questions addressed here are (i) how problematic are the responses and (ii) where are the areas of growth and adaptation. Each of the 10 domains figures prominently in response to bereavement and have received attention in the literature.

Table 3.1 An overview of the Two-Track Model of Bereavement (based on Rubin et al., 2012)

Track I: Biopsychosocial Functioning	*Track II: Relationship to the Deceased*
1. Where are the difficulties in biopsychosocial functioning?	1. What is the state of the desire to reconnect with the deceased affectively and cognitively?
2. Where are the strengths and growth manifest?	2. What is the nature of the ongoing relationship to the deceased? Is the death story integrated?
1. Anxious affect	1. Reconnection wishes and longing for the deceased
2. Depressive affects	2. Imagery, memory, physical experience of the deceased
3. Somatic concerns	3. Degree of emotional involvement and closeness
4. Indications of traumatic response (e.g. PTSD)*	4. Strength and frequency of positive perceptions and affects associated with the deceased
5. Familial relationships	5. Preoccupation with loss event, deceased, or both
6. General interpersonal relationships	6. Strength/frequency of negative perceptions and affects associated with thinking of the deceased and the relationship
7. Self-esteem and self-system	7. Presence of conflict surrounding the deceased, the relationship, the loss event, or all of these
8. General meaning structure: What has changed? One's view of the world, its value, religious worldviews etc. may be affected (e.g. 'I can no longer believe in a god'; 'Life has lost its meaning for me').	8. The loss trajectory: features of response to loss (e.g. shock, searching, disorganisation, reorganisation)
9. Work or similar roles	9. Upset of self-system re: the deceased
10. Investment in life tasks	10. Progress toward memorialisation and transformation of relationship with deceased

*Post-traumatic stress disorder

Track II is focused on the psychological construction and relationship to the deceased. Key questions here include (i) to what degree does the bereaved individual seek out and focus on the relationship to the deceased; (ii) what is the flow of the bereaved's experiences. This latter question relates to domain 8, what the TTM calls the 'loss trajectory': Rubin et al. (2012) distinguish between the stages of the Parkes-Bowlby model and *dimensions* of the response to loss (see Chapter 1). Instead of rejecting the stage approach, the model *reconfigures* the stages in a way that addresses the most salient feature of each 'stage' as an independent dimension for evaluation throughout the bereavement experience and as a reflection of how the bereaved person is constructing the loss experience. (The question arises as to why this appears in Track II rather than Track I?) Two further, inter-related Track II question concern who the deceased is and what s/he represents for the bereaved – and vice-versa.

Evaluation of the TTM

As shown in Figure 3.3, the TTM complements the DPM: Track I corresponds to the restoration-orientation, while Track II corresponds to the loss-orientation. While not identical, they can be regarded as focusing on how the bereaved person reacts to, and copes with, *primary* loss (Track II and loss-orientation) or *secondary* losses (Track I and restoration-orientation).

While the thrust of attachment theory and research is on how attachment style affects response to the death of an attachment figure, it's also important to reverse the question by asking how bereavement affects attachment to the deceased attachment figure. While the attachment figure no longer exists literally or physically in the world,

> Death does not sever the relationship with the deceased; thus today we refer to the 'continuing bonds' paradigm as predominant in loss.
>
> (Rubin et al., 2012, p. 24)

Track II of the TTM clearly belongs squarely within this 'continuing bonds' paradigm, which we discuss in the next section.

Continuing bonds: Attachment after death

Freud and Bowlby on the need for detachment

As we noted in Chapter 1, Bowlby (1980) used the term 'reorganisation' to replace the earlier 'detachment' to refer to the final stage of adult grief (based on adults' ability to talk about their troubling experiences and to deal cognitively with loss). This is important because it reflects Bowlby's belief that many grievers do not, and do not wish to, 'detach' defensively from their lost attachment figure; instead, they rearrange their representations of self and the deceased so that a continuing bond *and* adjustment to life without him/her are both possible (Shaver and Fraley, 2008).

The distinction between detachment and reorganisation is related to the debate between clinicians regarding whether or not Freud advocated *complete* detachment ('decathexis') from mental representations of lost loved ones. Bowlby's 'reorganisation' allows for the fact that bereaved individuals need to do considerable cognitive and emotional work to update their inner working models of themselves and their relationships – but without having to detach completely from the deceased. Shaver and Fraley (2008) explain the difference in their ideas about detachment in terms of the difference between Freud's 'psychic energy' model of the mind and Bowlby's 'cybernetic' model: the former requires that mental 'bonds' to one person need to be broken before bonds with other people can be established.

Klass et al.'s Continuing Bonds

Klass et al.'s *Continuing Bonds: New Understandings of Grief* (1996), an edited collection of original articles, is, arguably, the most frequently cited source of rejection of the 'detachment hypothesis', i.e. the view (originating with Freud) that the deceased loved one must be 'given up' in order for healthy mourning to take place and for new attachments to be formed. However, the editors and most of the chapter authors mistakenly bracket Freud and Bowlby together as advocating the detachment hypothesis, and define themselves in contrast or opposition to attachment theory in the process (Fraley and Shaver, 1999). As we noted above, Bowlby did *not* advocate complete detachment, and so Klass et al. have distorted intellectual history; they have also misread many of their own research findings in the process (Fraley and Shaver, 1999). Since 1999, the discussion of *Continuing Bonds* has itself continued and in 2006 the journal *Death Studies* published two special issues on the topic (Shaver and Fraley, 2008).

According to Bowlby (1980), the grief reactions that many psychoanalytically-oriented therapists apparently viewed as immature or pathological – searching, yearning, and sometimes expressing anger or ambivalence toward the lost attachment figure – are aspects of the normal functioning of the attachment system. He strongly disapproved of characterising such reactions as childish, irrational, or inappropriately dependent. As Shaver and Fraley (2008) observe, even Freud himself, at least in his personal correspondence, did not agree with the extreme position that later writers attributed to him. They refer to the common experience of bereaved individuals who are 'caught out' by memories of the lost loved one that seem to take them by surprise (what C. S. Lewis (1961) described as 'a sudden jab of red-hot memory', p. 6). This kind of 'jab' is a normal part of coming to terms with a loss that is not yet fully represented in all of a bereaved person's unconscious and preconscious memories; in turn, these memories are part of the internal working models of the lost attachment figure. The emotional charge associated with these unexpected memories typically decreases over time (in Lewis's terms, they become less 'red-hot') – partly due to habituation and desensitisation, partly to being reorganised into more realistic, updated working models (Shaver and Tancredy, 2001). But this does not mean that the bereaved person's attachment to the deceased is erased from memory – far from it (Shaver and Fraley).

According to Stroebe and Schut (2005), the process of working through grief can be interpreted as one of emotional *neutralisation* – not forgetting. Horowitz (1997) described this process of repeatedly confronting one's changed reality and outdated working models until an attachment figure's loss is fully represented in memory and integrated into updated working models. Bowlby (1980) stated that:

> Failure to recognise that a continuing sense of the dead person's presence . . . is a common feature of healthy mourning has led to much confused theorising . . . findings in regard both to the high prevalence of a continuing sense of the presence of the dead person and to its compatibility with a favourable outcome give no support to Freud's 'its [mourning's] function is to detach the survivor's memories and hopes from the dead' (*SE* 13, p. 65).
>
> (Bowlby, 1980, p. 100)

As Shaver and Fraley (2008) say, not only was Bowlby talking about continuing bonds (CBs) 16 years before the publication of *Continuing Bonds*, but the editors and many of the contributors to that publication seriously misrepresented Bowlby's account.

Subsequent theory and research into CBs

The *Continuing Bonds* book stimulated a large number of research studies. In a review, Boerner and Heckhasuen (2003), agreeing with Fraley and Shaver (1999), concluded that different types of connections with the deceased may be more or less adaptive. In another review, Stroebe and Schut (2005) concluded that it was impossible to tell whether CBs (at least as measured) were generally beneficial or detrimental in coping with bereavement. In most studies, CBs (at least as measured) were associated with grief severity, rather than resolution.

Developing Fraley and Shaver's (1999) suggestion that CBs can be either secure or insecure (in particular, part of unresolved/disorganised attachment), Field (2006) points out that there's a huge difference between (a) thinking positively about a deceased attachment figure's admirable and loving qualities and incorporating some of these into oneself, and (b) being haunted by the deceased's sudden (imagined) appearance or being confused about whether s/he is or isn't still available in the physical world. Most empirical studies focus on concrete aspects of CBs (such as keeping the deceased's clothes or possessions or keeping him/her in mind in various ways); as such, they don't help to distinguish healthy from unresolved grief. From the perspective of the Adult Attachment Interview (AAI) (see Chapter 2), the aim of such studies would be to determine how a person represents, relates to, and talks about (coherently or otherwise) a particular deceased attachment figure (Shaver and Fraley, 2008).

The effects of CBs on adjustment may depend on the length of time since bereavement. For example, Field et al. (2003) reported that more frequent CBs experiences at five years after loss was associated with more severe grief symptoms. Field and Friedrichs (2004) reported a positive relationship between CBs and positive mood at 24 months following bereavement, but not in the early bereavement period. These results suggest that having an emotional tie with the deceased can be comforting once the acute period of grief has passed (Ho et al., 2013).

Internalised versus externalised CB

The Continuing Bonds Scale (CBS: Field et al., 1999; Field et al., 2003) accounts for different ways of maintaining a tie with the deceased: memories, retaining possessions, sense of presence, identification with and internalisation of the deceased, the deceased as a standard, and reminiscence of the deceased. Field and Filanosky (2010) expanded the CBS to comprise two sub-scales: *internalised* and *externalised* CB. The internalised CB subscale comprises items relating to the use of the deceased as an autonomy-promoting secure base; the externalised CB subscale comprises items relating to illusory types of contact with the deceased, including visual, auditory, and tactile hallucinations (i.e. they refer to experiences of the deceased as somehow being present).

Field and Filanosky (2010) found that externalised CB was *positively* associated with both the violent death of the loved one and the bereaved's sense of responsibility for the death (i.e. the greater the one, the greater the other). Internalised CB was *negatively* associated with these factors (the greater the one, the lesser the other) but *positively* associated with personal growth.

Yo et al. (2013) cite a number of studies which have found that having a CB is normative among Chinese bereaved people. In their own study of 71 Chinese people living in Hong Kong who had lost a spouse in the previous 12–36 months, they demonstrated that a stronger reliance on either an internalised or externalised CB is associated with more severe grief symptoms following the loss of a loved one, but that only externalised CB is associated with having an anxious attachment style. Although not a main focus of the study, Yo et al. also found that religious bereaved people had less CB and were less likely to display an avoidant attachment style. Indirectly supporting their findings, Benore and Park (2004) had previously found that religious belief in a soul that is separate from and persists after the death of the physical body, also allows for the possibility of *continued attachment* (a similar concept to CB) with the deceased.

Drawing on the DPM, Yo et al. suggest that those anxiously-attached individuals who are 'stuck' with an externalised CB need to engage in oscillation: they need help to attend to restoration tasks, to reduce their heavy reliance on externalised CB, to decrease their ruminations about the deceased, and to reappraise their lost relationship more positively. They also refer to Malkinson et al.'s (2006) discussion of the practical implications of the TTM: the bereaved can at the same time maintain a relationship with the deceased *and* adapt to a life in which the deceased is absent. Applied to Yo et al.'s (2013) findings, the TTM implies that a therapist could reduce externalised CB and increase internalised CB *at the same time*.

The idea that death does not sever the relationship to the deceased but transforms it took hold after the publication of *Continuing Bonds*. The general acceptance of the CB paradigm is a welcome development in the theoretical and clinical under-standing of bereavement (Klass et al., 1996). Just as importantly, much CB-related research has focused on the parent-child bond: the ongoing relationships of chil-dren to their deceased parents – and siblings – has provided a dramatic alternative to the more typically studied loss of a spouse (Rubin et al., 2012: see Chapter 6).

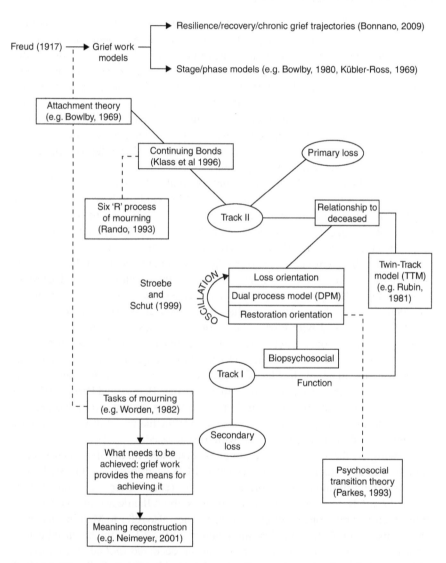

Figure 3.3 Diagrammatic summary of the major theories/models of grief, showing their interrelationships

Summary and conclusions

- Stage/phase theorists recognise that their proposed stages are neither invariant nor inevitable. At best, these accounts are merely descriptive rather than explanatory.
- The concept of 'grief work' stems from Freud's claim that the bereaved person needs to emotionally detach form the deceased. According to the *grief work hypothesis* (GWH), one must confront the experience of bereavement in order to come to terms with loss and avoid detrimental health consequences.
- The concept of grief work is built into Lindemann's account of *acute grief*, and Bowlby's stage account.
- The GWH has been criticised on many counts, including lack of supporting evidence, its lack of application across gender and culture, and its focus on primary loss to the exclusion of related – and inevitable-secondary losses
- Also influenced by the GWH, Worden's *tasks of mourning* portrays grief as a much more active process than what's implied by the stage/phase approach.
- Like all 'grief work' accounts, Rando's Six 'Rs' of mourning present a *normative* process of adjustment to loss. However, it also draws attention to secondary losses.
- According to Parkes's *psychosocial transition theory*, grief involves adapting to change, in particular to a revised *assumptive world*. Almost by definition, psychosocial transitions (PTs) involve many simultaneous dysfunctions in several areas of functioning (i.e. secondary losses).
- Traumatic losses, which, by definition, are unexpected and (often) untimely, are especially difficult to adjust to; they commonly involve the twin phenomena of avoidance and intrusive recall.
- Stroebe and Schut's *Dual-Process Model* (DPM) was partly a response to dissatisfaction with the GWH; while the latter sees grief as exclusively *intrapersonal*, the former acknowledges its *interpersonal* dimension.
- The DPM was intended to provide a model of *coping* with loss, as well as an account of *individual differences*.
- The DPM makes a fundamental distinction between two categories of bereavement-related *stressors*: those that are *loss-oriented* (the primary stressors) and those that are *restoration-oriented* (the secondary stressors). *Oscillation* between these two is a dynamic process and makes for 'normal' grieving. 'Time-out' from both is also part of the coping process.
- Pathological/complicated grief can be regarded as disturbances of oscillation. In attachment theory terms, for example, anxious-avoidant individuals would tend to focus on the restoration-orientation, while anxious-resistant/ambivalent individuals would focus on the loss-orientation. These individuals are *hypoaroused* and *hyperaroused*, respectively.
- The DPM accommodates gender differences better than earlier models: women appear to be more loss-oriented, and men more restoration-oriented; these correspond to *intuitive* and *instrumental* grievers, respectively.

- In Rubin's Two-Track Model (TTM), Track I (*biopsychosocial functioning*) corresponds to the restoration-orientation of the DPM, while Track II (*relationship to the deceased*) corresponds to the loss-orientation.
- Track II of the TTM belongs within the *continuing bonds* (CB) paradigm.
- Bowlby's use of 'reorganisation' for the final stage of adult grief reflected his belief that many grievers, quite normally, maintain a bond with the deceased. The CB approach represents a rejection of Freud's 'detachment hypothesis'.
- The Continuing Bonds Scale (CBS) distinguishes between *internalised* and *externalised* CB.
- The idea that death does not sever the relationship to the deceased is widely accepted. CB-related research has helped to shift the near-exclusive focus of earlier theories/models on spousal bereavement to child and sibling bereavement.

Chapter 4

The social context of grief

The chapter will address the following questions:

- How does consideration of the social context of grief differ from stage/phase accounts of grief?
- How do these two approaches complement each other?
- How can we characterise Western society's attitude towards death?
- What is meant by the '*medicalisation*' of grief?
- What is meant by the '*normalisation*' of grief?
- How is grief related to social structure?
- Is death the final taboo in Western society?
- In what ways has death become '*professionalised*' in Western society?
- What are the major kinds of effect that death has on the family?
- What are the main features of *family systems theory* (FST)?
- How can families best support their members in the face of bereavement?
- What are some of the potentially harmful ways in which families respond to bereavement?
- What are the social functions of funerals?
- How can funerals help bereaved individuals? What makes a 'good' funeral?
- What is meant by '*disenfranchised*' grief (DG)?
- What different kinds of DG are there?

In Chapters 1–3, the focus has been on grief as the physical, cognitive, emotional/affective, spiritual, and behavioural reactions of bereaved *individuals*. The discussion has been based on an implicit view of the bereaved person as a self-contained entity, almost totally unaffected by the surrounding social world. Although the sensitivity, responsiveness, and availability of the attachment figure represent crucial influences on the particular attachment pattern or style an individual develops, these patterns/styles reflect the underlying inner working model (IWM) of relationships in general and of specific attachment figures. By definition, these IWMs are private, largely unconscious, features of individuals.

This view of grief as essentially a *subjective* (private) experience (which is expressed overtly to varying degrees) reflects the dominance of Psychology in the twentieth century. By contrast with sociology, which focuses on social institutions and society as a whole, most Psychology (even Social Psychology) takes the individual as its focal point. Turning Psychology on its head, anthropology *starts* with the outward expression of grief (mourning) (see Chapter 5).

We also noted in Chapter 1 that 'grief'/'grieving' is often used synonymously with 'mourning' (although 'grief work' is often a more accurate synonym). However, we also saw that 'mourning' is used in a very different sense, namely to denote 'the culturally patterned expressions or rituals that accompany loss and allow others to recognise that one has become bereaved' (Doka, 1989b, p. 127), with funerals being the classic example. If we replace 'culturally' with 'socially' in Doka's definition, that should provide a good idea of the focus of this chapter: we are moving from what goes on inside the head of the bereaved individual (including differences between individuals) to widely-shared attitudes and practices surrounding death within whole societies or, more commonly, sub-groups within those societies. While the focus of this chapter will be on Western societies (such as the UK and US), Chapter 5 will focus on how these attitudes and practices differ between cultures and sub-cultures, with religion playing a major role.

In-between the individual mourner and the sub-group(s) within the society as a whole to which s/he belongs is the family unit. It has become something of a truism among those who study bereavement, and those professionals who support people through their grief, that it is the family that is bereaved, rather than the individual. In other words, in order to understand and support an individual family member, it is necessary to know how the whole family *as a system* (or unit) has been affected by the bereavement.

Having defined grief as a *universal* response to bereavement (e.g. Archer, 1999), Chapter 5 will consider the extent to which both the experience and expression of grief is culturally determined. All cultures and sub-cultures have to deal with death, psychologically, practically, and socially, and this chapter will emphasise the most widely practised rituals of mourning. But to understand those rituals, we need first to understand the widely-held attitudes towards death itself which form a major part of the social context of grief.

Western society's attitude towards death

According to Prior (1989), during the 19th century grief was regarded as a condition of the human soul or spirit rather than of the body; in this sense, it could neither be *normalised* nor *medicalised*. But all that was to change, beginning with Freud, who was the first to distinguish between normal and pathological responses to bereavement (in *Mourning and Melancholia*, 1917: see Chapter 3). Other psychoanalytic writers built on Freud's ideas, including Melanie Klein (1940) and Lindemann (1944).

The medicalisation of grief

According to Klein (1940), all grief is in a sense pathological insofar as it imitates the manic-depressive state, though for most people this is transitory. Lindemann (1944) was the first to place the study of grief on an empirical footing and the first to establish a 'symptomatology' of grief; as described in Chapter 3, he identified the symptoms of acute grief, which he regarded as a distinct syndrome with both psychological and somatic (bodily) symptoms. He distinguished between those people suffering from normal and morbid (pathological) grief in terms of intensity and duration; grief *management* was discussed exclusively in terms of the principles of clinical medicine.

An even more extreme attempt to reduce grief to a bodily disease was taken by Engel (1961) in his paper 'Is grief a disease?', in which he directly compared grief to pathogenic bacteria. Prior also quotes Parkes (1975), whose later writings suggest a rather different view of the nature of grief.

> On the whole, grief resembles a physical injury more closely than any other type of illness But occasionally abnormal forms arise, which may even be complicated by the onset of other types of illness.
>
> (Parkes, 1975, p. 19)

The normalisation of grief

While it should be clear by now what Prior means by 'medicalisation', what about 'normalisation'? She cites a number of writers who have identified *stages* or *phases* of grief, including Parkes, Bowlby, and Kübler-Ross, and she describes these accounts as adopting the *developmental metaphor*: grief is (implicitly) likened to stages of development that children naturally go through (as in, for example, Freud's stages of *psychosexual development*, Erikson's stages of *psychosocial development*, and Piaget's stages of *cognitive development*: see Gross, 2015). Although only meant as averages or approximations, each of the stages is reached at a particular age. So, by analogy with these developmental stages, grief is seen as *unfolding* (naturally) within the human (mainly adult) psyche (Prior, 1989).

Grief and social structure

Prior (1989) claims that both Lindemann and Bowlby gave a 'hesitant nod' to the role of *social influences* when assessing the impact of grief, but most writers seem to have ignored the work of Emile Durkheim, the influential nineteenth-century French sociologist, social psychologist, and philosopher. Durkheim and those influenced by him argued that the intensity of grief was *not* the product of some inner unfolding, but rather caused by social processes which tended to channel grief into some directions while deflecting it away from others. Important exceptions to the general exclusion of social influences are Marris's (1958) study of 72 London widows, and Gorer's (1965) study of bereaved individuals drawn from a number of age, gender, social class, and regional groups (see Chapter 1).

While both Marris and Gorer continued to assess grief in terms of 'normal stages' and timetables (see Chapter 1), they did supplement these with discussion of the role of social structure. For example, Marris acknowledged that sociological factors impinged on the intensity and duration of grief:

> The severity of grief depends, then, on the degree of [social] disruption: and it can be at least crudely predicted from the emphasis which a society places upon different relationships.
>
> (Marris, 1974, p. 38)

In that sense, the loss of babies and (widowed) old people, for example, is less disruptive than the loss of those in economically active groups and/or the married (Prior, 1989). Similarly, Durkheim argued that the intensity of grief (individual or group) depended on a socially constructed formula, rather than an innate or natural tendency. This 'formula' is reflected in Marris's 'degree of disruption' and is also consistent with anthropological studies of rituals surrounding funerals and burial rites. One example is Radcliffe-Brown's (1922) study of the Andaman Islanders (in the Bay of Bengal), for whom social bonds were asserted and emphasised in public declarations: without the bond, there could be no weeping. So, children who had not yet been awarded a social personality, were 'little mourned', and 'a stranger who dies or is killed is buried unceremoniously or is cast into the sea' (Radcliffe-Brown, 1922, p. 109). Another example is described in Box 4.1.

**Box 4.1   Burial rituals among the Nyakyusa
(G. Wilson, 1939; M. Wilson, 1957)**

- Among the Nyakyusa people (of Tanzania and Malawi) burial is a 'lively event', but there are marked differences between the reactions of males and females; broadly speaking, 'the women wail and the men dance' and the funerary ritual emphasised male strength and courage as opposed to female fear and trembling.
- While the women wept the whole time, the chief mourners – who were *obliged* to show grief – wept only once or twice.
- Also, the length of the mourning period depended on the status of the deceased: the higher the status, the longer the mourning.

What these anthropological and historical examples do is to illustrate the point that:

> grief, at least in its public manifestations, is socially variable and that the social location of a deceased person has much to do with the manner in which

grief is expressed. . . . All public expressions of grief act as a mirror in which private feelings are reflected.

(Prior, 1989, p. 152)

Is death the final taboo?

Gorer, who described himself as an anthropologist, reached the rather curious conclusion that modern mourning practices are marked by a total lack of ritual. In the England of the 1960s, 'The most typical reaction [to death] is the denial of mourning' (1965, p. 113). If problematic experiences such as bereavement are not handled ritually, individuals will incur psychological problems, and death will resurface socially in the form of an obsession with horror comics, war movies, and disasters (what he'd previously (1955) called 'the pornography of death').

Gorer's *Death, Grief and Mourning in Contemporary Britain* (1965) and Aries's *The Hour of Our Death* (1981) represent by far the most often quoted academic advocates of the view that death is taboo and uniquely badly handled by modern society (Walter, 1993). Walter believes that Gorer's argument helps explain how the media can be obsessed with death even at a time when individuals find it impossible to talk about their own personal grief, and how death can be taboo but his bereaved interviewees were so eager to talk (he'd given them 'permission' and an opportunity).

Gorer's taboo thesis could even explain the flood of academic material on death that has developed, especially in the US since the 1950s and that continues (for example, the second edition of the *Handbook of Thanatology* was published in 2013). Walter describes these publications as 'death at a remove, death abstracted, intellectualised, professionalised and depersonalised' (Walter, 1993, p. 294). Gorer has been widely criticised, partly for romanticising Victorian mourning rituals, and it has been suggested that the modern denial of death began in the early 19th, not the 20th, century (Walter, 1993).

Like Gorer, Aries argues that death is inevitably problematic. Along with sex, it is one of the major ways in which 'nature' threatens 'culture', making it necessary to 'tame' it; society traditionally achieves this through religion and ritual. But over the past few centuries, individualism, romanticism, and secularism have undermined the rituals, and the modern individual is left naked before death's obscenity. Today, we are the heirs to both a Victorian romanticism which made the loss of the loved one unbearable, and of a twentieth century denial that forbids (Aries, 1974) or at least conceals (Aries, 1981), death. This 'inheritance' can explain the apparent opposing trends in the US: (i) the denial of death implicit in American hospitals and in the lack of mourning; and (ii) the continuing tradition of Americans viewing the body (Aries, 1981).

While Aries has also had his critics, at least he and Gorer have put the subject on the academic (if not the British sociological) map (Walter, 1993). Walter proceeds to outline seven alternative modifications or critiques of the taboo thesis, aimed a helping us to understand the complexity of changing attitudes and practices toward death. Some of these are summarised in Box 4.2.

Box 4.2   Modifications of the death as taboo thesis (Walter, 1993)

1. *Taboo plus coda:* While accepting the basic argument that death has become something of a taboo since the end of World War I, at least among the middle classes, we should add that it's now ceasing to be – not least because of the work of scholars such as Gorer and Aries, i.e. it needs updating and modifying along social class and gender lines.

2. *Not forbidden, but hidden:* While the original taboo thesis and the first modification (*taboo plus coda*) are about *culture*, Blauner (1966) focuses on *demographic structure*. In the modern world, most deaths are of elderly people; in past generations, the vast majority of adults who died did so in the prime of life. The result is that we miss the deceased *less* than in previous centuries; this means that we don't need elaborate rites of passage, nor even beliefs in an afterlife. However, if fulfilled death in old age is the norm, the more unprepared we are for atypical deaths (of children and adolescents, non-elderly spouses, traumatic deaths etc.). Bereavement support is offered to increasingly *isolated* mourners who have suffered these *categories* of loss.

3. *Limited taboo:* It is not modern society *per se*, but particular key occupational groups within it, that find death peculiarly difficult to handle. Doctors and public health officials are dedicated to keeping people alive and healthy, so death represents *failure* from their perspective. In addition, the media have extraordinary power to interpret death for us, and yet, surely, for those who work in the media world of youth and glamour, death is also an embarrassment.

4. *Universal taboo:* Becker, in his classic *The Denial of Death* (1973), argues that the denial of death is not a modern condition, but the *human* condition. Both social life, and the life of individuals, would be impossible if we did not repress our death terror. (This is discussed further in Chapter 8.)

5. *Individual and society:* In traditional societies, where identity is rooted in the group more than in the individual, death does not threaten the individual to the extent that it does in advanced societies; in the former, death threatens groups and their culture – hence the need for communal death rituals. The reverse applies in modern societies, where identity is invested largely within the individual who is indeed threatened by death. Communal and religious death rituals that once functioned to affirm culture fall into disuse; individual therapy and one-to-one bereavement counselling aim to support bewildered individuals. Modern cultures deal with death well – it's *individual* members who struggle with it.

The professionalisation of death

In discussing the way that death was dealt with in Staithes, a small coastal town in North Yorkshire in 1900, Clark (1982/1993) compares it with modern practices in that same town. Perhaps the most significant innovation he observes is the emergence of a number of specialist organisations which are concerned with the processes of death and dying. This is a transformation that has stripped the family of one of its traditional functions: some of the familial and communal rituals previously associated with the death of a villager have disappeared beneath a general trend of *professionalisation*.

For most villagers, contact with death takes place at a distance or through intermediaries, in the form of bureaucratically-organised agencies which perform the tasks and duties previously performed by the family or community. The very existence of these agencies implies that competence to deal with the practical matters associated with death requires professional training; this means that any relevant skills that families might have are inferior. Professionalisation has thereby resulted in a vastly different set of responses to the problem of death. The 'undertaker' has now become a 'funeral director', implying a much more professional set of skills and responsibilities.

Clark and others (e.g. Mauksch, 1975) point out that while most people used to die at home, we are now most likely to die either in hospital, a geriatric unit, or a residential home. When death occurs in one of these institutions, the body is commonly removed to the funeral director's memorial house, rather than to the deceased's home; preparation of the body and laying-out is also undertaken by the funeral director rather than by the traditional female specialists in the village. It is also usual for the funeral director to arrange for publication of details in the death and obituary column of the local newspaper, another function taken over from members of the village community. Similarly, making the coffin, once a task for the local joiner, is now arranged by the funeral director, as may be the ordering of flowers and wreaths, as well as arranging the funeral tea by outside caterers.

This professionalisation of death – and the facts regarding where most people die – can be seen as one way in which death is *hidden* (see Box 4.2). It goes hand-in-hand with what is sometimes called the *sanitisation* of death: the 'messy reality' of death which used to be dealt with by the family and the community as a whole is now removed from those social groups to the professionals, in particular hospital staff and funeral directors. Depending on the details and circumstances of the death, it is probably the norm for even the closest relatives to not actually see the deceased's body; we take it on trust that the body in the coffin is that of our loved one because we have given up what were previously the responsibilities and duties of the family to the 'death professionals'.

Death and the family

Having discussed how families are no longer involved in the practical aspects of death (at least in Western countries), we now turn to the social psychological impact of death on the family. According to Cook (2013):

> Death is a family event. It occurs within the context of existing relation-
> ships and family dynamics. While grief is often viewed as a personal experi-
> ence, it occurs in two realms simultaneously – the intrapsychic level and the
> interpersonal level.
>
> (Cook, 2013, p. 171)

Personal grief always occurs within a social context and is embedded in a web of
complex relationships; in most societies, the closest relationships and attachments
are found within *family systems*, be it the *nuclear* family (parents and biological offspring) typical of Western cultures or the *extended* family, more typical of
non-Western cultures (see Chapter 5). However, this distinction between nuclear
and extended families represents a gross oversimplification, as discussed in
Box 4.3.

Box 4.3   The complex variety of Western families

- While a husband and wife and their (2.5) biological children used to be
  the norm in Western countries, changes in both technology and social
  attitudes and behaviours mean that such family groupings are probably in
  the minority.
- If *single-parent* families represent one end of a continuum, *blended* families
  could be seen as representing the other end: two parents who have previously been divorced or had children with a previous partner raise one or
  more of their children from those previous relationships together within
  a single family grouping. There may be full-, half-, and step-siblings all living
  under one roof.
- While *adoption* has been taking place for many generations, *assisted repro-
  duction families* are a relatively recent phenomenon. This can take a variety of forms, including *in-vitro fertilisation* (IVF), *surrogacy* (both *non-genetic*,
  which uses the egg of the mother who will raise the child, and *genetic*,
  where the surrogate mother both 'hosts' the baby and provides the egg),
  and *donor insemination*.
- It is now possible for a child to have *five* parents: an egg donor, a sperm
  donor, a surrogate mother who hosts the pregnancy, and the two social
  parents whom the child knows as mum(my) and dad(dy) (Golombok, 2010).
- Since the 1970s, many of the beneficiaries of donor insemination and surrogacy have been lesbian couples and (more recently) the increasing number of gay couples (who are also increasingly adopting).

Family systems theory

According to *family systems theory* (FST), families are whole entities, both unique and greater than the sum of its individual family members (Cook, 2013). Individual behaviour cannot be understood in isolation but only within the context of the social group(s) to which the individual belongs: while the experience of grief is a personal event for individuals, it is also a *systems* event for the family.

In order to understand how bereavement affects the family system, we must consider individual family members, their relationships to each other, their individual relationships with the deceased, and their relationships and interactions with other individual and systems outside the family. Family systems comprise *subsystems*, such as marital, sibling, and parent-child relationships. As illustrated in Box 4.3, the subsystems of 'modern' families (especially blended families) are now far more numerous and complex compared with past generations. The death of a family member can have a powerful impact not only on the family system as a whole but also on the subsystem(s) which the deceased belonged to (Cook and Oltjenbruns, 1998).

A death changes the family system's equilibrium, often disrupting its functioning and affecting available emotional and physical resources. For example, the death of a spouse may alter the extended kinship network (such as the surviving spouse's relationships with his/her children), the death of child may alter perceptions of the future (including the parents' relationship with each other), and the death of a parent or breadwinner can threaten a family's sense of security (Hansson et al., 1999). (See Chapter 6.)

The effects of especially difficult losses can be transmitted through multiple generations (see Chapter 7). When secrecy and taboos surround a particular death, families can become more vulnerable to future losses. Understanding multigenerational patterns of interaction and communication around loss can provide a better understanding of current family functioning and coping styles (Cook, 2013).

The importance of timing

The *timing* of a bereavement in the family lifecycle can be a critical factor in how the family adjusts to the loss. Deaths that are untimely, such as those involving children, adolescents, or non-elderly adults (whether sudden or not, and whether traumatic or due to natural causes) are especially difficult. Surviving family members may not know anyone within their social networks who has experienced such untimely losses; this may add a sense of isolation to their grief, which may be reinforced by their peers not knowing how to offer appropriate and effective support (see Chapter 6 and 7).

Loss can also coincide with other major life events that pose unique challenges. For example, loss of a spouse can occur near the time of birth of a first child (such as when a serving soldier is killed on active service or a police officer is killed on duty), or when the family is facing financial difficulties due to redundancy/

unemployment. Multiple stressors, developmental demands, and related losses can produce overload and compromise the family's ability to cope with the bereavement (McGoldrick and Walsh, 2005).

Healthy family processes following bereavement

Cook and Oltjenbruns (1998) and others have discussed the importance of (i) families sharing the loss; (ii) maintaining open communication; (iii) reorganising and regaining equilibrium; and (iv) making effective use of available support systems and external resources:

(i) *Sharing the loss* relates to funerals, memorial services, and other post-death ceremonies that can serve as meaningful occasions for family members to come together to acknowledge and share the loss of a loved one. These are discussed in more detail below (pages 80–84).

(ii) *Maintaining open communication*, both before and after a death, allows family members to share deep feelings and create stronger bonds, but they must be accepting and supportive of the range of feelings that may be expressed. This can be seen as a symbolic, transactional process of creating and sharing *meaning*; it is transactional in the sense that family members have an impact on each other (Galvin et al., 2004). Certain types of loss, such as suicide, may evoke strong feelings of anger and shame that may be particularly difficult to share with others; lack of open communication has been shown to increase the possibility of blame, guilt, and conflict (Vess et al., 1985).

(iii) *Reorganising and regaining equilibrium* involves an age-appropriate redistribution of roles and responsibilities following the death of a family member; together with moving house, changing jobs, or looking for employment, these are all *secondary* losses, some of which may result from an unexpected death. Open family systems, in which information is freely exchanged, are better able to reorganise in new and effective ways which support and acknowledge individuals while maintaining functioning of the whole family unit.

(iv) *Making effective use of support systems and external resources* involves accessing and accepting the support of extended family and friends, religious institutions, community and mental health services, and formal support organisations such as Compassionate Friends (in both the UK and US) and Cruse Bereavement Care (in the UK). Churches, mosques, synagogues, and other religious centres provide time-honoured rituals surrounding death that can provide comfort for families and connect them with others who share their belief system (Cook and Dworkin, 1992: see below).

Factors that affect coping

In the case of bereaved children, *protective factors* include the efficacy of preventative interventions on strengthening parenting (Sandler et al., 2008), positive parenting (Haine et al., 2006), and the surviving parent's warmth and ability to provide consistent discipline (Lin et al., 2004). Traylor et al. (2003) reported that higher levels of family affect and family cohesion predicted fewer manifestations of grief over time.

Risk factors for poor outcomes after loss include internal family factors (e.g. poor communication, and conflict in interpersonal relationships), as well as details of the loss itself. Also, concurrent stressors unrelated to the death can make coping with the loss more challenging, such as being made redundant, caring for ageing parents, and personal health problems. Death by accident, murder or suicide, all of which are, by definition, sudden and unexpected – and so impossible to prepare for – are more likely to produce complicated grief (see Chapter 7). This may be the result of the difficulty that family members have of *making sense* of, and finding *meaning* in the loss (Currier et al., 2006: see Chapter 8).

Anticipated deaths may involve major stressors over protracted time periods; these may include having to give up work and the financial consequences of this, a change to the family routine, spending a lot of time travelling to and from hospital, and perhaps having to adapt the home in order to accommodate the sick person. These may exacerbate already-existing issues within the family and accentuate tensions. *Anticipatory grieving* may take place, both for the person who is going to die and all the associated secondary losses; different family members may grieve most for different anticipated losses (those which are anticipated or may have already occurred), and, without open communication about these, both individual and family grief may become more complicated.

Positive and negative outcomes

Dyregrov and Dyregrov (2008) found that many couples report increased closeness following a loss, while a larger number report growing apart. For example, Gilbert (1989) reported that the majority of couples who had experienced either a foetal or infant death also experienced marital discord following the loss; they were described as displaying 'incongruent grieving'. These differences in *how* each partner grieves may be along gender lines. As we noted in Chapter 1, women are more likely to display *intuitive* grief, and men *instrumental* grief; women may mistake instrumental grief for an *absence* of grief, which, in turn, may cause conflict and resentment between them (Doka and Martin, 2010). Men are more likely to channel their grief into activities, some of which may detrimental to their health, such as excessive drinking (Umberson et al., 1992).

Over and above any such gender differences, each family member's grief is unique, reflecting not just the unique relationship with the deceased, but his/her developmental level, personality and coping skills, prior experience of loss, and many other factors. Also, the manifestations and duration of any one member's grief may be quite different from those of another (the *dissynchrony of grief*) (Cook, 2013). A 'classic' demonstration of this dissynchrony is the case of parents who have lost a child: they may be so absorbed in their individual grief that they fail to reach out to each other (see above) or to provide emotional support for their remaining children:

In these instances, a surviving child may become parentified and be the one to attempt to care for all other family members, thus compromising his or her own development.

(Cook, 2013, p. 177)

However, other studies have reported positive outcomes. For example, Brabant et al. (1997) interviewed parents 1–8 years following the death of a child: most expressed feeling more sensitive and more spiritual as a result of their loss, and also perceived themselves as better people. Most also expressed a change in values, including a desire to help others more and placing a higher priority on family and less on money and work.

Despite the pain associated with loss, families often report finding meaning in their suffering. Many families report positive changes, often expressed as truths realised or lessons learned (Nadeau, 2008). Positive outcomes can also relate to changed self-perceptions, such as seeing oneself as stronger and more mature. Others have reported being more caring for others, more open in sharing feelings, and better communicators (Calhoun and Tedeschi, 1990). Three-quarters of the widowed persons studied by Utz (2006) reported having become more self-confident as a result of having to manage on their own since losing their spouse.

Klass (1986) observed that death creates new bonds in some families as individual members pull together to cope with their shared loss. Surviving a common loss as a family can produce a renewed sense of closeness and unity, a better understanding of each other's strengths, and enhanced communication and flexibility (Cook, 2013).

Funerals and other death-related ceremonies

Every known culture has rituals to mark death, to acknowledge the life of the deceased, provide support for survivors, and facilitate ongoing life after such loss (Imber-Black, 2005). Whether formal or informal, such rituals can be of therapeutic value, helping to facilitate emotional healing and family cohesion. Funeral rituals can help to assist in accepting the reality of the loss (e.g. Parkes and Prigerson, 2010), serve as an affirmation of faith, religious beliefs, and/or philosophy of life, facilitate emotional expression, provide a context for emotional support from family, friends, and the wider community, and to reconnect to a greater sense of family and the integration of personal and family identity (Cook, 2013).

Cook (2013) defines a ritual as a specific behaviour or activity that gives *symbolic expression* to feelings and thoughts. Actions that occur many months or even years following a death can be thought of as rituals, such as going through the deceased's personal belongings or taking off a wedding ring; these have important symbolic significance, even if performed privately with no one else to witness them. Rituals can also provide a context for *reminiscence*, which can be performed privately, but when shared with another person this can represent an important aspect of social support. Rosenblatt and Elde (1990) found that reminiscence was common among adults who had lost a parent, especially between siblings.

Funerals and grief work

Compared with the UK, it is quite common for relatives in the US to view the body before the funeral in a chapel of rest in order to 'pay their respects' and say 'Goodbye'. The financial costs associated with this practice have led some US critics to accuse funeral directors of exploitation, quite apart from the pointlessness of trying to make a corpse look 'life-like' or producing an illusion of sleep (Parkes and Prigerson, 2010).

However, Parkes and Prigerson (2010) demonstrate that physical death and social death do not take place simultaneously: 'Grief is a process of realisation, of 'making real' the fact of loss. This process takes time . . .' (p. 205).

Anything that forces reality-testing in the early post-bereavement period is likely to cause problems, especially in the case of sudden and traumatic death; these problems may include panic attacks, the massive shutting off of emotion, and/or the repetitious reliving of the traumatic events as in PTSD. However, the disturbing memories of a painful death or a mutilated body can be mitigated to some degree by positive memories of the funeral (Parkes and Prigerson, 2010).

For many of the young widows in the London Study (Parkes, 1970, 1972), the funeral service (within a week of bereavement) took place too soon after the death to be of great positive psychological value (a successful *rite de passage*). However, it brought family and friends together to be close to the widow, and over half of the participants referred to the support this provided as a positive experience.

About half the widows in the London Study, and two-thirds of the Boston widows in the Harvard study (Glick et al., 1974; Parkes and Weiss, 1983), described their husbands' funerals in positive terms. By contrast, those who expressed negative or mixed feelings were clearly unprepared for the forceful way in which the funeral, and particularly the committal (burial or cremation), brought home the reality of their bereavement; this was especially true in the case of cremation (see below).

Agreeing with what Parkes and Prigerson say about the importance of reality-testing, Roy and Jane Nichols (1975), husband and wife funeral directors in the US, state that:

One of the most important purposes [of the funeral] is to facilitate grief work. Grief begins with acceptance, with facing up. People need to come to grips with the reality of the death. This acceptance must not only be intellectual, it must also be emotional.

(Nichols and Nichols, 1975, pp. 90–91)

Burial or cremation?

In his account of how death was dealt with in Staithes in the early 1900s and more recently (see above), Clark (1982) states that perhaps the greatest innovation was the introduction of cremation as an alternative form of disposal of the dead. Nevertheless, and despite cremation being the cheaper option, most modern-day funerals in Staithes still involved burial; Clark believes that this reflected an aversion to cremation, combined with a deep-seated preference for the traditional ritual.

Although funerals may be more for the living than the deceased, whether cremation or burial takes place may reflect the expressed wishes of the deceased. In the London Study, although some widows subsequently visited the crematorium, entered their husband's name in the Book of Remembrance, and attended memorial services, there was a tendency to feel less close to him at the crematorium than at the cemetery. Several widows regarded this as a distinct disadvantage of cremation. (Of course, in some parts of the world, notably the Indian sub-continent, cremation is the norm: see Chapter 5.)

Where do the dead 'go'?

Traditionally, in all major religions, what matters most is the *destination of the soul* (Orbach, 1999). According to Parkes and Prigerson (2010), most funerals and similar rituals end by indicating a location for the dead, a grave, shrine, columbarium, or similar place where bereaved people can 'visit' them, communicate with them, and, to some degree, continue to care for them. While such places are a poor substitute for the physical presence of the dead loved one, they often give comfort and are seen as mitigating some of the pain of separation (Yamamoto et al., 1969).

This sense of the dead having a physical, tangible location may help to explain the resistance among residents of Staithes to opt for cremation (see above). While the buried ashes can be visited at the crematorium, for many bereaved people this is probably a poor substitute for visiting the grave, which at least once contained an intact body, and can be tended to as a way of 'taking care' of the deceased. It's also easier to leave flowers and other 'gifts' or tributes' at a graveside than at the crematorium. In Judaism, the erection of the headstone 12 months following the burial marks the official end of mourning, a major *rite de passage* in its own right (see Chapter 5).

The makings of a good funeral

According to Holloway et al. (2013), there has been renewed public interest in funerals in the UK over the past decade.

> From the subdued funerals of the mid-twentieth century, the early part of this century has seen a steady expansion in the types of funeral and options available. For a society which supposedly avoids discussing death, we have

shown ourselves surprisingly interested in one of the central events around an individual death.

(Holloway et al., 2013, p. 30)

They go on to say that both academic and popular commentators agree that funerals in late-modern Western societies reflect personalisation, secularisation, consumer choice, and individual stories. Table 4.1 contrasts the major features of traditional and post-modern funerals (often dubbed 'DIY' funerals).

During the 1980s there was a reaction against the impersonal way in which many religious funerals were conducted (Littlewood, 1992) and the meaning-lessness of the Christian liturgy for the majority of mourners (Bowman, 1975). However, the increasing popularity of 'DIY' celebratory funerals has itself been criticised, for example (i) the abandonment of the traditional ritual has left mourners unable to express or manage their grief (Coward, 2002; Valentine, 2006); and (ii) contemporary ceremonies are spiritually barren and ignore the spiritual needs of diverse cultural groups who may be attending (Collins and Doolittle, 2006).

These changes in the nature of funerals have taken place in parallel with a growing debate regarding the nature and place of religion and spirituality in modern society. What is increasingly referred to as 'humanistic spirituality' (Holloway et al., 2011) emphasises personal expression, life-enhancement, and individually-customised meanings over handed-down, traditional religious belief systems, all of which may or may not involve belief in some external power or divine being (Holloway and Moss, 2010). Ironically, these seemingly *secular* practices may have become new forms of religiosity and spirituality (Heelas and Woodhead, 2005; Davie, 2007).

Holloway et al. (2013) conducted a qualitative study of 46 funerals that took place predominantly in the north of England; a significant number of the deceased came from large council housing estates. The celebrants/officiants were mainly either 'Humanist' (12) or Church of England (14); the next largest were Salvation Army (5), Methodist (4), and Roman Catholic (3) and 'Civil' (3). The remaining

Table 4.1   Major features of traditional and post-modern funerals

Traditional funerals

- Commend the departed.
- Symbolically mark their passing on.
- Acknowledge the individual's life within a wider existential frame for understanding life and death.

Post-modern funerals

- Serve the needs of the bereaved.
- Celebrate the life lived.
- Take the form of personally customised tributes.

five celebrants/officiants were Jehovah's Witness, Independent Evangelical, Spiritualist, Jewish, and Interfaith Memorial Service (one each).

The fundamental research question which the study was aimed at exploring was 'how meaning is sought, ascribed and expressed through the funeral, and whether and for whom and through what forms, this can be termed 'spiritual'' (Holloway et al., 2013, p. 33). A major conclusion from the study is that the contemporary funeral is a *psycho-social-spiritual* event.

Holloway et al. (2013) cite Parkes's (1990) observation that the funeral is an illogical act for rational people yet remains remarkably preserved in all societies. The reason for this surely lies in the enduring individual and social need for the living to manage the transition from life to death. A *physical procedure* (disposal of the body) is encapsulated in a ritual *social process* (the funeral) which demands a *philosophical response* on the part of the individual regarding the relationship between life and death; each of these elements is highly emotional and this is the crucial link to the main research question.

Contemporary understandings of *spirituality* combine physical, social, philosophical, and emotional responses to the question of what it means to be human (Holloway and Moss, 2010: see Chapter 8). Likewise, the funerals that Holloway et al. studied combined meanings that have deep personal resonance with meaning that is experienced in the community and is located within wider religious, quasi-religious, and philosophical frameworks, including transcendental elements. The funeral directors and celebrants involved all acknowledged that changes in how they understand and do their job reflect changes in the nature of funerals. However, both sets of funeral professionals also described the funeral as designed to help people find meaning at a time of existential challenge.

It is a gross over-simplification to see modern funerals as exercises in individual self-affirmation, lacking tradition and traditional sources of meaning (Holloway et al., 2013). However,

> instead of *meaning-taking* derived from handed-down beliefs, forms and rituals, this study found a process of *meaning-seeking and creating*, which results in meaning-taking only after each unique funeral has been created and taken place.
>
> (Holloway et al., 2013, p. 50; emphasis in original)

At the heart of the funerals in Holloway et al.'s study was the mourners' active participation in the co-creation and enacting of the funeral as a meaningful event. This accounts for their conclusion that contemporary funerals do indeed have a spiritual dimension.

> Our study showed clearly that meaning transforms and transcends the ordinariness of life and the challenge of death, and it is that *process* of meaning-seeking, creating and taking which shapes these personalised funerals.
>
> (Holloway et al., 2013, p. 50; italics in original)

This is what makes for a 'good funeral'.

Disenfranchised grief

A phenomenon that illustrates beautifully what is meant by the social context of grief is *disenfranchised grief* (DG). However a particular individual may be affected by someone's death, his or her grief may not necessarily be recognised and accepted by other people as valid, justified, appropriate, or 'fitting': DG refers to an individual's grief that is *not* validated by others.

According to Doka (2002), DG occurs when 'Survivors are not accorded a 'right to grieve''(2002, p. 5). DG isn't merely unnoticed, forgotten, or hidden; it's socially disallowed and unsupported (Corr and Corr, 2013, p. 143). The right to grieve entitles a bereaved person to grieve in a way and when s/he needs or chooses to, free of interference from others. Just as no one is obliged to grieve or do so in a particular way, so others are obliged to honour the right and refrain from interfering in the experience and efforts of grieving. DG is a form of interference which violates the mourner's right to grieve (Attig, 2004).

Attig (2004) regards the right to grieve as a matter of human dignity and DG as a denial of a human right; this makes it:

> not simply a matter of indifference It is more actively negative and destructive as it involves denial of entitlement, interference, and even imposition of sanction . . . disenfranchising behaviours interfere with the exercise of the right to grieve by withholding permission, disallowing, constraining, hindering, and even prohibiting it.
>
> (Attig, 2004, p. 198)

The scope of DG

Doka (1989a, 2002) states that grief can be disenfranchised in three major ways:

1   *Relationships* may be disenfranchised if they are non-traditional (e.g. homosexual or extra-marital); are thought not to be close enough (e.g. are not with spouses or first-degree relatives – parents and siblings); have remained unsuspected or secret; or are viewed as acceptable although their full implications are not appreciated (e.g. with friends, in-laws, work colleagues, or ex-spouses). While homophobia is still all-too common in Western countries (and in certain parts of the world, notably certain countries in Africa, Asia, and Latin America, homosexuality is illegal and outlawed), the introduction in the UK of civil partnerships (in 2004) and full married status (in 2014) has helped to 'reclassify' grief for a same-sex partner/spouse as legitimate (i.e. it has become enfranchised). This illustrates the dynamic nature of social influences on grief: the social context of grief is a constantly changing one.
2   *Losses* may be disenfranchised when there is a failure to recognise that a death has been experienced as a significant loss, as in the case of birth terminations

(abortions), miscarriages, loss of body parts (e.g. amputations), loss of pets or companion animals, the psychological/social deaths of Alzheimer's sufferers, prisoner deaths, or deaths on the 'losing' side in a war. (Most of these are discussed in Chapter 6.)

3   *Grievers* may be disenfranchised when there is failure to acknowledge that some people are *capable* of grieving (e.g. young children, elderly people, and people with learning disabilities). Cook (2013) observes that in some cultures, children are an integral part of all family rituals surrounding death, while in others they are rarely included – and often, positively excluded (see below).

Doka (2002) added two further categories:

4   *Circumstances of the death* may be disenfranchised if they inhibit either seeking or receiving support from other people (e.g. suicides, deaths from AIDS or other stigmatised diseases, deaths induced by excessive use of alcohol, deaths involving mutilation, executions). (Again, see Chapter 6.)

5   *Ways individuals grieve* may be disenfranchised when styles of experiencing and expressing grief clash with the experience of others (e.g. when *instrumental* grievers fail to show a strong affective response, *intuitive* grievers show excessive emotion, or culturally-engrained stoicism or wailing violate the grieving 'rules' of a given society) (see Chapters 1 and 5).

An example of DG that doesn't seem to fit any of the above categories or definitions is the grief of *grandparents*; or, as Doka (1989) puts it, *overlooking* grandparent grief is a form of disenfranchisement. Until recently, clinical and research interest has largely overlooked the bereavement responses of grandparents. Whereas bereaved parents' attention centres on the dead child, bereaved grandparents focus their attention on the suffering of their own children – the parents of the deceased child (Ponzetti, 1992). However,

> Ignoring the role of grandparents in the lives of families during bereavement does not match the cultural experiences of many groups of people – whether in the culturally rich amalgam that is the United States or in the rest of the world.
>
> (Balk, 2013, p. 163)

(See Chapter 5.)

Corr (2002) has expanded the scope of understanding of what can be disenfranchised beyond aspects of bereavement:

•   *Grief reactions and expressions of them* can be disenfranchised when some people actually insist that it is inappropriate for the bereaved to even *experience* the feelings, somatic effects, thoughts, and behaviours that come over them as they spontaneously react to the death of a loved one – as if it were possible to short-circuit reflex responses. Alternatively, certain feelings and thoughts might be approved – but not certain behaviours.

- *Mourning* can be disenfranchised when the significance of rituals in response to loss is dismissed or the bereaved are discouraged from attending or partici-pating in them; or when others discount the efforts of the bereaved to cope with loss and the pain it causes or to contend with the hardship involved in meeting new challenges (i.e. secondary losses). Rather than supporting the bereaved, other people might encourage them to repeatedly go over the cir-cumstances of the death or dwell on their pain.
- *Outcomes of grieving/mourning* can be disenfranchised when some respond negatively to mourners who, for example, grieve for 'too long', fail to return to 'normal' or move on, fail to 'get over it' and make new relationships, or still seem attached to the deceased (see Chapter 3).

However it occurs,

> The problem of disenfranchised grief can be expressed in a paradox. The very nature of disenfranchised grief creates additional problems for grief, while removing or minimising sources of support.
>
> (Doka, 1989, p. 7)

Many situations involving DG involve intensified emotional reactions (such as anger, guilt, or powerlessness), ambivalent relationships (as in cases of abortion or between ex-lovers), and concurrent crises (such as those involving legal and financial problems) (Corr, and Corr, 2013).

> Disenfranchisement may remove the very factors that would otherwise facili-tate mourning (such as a role in planning and participating in funeral rituals) or make it possible to obtain social support (for example, through time off from work, speaking about the loss, receiving expressions of sympathy, or finding solace within some religious tradition).
>
> (Corr and Corr, 2013, p.144)

Attig (2004) cites Neimeyer and Jordan's (2002) characterisation of DG as a form of 'empathic failure', a failure to understand the suffering and hurt of the bereaved, the gravity of what has happened, or the resulting anguish and loss of meaning in the mourner's life. This makes it hurtful and destructive. But Attig (2004) believes that DG also represents a *political failure*, including the abuse of power, which, in turn, often results from misuse of *authority*. For example, DG is an abuse of *authority as expertise* when others presume to know, but do not actually understand, a mourner's suffering or efforts to overcome it and decide what is best for him/her; they may limit the mourner's options in grieving, con-trol his/her ways of expressing grief, or sanction his/her efforts to overcome suffering.

Box 4.1   A case study in the abuse of authority in relation to DG

Attig (2004) gives the example of a church minister who conducted the funeral service of Elsie, a much loved 86-year-old woman, in the way that he thought appropriate. He knew next-to-nothing of either the needs or desires of her two sons, presumed authority to choose how the ritual and ceremony would unfold by adhering to the most rigid denominational protocol and ignoring the fact that most of those who attended the funeral were not members of his church. Also, instead of talking about Elsie's life, he gave a sermon; prior to the funeral, he had refused to allow Elsie's sons to tell him about their recollections of their mother. Consequently, he dismissed the experiences and needs of the bereaved, added unnecessarily to their distress, and denied the mourners opportunities for meaningful participation in ritual. The resulting funeral service was largely meaningless.

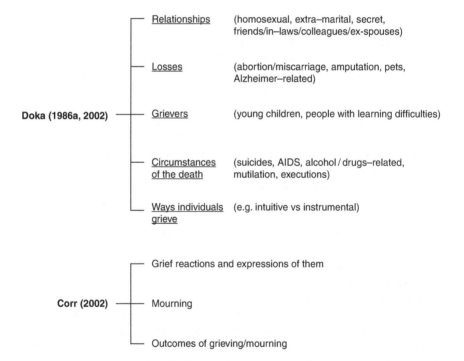

Figure 4.1 The scope of disenfranchised grief (DG)

Summary and conclusions

- Most theories/models of grief focus on its *subjective/ intrapersonal* features, reflecting the dominance of 20th-century psychology. But individual grief is experienced within widely-shared attitudes and practices surrounding death; these may apply to an entire society or sub-groups within them.
- The family unit represents the meeting place between individuals and the wider society; in order to understand and support an individual family member, we need to appreciate how the *family as a system* is affected by the bereavement.
- In the 20th century, grief became *medicalised* (e.g. Engel) and *normalised* (as reflected in stage/phase theories/models).
- Most grief theorists have ignored the work of Durkheim, according to whom the intensity of grief is caused by *social processes* and a socially constructed *formula*, rather than innate or natural tendencies. Similarly, Marris claims that grief severity depends on the degree of *social disruption* caused by the loss.
- These social influences are seen in anthropological studies of rituals surrounding funerals and burial rites (e.g. the Andaman Islanders and the Nyakyusa people).
- Both Gorer and Aries argue that death is taboo (the *taboo thesis*). At the same time, the media are obsessed with death and there is considerable academic/ research interest in the topic. In Western society, death is now largely denied.
- Walter proposes modifications or critiques of the taboo thesis. One of these is Becker's claim that the denial of death is not a modern condition but part of the *human* condition.
- In modern Western societies, death has become *professionalised*: some of the familial and communal rituals previously associated with bereavement have been taken over by hospitals and funeral directors. Death is largely hidden and sanitised through the involvement of professionally qualified strangers.
- Death occurs within the context of existing family relationships and dynamics. There is now a wide variety of family systems, including nuclear, extended, single-parent, and blended.
- According to *family systems theory* (FST), the death of a family member can have a powerful effect on both the family system as a whole and the subsystem(s) to which the deceased belonged. The family's functioning may be disrupted and the effects of particularly difficult (*untimely* or *traumatic*) deaths can be felt through later generations.
- Sharing the loss, maintaining open communication, regaining equilibrium, and making effective use of support systems and external resources all help the family to cope with a bereavement.
- While sudden and/or traumatic deaths cannot be prepared for, anticipated deaths may involve major stressors (i.e. secondary losses) over extensive time periods.

- Negative outcomes may include *incongruent grieving* (as when one bereaved parent displays intuitive grief and the other instrumental) and *dyssyncrony of grief* (as when bereaved parents neglect their other children).
- Positive outcomes may include increased sensitivity and spirituality, changed values, increased self-confidence, and finding meaning in suffering. Family members may also become closer.
- Funeral rituals serve a number of important functions, including helping mourners accept the reality of the loss (a major feature of grief work), providing a context for emotional support, and giving symbolic expression to thoughts and feelings.
- Funerals also provide a location for the deceased, but cremations make this more difficult to achieve than visiting the grave.
- In late-modern Western societies, funerals have become much more personalised and occasions for celebrating the life of the deceased. Instead of funerals being prescribed by handed-down beliefs, mourners now actively help to create the funeral as a *psycho-social-spiritual* event (Holloway et al.).
- *Disenfranchised grief* (DG) illustrates the social context of grief. Many situations involving DG involve intensified emotional reactions, ambivalent relationships, and concurrent crises. Attig regards DG as a denial of a basic human right and also an abuse of power (as in abuse of *authority as expertise*).

Chapter 5

Cultural and religious aspects of death and dying

The chapter will address the following questions:

- What is the relationship between grief and culture?
- Is it possible to experience grief outside of any particular cultural context?
- What do we mean by 'culture'?
- Why is it important to identify the different sub-cultures that exists within a particular country?
- How do different cultures define loss and death? What bereavement-related behaviours are prescribed by different cultures?
- In what ways does culture 'police' grief and grieving?
- What roles does religion play in death and mourning?
- What is the difference between 'official' and 'lived' religion?
- How do major world religions (Christianity – including Roman Catholicism – Islam, Hinduism, Sikhism, Buddhism, and Judaism) deal with dying, death, and grief?

According to Rosenblatt (2008b), 'No knowledge about grief is culture free' (p. 207). La Roche (2012) notes that focusing on culture as if it could be isolated from other aspects of human experience can easily lead to an approach based on social stereotypes; this, in turn, could lead to racial profiling. Further, for many of the world's communities, understanding relationships between life and death incorporates culturally specific, historically evolving religious traditions (Klass, 1999).

> Societies have traditionally taken tremendous care with the shared transformation of life into death, because of their responsibility to preserve everyday life's continuity and stability in the face of death's many disruptions.
>
> (Shapiro, 2013, p. 197)

Cultural beliefs and practices concerning death and its aftermath derive from a cosmology of shared worldviews incorporating death into interdependent, intergenerational lifecycles under highly specific circumstances for everyday survival. Who died, how they died, who remains to mourn and remember them, and what assistance they should expect from their community, are interpreted in light of cultural under-standings of death, its timing and circumstances, and its place in connecting the demanding present to an ancestral past and a hoped-for future (Shapiro, 2013).

The cultural dimension of death and grief has been studied by anthropologists for a long time; they have demonstrated how a community's rituals and beliefs facilitating the passage between life and death throw light on its beliefs and prac-tices. Moments of transition (such as from life to death) help us to understand how culture works: for most of us, in our everyday activities, culture is 'invisible' precisely because it is all around us and it is a major part of our assumptive world (see Chapter 3). As Shapiro (2013) puts it, it is as 'natural and unremarkable as the air we breathe or as the solid ground beneath our feet' (p. 201).

Some definitions: Culture and ethnicity

From before birth, we are socialised into our culture, which Valsiner (2012) defines in terms of four interdependent dimensions which together represent the context for human development:

• landscape and the natural world;
• economic activities for survival;
• human roles and relationships;
• cultural symbols and meanings.

Human symbolic activity guided by culture allows us to organise and symbolize our understanding of our environments, so that we are both shaped by them and shapers of them.

Throughout human development, both expected and unexpected lifecycle transitions (*normative* and *non-normative shifts*, respectively: Kloep and Hen-dry, 1999) create disruptions and discontinuities; we bridge these disruptions and discontinuities by drawing on the relationships, environments, private and shared meanings that offer stability and continuity (ways of making the new and unknown safe and familiar) (Shapiro, 2013). Cultural anthropologists use the con-cept of *liminality* to describe rituals of transition as culturally-sanctioned spaces of transformation that bridge one state or stage and the next.

> Cultural death and grief rituals are designed first and foremost to reassure the broader society that a community's life goes on after a member's death.
>
> (Shapiro, 2013, p. 202)

However, in culturally diverse societies, as well as in traditional societies that are becoming westernised, the relationship between culturally-sanctioned death and grief rituals and an individual or family's grief experience may be *discordant* (i.e. there may not be a perfect fit) (Shapiro, 1996). This has important implica-tions for any bereavement support that may be offered in such cultures: the person offering the support needs to understand the cultural norms relating to death and grief that apply to the person being supported.

According to Klass and Chow (2011), in the study of bereavement, 'culture' and 'ethnicity' refer to the same thing. The members of an *ethnic* group identify with each other as sharing common genetics, history, religion, language, geographic origin, governmental organisation, or physical appearance. Each of these elements may be flexibly applied and can change, sometimes rapidly, over time. *Culture* (from the Latin 'to cultivate') has many connotations, but in the context of bereavement and grief, Klass and Chow use it to refer to how a people or groups of peoples construe their world.

> Culture provides the templates for how people represent their experience and is, thus, the basis for their actions.
>
> (Klass and Chow, 2011, p. 342)

Cultural definitions of loss and grief

There are striking similarities in grieving across the diversity of human cultures (Rosenblatt, 1993). For example, across cultures, most people seem to grieve the loss of someone close; in almost all cultures, many people will feel that a person who has died continues in some way beyond death (Rosenblatt et al., 1976). This belief in the continuation of the deceased's relationships with the living beyond bodily death is one of three major types of response to bereavement and mourning rituals that Bowlby (1980) identifies based on the work of major anthropologists. The other two are:

(a) the belief that the bereaved are expected to feel angry with those responsible for the death;
(b) prescribing a time when mourning should end.

All three are described below.

Continuation of relationship with the deceased

In many cultures these continuing relationships are considered to be wholly beneficial, in which case rules and rituals are aimed at preserving them; in others (especially the more isolated, remote ones, least influenced by Western culture), relationships with the dead are regarded as more-or-less harmful; here, rules and rituals are aimed at protecting the living and despatching the dead. Nevertheless, according to Malinowski (1925) every society conceives such relationships as more beneficial than harmful. Either way, a sense of the persisting presence of the dead person is socially sanctioned and appropriate behaviour prescribed. This is nowhere more dramatically demonstrated than in Japan, as described in Box 5.1.

Box 5.1   Mourning a husband in Japan

- In both the Buddhist and Shinto religions, there is a deep-seated respect for ancestors, who are normally referred to by terms used to designate divine beings; it is believed that their spirits can be recalled.

- Mourning rituals are prescribed which encourage a continuing relationship with any person who has died: every family erects an altar in the living room, with a photograph of the deceased, the urn containing the ashes, flowers, water, rice, and other offerings.

- A widow's first duty after losing her husband is to build an altar, which she visits at least once daily to offer incense. She is also encouraged to visit it at other times, to ask his advice or share her feelings – positive and negative – with him. In this way, the relationship is maintained through his transformation from living man to revered ancestor.

The bereaved are expected to feel angry with those responsible for the death

In most non-Western communities, more children, adolescents, and young adults die than elderly people; in other words, most deaths are *untimely*, and the more untimely the death is felt to be, the more likely someone is held to blame, resulting in anger towards that person or persons. Most cultures define whom it is appropriate to blame, which may be third parties (commonly members of a nearby village or tribe), the self, or the deceased. Complaints against the dead for having deserted the living are known and sanctioned in many societies. *How* the anger may be expressed is also prescribed. While in some societies active expression of anger is an established part of the funeral rites (and may involve verbal or physical attacks on the deceased), in others this is forbidden. In some cases, directing anger against the self is not only permitted but prescribed; for example, among Moroccan Jews it has been a long-established custom for women mourners to tear their flesh with their finger nails until they bleed.

Prescribing a time when mourning should end

Bowlby (1980) draws on Mandelbaum's (1959) account of the Kota, one of the remnant tribal peoples who live in a remote area of India and whose funeral rites (at least up to the early 1950s) still followed much of their ancient form. These are described in Box 5.2.

Box 5.2   The double-funeral of the Kota

- The Kotas hold *two* funeral ceremonies, the Green and the Dry.
- The Green takes place soon after the death, where the body is cremated; only close relatives and friends attend.
- The Dry is a communal occasion held at intervals of a year or two to commemorate all the deaths that have occurred since the last Dry funeral; all the Kota people in the area attend.
- In the period between the Green and Dry funerals, the deceased is considered to still play a social role: a widow is held to remain her late husband's wife, so that should she become pregnant, the child is regarded as his with all the social rights that that confers.
- Not until the Dry funeral does the dead person's spirit depart and his/her social status cease.
- Mandelbaum sees demonstration of family cohesion and reaffirmation of kin relationships beyond the family as two major social functions of these funeral customs (see Chapter 4). Every participant is given a renewed sense of belonging to a social whole – the entire community of Kotas.
- At the same time, the personal and emotional responses of the bereaved are recognised and sanctioned, and in due course they are encouraged to return to normal social life.

Rosenblatt (1975) reports that many societies prescribe customs which seem to have the effect of helping widows to remarry and resume an apparently normal married life; examples include practising a taboo on the name of the deceased, destroying or disposing of his property, and changing residence. 'Officially' some of these customs may relate to fear of ghosts or contamination, or to actually honour the deceased. But Rosenblatt believes that their *true* purpose is to impel a widow through the transition from widowhood to a new married life.

Having acknowledged what different cultures have in common, Rosenblatt (1993) also points out that cultures differ widely in how they define death and appropriate expressions of grief. Indeed, Klass and Chow (2011) argue that we cannot experience our world outside the cultural framework we bring to it. They take this to imply that the distinction between *grief* as an internal, subjective process and *mourning* as its social expression is false (see Chapter 1). They quote Fontana and Keene (2009), who noted, 'It is really difficult to provide specific examples of grief, since the moment it is expressed it becomes mourning' (p. 162).

Thus there is no death that is not experienced within cultural categories and no grief that is not felt and expressed within cultural guidelines and expectations.

(Klass and Chow, 2011, p. 342)

Similarly, Rosenblatt (1993) argues that culture is such a crucial part of the context of bereavement that it is often impossible to separate an individual's grief from culturally required mourning. For example, in cultures with a belief system that says 'do not grieve because grief will cause the ghost of the deceased to take you away' or 'do not grieve because the deceased has gone to a better life', it is difficult to assess accurately what seems to be muted grief. It is difficult to distinguish where the rules that demand muted grief end and 'real' grief begins. Similarly, when the rules say 'cry' and people cry, how do we tell whether the crying is genuine, deeply felt, and likely to occur in the absence of the cultural demands for crying, or merely conformity with those cultural expectations?

Presumably, what people do in grieving feels real to them, and their expressions of grief in accord with cultural rules validate the rules and become part of the context of grief for others.

(Rosenblatt, 1993, p. 104)

Klass and Chow discuss the relationship between grief and culture/ethnicity in terms of three general themes: (i) bereavement is experienced within a cultural framework; (ii) culture polices grief; and (iii) culture affects how grief is handled.

Bereavement is experienced within a cultural framework

This distinction between *grief* and *mourning* may be seen as a peculiarly Western one, symptomatic of a more widespread phenomenon:

There seems to be good evidence that the definition of grief that gradually developed in the middle of 20th-century Europe and North America is part of the spread of the Western idea of mental health and illness.

(Klass and Chow, 2011, p. 343)

One implication of this development is that cross-cultural studies of grief may well be reporting only on how European and North American ideas have become assimilated into Asian, South American, Middle Eastern, or African cultures (Klass and Chow, 2011).

After examining how new words are being used in China to describe grief, mourning, and other bereavement-related phenomena, Klass and Chow conclude by saying that culture is how people construe their world:

Culture provides the templates for how people represent their bereavement and, thus, the basis for their feelings and actions. Culture provides the words by which people recognise and articulate their experience.

(Klass and Chow, 2011, p. 344)

Culture polices grief

Klass and Chow maintain that the radical individualism of modern consumer society seems to impose few restrictions placed on grieving. The popular mantra among bereavement counsellors that 'there is no right way to grieve' may be misleading: individuals grieve and maintain their bonds under the watchful eyes of their family and friends as well as those with religious and political power.

All cultures regulate their members' mourning, subtly or openly, implicitly or explicitly. In terms of Neimeyer's *constructivist model* of bereavement (Neimeyer, 2001: see Chapter 8), *individual* grief narratives are subjected to a *dominant* grief narrative. Society controls and instructs the bereaved how to think, feel, and behave, and those who don't conform to social expectations are labelled as 'abnormal' (Walter, 1999). In contemporary psychotherapeutic culture, abnormal grief is described as *complicated*, a term that largely replaced the former 'pathological' which made some bereavement counsellors uncomfortable (see Chapter 7). Complicated grief can describe those who are seen as grieving too long, grieving at the wrong time, or not grieving at all. Klass and Chow identify two major aspects of culture's policing of grief: (i) how grief is *expressed;* and (ii) how *continuing bonds* with the dead are managed.

Policing grief's emotions

Emotions must be expressed in ways that are congruent with larger behavioural codes, and different cultures differ widely regarding which emotions are acceptable and how overtly they may be expressed. How, or how much, emotional expression is 'appropriate' is often related to gender roles. In a review of anthropological studies, Rosenblatt et al. (1976) concluded that 'where there are differences, women seem to cry, to attempt self-mutilation more than men; men seem to show more anger and aggression directed away from self' (p. 24). This corresponds to Doka and Martin's (2010) distinction between *intuitive* (female) and *instrumental* (male) grieving (see Chapter 1).

Although gender roles may be the most obvious example of how emotional expressions are policed, *national character* may also be at stake (Walter, 1997). Klass and Chow (2011) give the example of the outpouring of grief following the death of Diana, Princess of Wales. Media commentators were ambivalent about an un-British expressiveness that seemed to contradict the 'stiff upper lip' stereotype. While the Windsors followed the coffin showing almost none of the deeply conflicting feelings her death must have evoked, the public, for whom she was their 'queen of hearts', wept and embraced openly (Biddle and Walter, 1998).

Policing continuing bonds

As we saw above, Japanese widows maintain their relationship with their dead husband via the altar. The dead as a whole pass easily from one world to another; they are both 'here' and 'there'. Chinese culture has a similar sense of ancestral bonds, though there it is based on Confucian beliefs.

During the 20th century, in the US and Western Europe, an original emphasis on continuing bonds (CBs) changed to a belief that these bonds should be broken (reflecting Freud's theory and the whole grief work approach), and more recently, back to advocacy of CBs (see Chapter 3). The mass slaughter of soldiers in the 1914–1918 World War overwhelmed the Victorian ideal of maintaining sentimental attachment between the living and the dead (Stroebe et al., 1992); by the end of the war, grief was being regarded as a private, individual process with few social customs to support it. Pathological grief was now defined in terms of failure to relinquish the useless attachment to the deceased.

A more extreme and controversial example of how the value and acceptability of ancestral bonds can change in changing political and economic circumstances is that of Communist China starting in the mid-1950s. In the Communist narrative under Mao Zedong, individuals were no longer to regard themselves as family members, but rather as workers, members of the proletariat. Funeral reform was high on the Communist Party's agenda: ancestor rituals were suppressed and loyalty to family was converted into loyalty to the State, and then to loyalty to Mao himself. In these and other ways, mourning and memory were assigned new meanings in keeping with the emergent dominant narrative of the state (Neimeyer et al., 2011).

Culture affects how grief is handled

Referring to Stroebe and Schut's (1999) Dual-Process Model (DWP)'s advocacy of a balance between loss-oriented and restoration-orientated coping (see Chapter 3), Klass and Chow (2011) cite observations in China which seem to indicate that there has recently been a disproportionate emphasis on restoration. Following the earthquake in Sichuan in 2008, tens of thousands of widows and widowers remarried shortly after their spouses' deaths. Also, a significant number of middle-aged mothers who lost their only child used reproductive technology to get pregnant soon afterwards. This inclination toward the restoration-orientation can also be seen among Chinese cancer patients; while accepting the fact of their illness, many reserve energy and resources for managing what is changeable.

Pressman and Bonanno (2007) found that Chinese bereaved people score (i) higher on measures of *avoiding* thinking about the deceased, which can help them focus on their daily tasks which they can control, and (ii) higher in searching for *meaning* in the bereavement process, which is related to restoration and functionality as it gives new direction for how to live after the death. Lalande and Bonanno (2006) reported that compared with US participants, Chinese bereaved people experienced more acute distress in the first few months but a faster improvement. This relatively more 'efficient' way of grieving might be related to the cultural value of pragmatism, the idea of moving on with life, and participation in ancestor rituals that restrict overt grieving to specific prescribed dates (Klass and Chow, 2011).

Sub-cultural or ethnic differences

Countries such as the US and UK are culturally diverse ('multicultural'), which means that we cannot just assume that what is 'normal' for one individual or family will also be normal for others. As Rosenblatt (1993) states, American popular culture may suggest that ethnic differences do not extend beyond food preferences and holiday celebrations. This may cause us to underestimate differences in relation to beliefs and practices regarding death and grief; this, in turn, may lead to intolerance and either failing to recognise the need of ethnic group members for emotional support or offering them an inappropriate form of support. For example, WASP (White Anglo-Saxon Protestant) Americans (and British) tend to 'psychologise' their emotional pain, while people in many other ethnic groups tend to 'somatise' theirs (Kleinman and Kleinman, 1985) (see Chapter 1). Hence, WASP people may find it difficult to support non-WASP-like grief.

Individuals who attempt to assimilate another culture's norms for bereavement, such as ethnic Americans trying to assimilate the WASP American norms that include self-control and suffering in silence (McGoldrick and Rohrbaugh, 1987), may experience guilt and depression, and, ultimately, may not effectively come to terms with a loss (Moitoza, 1982). Many people within such diverse countries may be *in transit* between cultures or grounded in more than one at the time of loss and may struggle to find an appropriate cultural footing for their grief. They may also be multicultural in the sense of feeling and expressing their grief in a way that fits no single culture: this blending may seem genuine and appropriate to them, but it may confuse others who are not similarly multicultural, again making support less likely or less helpful (Rosenblatt, 1993).

Each of the three themes explored by Klass and Chow above have implications for practice. For example, it may be that the striving for balance between loss- and restoration-oriented coping as recommended by the DPM isn't equally appropriate for all cultural/sub-cultural (or ethnic) groups. Also, in addition to the primary loss of the loved one, the bereaved person may need support in dealing with the *secondary stresses* induced by how family and friends are judging the (in)appropriateness of his/her grieving. Theories of grief and the techniques used to help the bereaved are themselves as culture-bound as any other aspect of bereavement (Klass and Chow, 2011).

Religion, death, and mourning

According to Klass (2013), issues in religion (and spirituality: see Chapter 8) are inescapable when we grieve and when we try to help the bereaved because religion is about human limitations. At their best, religions are about the boundaries between myself and others, between meaning and absurdity, between hope and despair, between life and death.

> Difficult bereavements bring us to the boundary between life and death, and so there the potential meaning of life and the potential meaningless of life becomes clear, the possibilities of both hope and despair are present, the boundary between me and the person who has died as well as the boundaries between me and other mourners become both defined and blurred.
>
> (Klass, 2013, p. 127)

While grief tests the assumptions about how the universe works and our place and power in it, religion may or may not be helpful to people as they try to come to terms with a significant death (Tedeschi and Calhoun, 2006). For some, their prior religious life might prove adequate, while for others their grief may seriously compromise their faith. All religions offer guidelines regarding how to dispose of the corpse (for example, should the body be burned because the true self has no further need of it?) as well as possible meanings for both physical and emotional suffering (for example, is suffering positive or negative?) (Klass, 2013).

Religion old and new

As Klass (2013) observes, in the past most people had access to only one or two religious traditions. If you were European, you were probably Christian (or Jewish if you came from certain parts of Eastern Europe); if you were Thai, you were probably Buddhist. With developments in communications technology and international travel, people have become increasingly exposed to all the world's (major) religious traditions. Examples of the meeting and mixing of religious traditions include Tibetan Buddhists living in New York and Pentecostal Christians living in Mexico City.

In traditional societies with only one religious tradition, religious rituals, symbols, and teachings prescribed (literally, *prewrote*) the mourner's inner experience. But with the rise of modernity, the old rituals lost much of their power; consequently, bereaved people today have an incredible range of symbols available to them: their *grief narratives* are *not* prewritten and they must engage in the difficult task of writing their narratives for themselves (Walter, 1994). This means that those trying to help the bereaved need to understand the symbols that mourners use for finding (or losing) meaning and the religious traditions that supply those symbols (Klass, 2013).

Official and lived religion

Another issue relating to helping the bereaved relates to the distinction between (i) the *official* version of the religion and (ii) the same religion as it is *lived* or enacted by the bereaved individual and his or her community. Klass (2013) regards this as a *practical* problem: accounts of how bereavement is dealt with by different religious traditions are typically written by religious leaders who are describing the official version or orthodox practice, rather than what people actually do. The official theology of a religion is only one element involved in how grief is narrated or expressed: in different cultural settings, the same religion often provides very different styles of grief.

Klass (2013) cites Wikan (1988), a Norwegian anthropologist, who studied mothers whose children had died in Egypt or Bali, both Muslim cultures. Officially, Islam teaches that every death has been predetermined, even predestined, but the teaching is interpreted differently in the two countries. In Egypt, emotions should be expressed, their God is close to them, compassionate, just and forgiving, while in Bali, the family, including the mother, should try to restrain their emotions and work to maintain a calm composure (especially in the presence of non-relatives); even among intimates, they will laugh and joke, and cheerfulness is mingled with mutely expressed sadness. While Egyptian Muslims believe that holding emotions in is bad for mental health, those in Bali believe that negative emotions can spill from the individual to the community and thus cause their spirits to weaken; this weakened state increases vulnerability to black magic that causes up to half of all deaths. Similar examples for Buddhism are described in Box 5.3.

Box 5.3   Differences in official versions of Buddhism

- One of the basic tenets of Buddhism is the realisation that all things are impermanent. The suffering in grief is the beginning of the path that will lead to enlightenment.
- 'All life is suffering' is the First Noble Truth.
- Yet in many Buddhist cultures, the religious rituals performed during the dying process and in bereavement are *not* aimed at realising the Noble Truth. Rather, the rituals are aimed at building merit, often by devotion to a Bodhisattva, that can then be transferred to the deceased to help them toward a better rebirth.
- Buddhism officially teaches that, to achieve enlightenment, we have as many lifetimes as we need. Reincarnation, rebirth to another lifetime, is a *literal reality*.
- Yet in Japan, although the doctrine of rebirth is still part of the tradition, the dead (including the great founders of the various Buddhist sects) become ancestors and stay part of the family – and so are *not* reborn (see Box 5.1).
- For American converts to Tibetan Buddhism, reincarnation plays almost no part in their grief, and merit plays no role in how they see themselves helping the bereaved or continuing their own bonds with the deceased. (Based on Klass, 2013.)

Similarly,

> When we investigate the official teachings of the religion about afterlife and continuing interactions with the dead, we are likely to find that they bear little resemblance to the heaven in which the bereaved hope to rejoin their dead family members or to the active interaction with the dead that the bereaved maintain.
>
> (Klass, 2013, p. 131)

Defining religion in a way that can help the bereaved

Klass (2013) outlines a way of defining the elements of religion, each of which can be both problematic and helpful in grief. To be useful, this definition (i) must apply to *all* the world's religious traditions; and (ii) will allow us to better understand the complexities of people living their everyday *intra*personal and *inter*personal lives – not just the official teachings.

Box 5.4   Klass's (2013) three elements of religion

1. Encounter or merger with *transcendent reality*, i.e. the sense that there is something beyond our everyday existence that we can, at least momentarily, experience as an *inner reality*. Our bond with the transcendental reality (such as God) is often connected with our continuing bond with the deceased.
2. A *worldview*, i.e. a higher intelligence, purpose, or order that gives meaning to the events and relationships in our lives. This is expressed in our assumptions regarding how the world works and what place and power we have in the universe. (See the discussion of *terror management theory* in Chapter 8.)
3. A *community* to which we belong, in which transcendent reality and worldview are *validated*.

A 'worked example' is, in the case of Islam:

1   Allah is the god who can be found but not understood by human intelligence.
2   The prophet Mohammed was given the revelation to which human life should conform.
3   The Umma is the community of all those who submit to Allah.

Buddhism has the three refuges: the Buddha, Dharma, and Sangha. Christianity affirms the trinity of (i) God the Father who is unknowable in Himself; (ii) God the Son who is in human form; and (iii) God the Holy Spirit who is the giver of understanding and foundation of the Church.

Based on his work as a professional helping the bereaved, Klass (2013) claims that these three elements are interconnected, such that as one changes, so the others will follow suit. For example, very often as the continuing bond with the deceased is comfortably established in the survivor's life, so the bond with the transcendent becomes less troubling, the meaning of his/her life becomes clearer, and troubled relationships in the community or family become less of a barrier. To be able to help the bereaved, we don't need to know 'how Muslims, Jews, Christians etc. grieve', all we have to do is to listen carefully and say as best we can how *this* individual or family relates to each of the three elements: 'we can let the bereaved be our world religions teachers' (Klass, 2103, p. 134).

How major world religions deal with death, dying, and grief

While only the bereaved themselves can tell us about their particular *lived religion*, in the rest of this chapter we shall take a look at some more 'official' versions of religious beliefs and practices regarding death, grief, and mourning rituals.

Christianity

Church of England

Anglicans (members of the Church of England) believe that those baptised into the Christian faith will share in Jesus Christ's resurrection and eternal life. Baptism is regarded as the outward sign of Christ's love and the ceremony has deep significance for believers (Green, 1993).

Baptism in infancy and childhood is associated with the naming of the child – the christening. If an infant dies not having been baptised, the family may feel that the child has been excluded from the family of God; this may cause the parents especially real distress. For this reason, if death is imminent, baptism may be arranged as a matter of urgency. In the absence of a priest, another Christian (who may be member of the hospital staff) may perform the ceremony. There is no age limit for baptism, and if someone dies unbaptised, the priest may offer a naming and blessing ceremony soon after death. This is particularly appropriate following a stillbirth (see Chapter 6); a certificate to commemorate the ceremony may be provided (Green, 1993).

For those already baptised, if death is imminent, the priest may be called to administer the sacrament for the sick (anointing ceremony) and offer prayers. Hospital chaplains and other clergy will offer prayer and comfort to anyone who requests it – including non-believers.

There is no religious objection to the giving or receiving of blood or organs, nor to the donation of the body for teaching or research; in this last case, the church would offer a memorial service, and a funeral service later following death when the body is finally interred. An Anglican body may be laid in the coffin with hands crossed over the chest, placed in an attitude of prayer, or supine with hands at the sides. Burial and cremation are equally acceptable.

If a patient dies in hospital, prayers may be said at the bedside at the point of death, or over the body in the ward or in the mortuary chapel. Last offices (washing and laying out of the body) are performed according to normal ward practice (Green, 1993).

Roman Catholicism

Catholic chaplains consider it their duty to visit Catholic hospital patients probably more so than do those of other denominations, and a priest is always available for the emergency administration of the sacrament. Patients who are able will wish to take Holy Communion (the sharing of bread and wine as an act of sharing with Christ) (Green, 1993).

As with Anglicans, baptism has great significance for Catholics of all ages, especially so when an unbaptised child is dying or has died (see above). Anyone, even a non-believer, may baptise in an emergency; the chaplain would register the baptism subsequently. For those already baptised, the sacrament of the sick is a symbol of Christ's healing and loving and it can be adapted to suit the circumstances. If the person is dying, the priest anoints him or her with consecrated oil on the forehead and hands ('extreme unction') which symbolises forgiveness, healing, and reconciliation. These sacraments are of enormous significance to believers (Green, 1993).

There is no religious objection to post-mortems, transfusions, transplants, or body donation, nor to non-Catholics handling the body, but the body should be treated with reverence at all times. Traditionally, in the UK and Ireland, Catholics are buried rather than cremated, but there is no religious prohibition to cremation. In some communities, especially among Irish Catholics, it is customary to display the body after death or at the funeral; if so, the body should preferably be embalmed. A Requiem Mass may be held at a later date to pray for the deceased and comfort the family and other mourners (Green, 1993).

Jehovah's Witnesses

Although they don't believe in the Trinity, Jehovah's Witnesses regard Jesus Christ as the Son of God and declare themselves to be Christians. They are well-known for their fundamental religious objection to the use of blood as part of medical practice (e.g. in transfusions), including both whole blood or its components (red cells, white cells, plasma, platelets). Blood samples may be taken for pathological testing provided any unused blood is disposed of. Most Witnesses carry a card which directs medical staff appropriately (Green, 1993).

Baptism is unusual before the age of 12; younger children are protected by the dedicated state of the parents and would not require urgent baptism, even *in extremis*. Baptised parents will not give permission for their child to receive a blood transfusion. There is no formal ritual for the dying, and both burial and cremation are acceptable. While the living body is dedicated to God, it has no particular religious significance following death. While post-mortem or organ/body donation are matters of individual conscience, most would probably object to donate major organs because blood would then flow through that organ (Green, 1993).

Rastafarianism

Central to Rastafarianism is the belief that Ras (Prince) Tafari, who became Emperor of Ethiopia (Haile Selassie I) in 1930, is a divine being, the Messiah of the human race, who will ultimately lead all black people to freedom. They do not regard themselves as Christians, but as the true Jews. It is a personal religion: there are no church buildings, set services, or official clergy.

The family may pray by the bedside of the dying person, but apart from this there are no last rites. Rastafarians believe in the resurrection of the souls after death, but not of the flesh. However, most would find both post-mortems and body donation extremely distasteful, and fear of contamination may make both blood donation and receipt of blood unacceptable. Burial is preferred but cremation is not forbidden. The funeral is plain and simple, unlike the elaborate funerals of other African-Caribbean communities; only intimate family and friends attend and there is no special mourning ritual. Family and friends are very supportive of the bereaved (Green, 1993).

Islam

'Islam' means 'submission' (to the will of God); followers of Islam are Moslems. The Islamic religion was founded by Mohammed (born AD 570) in Mecca (Makka), now in Saudi Arabia. Moslems believe in one God (Allah) and that Mohammed was his prophet or messenger (Black, 1987).

The dying Moslem patient may wish to sit or lie with his/her face towards Mecca; another Muslim, usually a relative, may whisper the call to prayer into the dying person's ear, and family members may recite prayers round the bed. In Islam, the body is considered to belong to God, and strictly speaking no part of a dead body should be cut out, harmed, or donated to anyone else. Post-mortems, therefore, are forbidden unless ordered by the coroner. Strict Muslims will not agree to organ transplants, and the subject should not be raised unless the family initiates it (Green, 1991).

After death the body should not be touched by non-Muslims; at the very least, others should wear disposable gloves if they have to touch it. Normal procedure involves straightening the body immediately after death; this is believed to ensure that it does not stiffen, making washing and shrouding easier. The head is turned to the right, so that the body can be buried with the face towards Mecca;

a sheet is used to conceal the entire body. The funeral should take place as soon as practicable, preferably within 24 hours; delay can be distressing for the relatives. Only burial is permitted. The bereaved are in mourning for three days after the funeral and visit the grave every Friday during the following 40 days (Black, 1987; Green, 1991).

Hinduism

The vast majority of Indians are Hindu, which is inextricably bound up with culture and social structure (see Chapter 4). It embraces a great tolerance of beliefs and practices, and different Hindu communities have different ways of expressing their faith and usually have their own local temple. Hinduism is *polytheistic*: numerous gods are worshipped, but each is the personification of a particular aspect of the supreme being that resides within each individual. The ultimate goal is the release of the individual's soul from the cycle of birth, death, and rebirth to join the supreme being (Black, 1987).

A devout Hindu who is dying may receive comfort from hymns and readings from the holy books (especially the *Bhagavad Gita*); some may wish to lie on the floor (symbolising closeness to Mother Earth). A Hindu priest may be asked to perform holy rites, which may involve tying a thread around the person's neck or wrist as a blessing, sprinkling blessed water from the Ganges over him/her, or placing a sacred tulsi leaf in his/her mouth. Hindus very much prefer to die at home and death in hospital can cause great distress (Green, 1991).

There are no religious objections to blood transfusions or organ transplants, provided permission has been obtained. While post-mortems are disliked, they are accepted. The family will usually want to handle the body themselves and to wash the body at home. As with Islam (and Judaism: see below), funerals should ideally take place as soon as possible, and in India this would be within 24 hours. Because all Hindu adults are cremated (infants and young children may be buried), in the UK there is likely to be a delay of several days due to pressure on crematorium capacity (Green, 1991). The ashes are scattered at sea, or over any large expanse of water (for which permission must be obtained). The family is in mourning until the thirteenth day following the cremation, when a special ceremony takes place (this applies equally to burials) (Black, 1987).

Sikhism

Sikhism ('Sikh' = 'disciple' or 'follower') originated in the 16th century in the Punjab, Northern India, as a reformist movement of Hinduism. The founder, Guru Nanak, tried to combine the best features of Hinduism and Islam. Sikhs believe in one God, each making his/her personal relationship with God and worshipping in their own way; after many cycles of rebirth, they aim to achieve true understanding and unity with God. Sikhism preaches the equality of all people, regardless of gender, caste, colour, or creed (Black, 1987; Green, 1991).

A dying Sikh may receive comfort from reciting hymns from *Guru Grant Sahab*, the holy book, or having them recited by any practising Sikh. There are no religious objections to blood transfusion, organ transplant, or post-mortems, and generally Sikhs are happy for non-Sikhs to tend the body. By tradition, the family is responsible for all ceremonies and rites associated with death, and many will want to wash and lay out the body themselves. Any hair (including beards) must not be trimmed, head hair should be kept covered, the face of the deceased may be displayed many times before the funeral (preferably displaying a peaceful expression), the whole body should be straightened and covered in a plain white sheet or shroud.

The body of a stillborn baby or late miscarriage should normally be given to the parents so that they can perform the normal funeral rites (cremation or burial); otherwise, Sikhs are always cremated. As with Hinduism and Islam, the funeral should take place as soon as possible following the death, and the ashes are scattered at sea or in a river. The family is in mourning for about 10 days, and the end of mourning is marked by a ceremony (Bhaug) held at the family home (Black, 1987).

Buddhism

Buddhism arose in the 6th century in Nepal, Northern India. It takes its name from the title 'Buddha' (The Enlightened One) given to its founder. Buddhists are now widely found in Sri Lanka, the Indo-Chinese peninsula, China, Japan, and Korea. In the UK, there are about 20,000 Buddhists (including native converts and refugees from Tibet and Vietnam) and three different 'schools', each with different traditions (Green, 1991).

Buddha is revered, not as a god, but as an example of a way of life. Buddhists believe in reincarnation, and so accept responsibility for how they exercise their freedom in life: the consequences of their actions may be felt in subsequent lives, which includes killing in any and every form (from killing insects, to abortion and euthanasia).

In relation to the dying, the most important consideration is the state of mind at the time of death; this will influence the nature of rebirth. Buddhists who are dying in hospital may seek a time of peace and quiet so that they can meditate; alternatively, they may seek counselling from a fellow Buddhist. There is no objection to blood transfusion, organ transplants, or post-mortems (Green, 1991).

There are virtually no formal or ritualistic requirements regarding how a corpse should be treated. Most important is that a Buddhist monk or minister is informed as soon as possible, ideally from the same school of Buddhism. Most Buddhists opt for cremation, and if the body or ashes are buried, the headstone should bear the Buddhist symbol of the eight-spoked wheel of the law. Where the rites cannot be observed, any burial service may take place; however, there should be no reference to Christian doctrine or the Deity, and Christian prayers should be omitted. A visiting and counselling service is usually offered by local Buddhists, and there also exists a Buddhist Hospice Trust (Green, 1991).

Judaism

In the UK today there is a wide range of observance amongst Jews, from the ultra-orthodox Hassidic Jews to those who belong to 'liberal' or 'reform' synagogues. *Sephardic* Jews originate from Spain, Portugal, North Africa, and the Middle East, while the ancestors of *Ashkenazi* Jews came from France, Germany, and Eastern Europe; they differ in terms of cultural heritage, liturgy, customs, and practices. Individuals from both backgrounds are to be found within all the groups (Orthodox, Liberal, Reform etc.). Many Jews retain a strong Jewish identity without necessarily being religiously observant. Even observant Jews may choose not to observe all the customs and rituals of Judaism, and may not even be familiar with the intricacies of specific Jewish laws (including some that are related to mourning: see below) (Katz, 1993).

'Where there is life, there is hope' is central to Jewish teachings and visiting the sick is a religious duty (*mitzvah*); this is to prevent the alienation and isolation of the sick as well as to pray for their complete recovery. This is related to belief in the sanctity of human life, from which follows the obligation/duty to heal the sick and to preserve human life, even if this conflicts with other religious obligations (such as the observance of the Sabbath: from sundown on Friday to sundown on Saturday) (Katz, 1993).

When approaching death, many Jewish people want to be visited by a rabbi, preferably their own; if possible, the dying person would (be helped to) recite psalms, in particular Psalm 23 ('The Lord is my Shepherd') and the special prayer (the *Shema*, the equivalent of Christians' 'The Lord's Prayer'). Also, if sufficiently conscious, s/he will recite 'confessional prayer on the deathbed', usually in Hebrew. Family and friends should be present to reassure the dying person that s/he is not alone when the soul departs. Once death has occurred, those present will recite the *Shema* (Katz, 1993).

The treatment of the body is seen as a religious act and strict rules must be observed. As with other religions, the body should be straightened, the eyes closed, and it should be covered by a white sheet; in addition, the feet should point towards the door. The body should be handled as little as possible and not left alone until members of the Jewish burial society come to collect it.

Box 5.5   The Jewish funeral

- As in Islam and Hinduism, burial should take place as soon after death as possible. Based on the belief that the body should be allowed to decompose naturally, cremation is forbidden (as are post-mortems or any disfigurement of the corpse unless required by civil law), but Liberal and Reform Jews may opt for cremation. Funerals cannot take place on the Sabbath or major festivals.

- Jews are buried in simple, plain wooden coffins, in designated burial grounds/cemeteries (quite separate from synagogue buildings).
- The chief mourners are first-degree relatives (children, parents, siblings), plus spouses. They deliberately tear an article of their clothing as an outward symbol of grief (*Kriya*); this permits the mourner to give vent to pent-up anguish via a controlled, religiously sanctioned act of destruction (Lamm, 1969). These torn clothes are worn throughout the week-long period of mourning (*shiva*) that follows the burial.
- Psalms and prayers are recited, and a eulogy given by the officiating rabbi, in the cemetery prayer hall with the coffin present on the trolley that will be wheeled down, in a slow procession, to the grave. At Orthodox funerals, the males present take it in turns to shovel earth onto the coffin (usually three times) until it is completely covered.
- The mourners return to the prayer hall (having ritually washed their hands before entering) and more prayers are recited, including the Memorial Prayer (*Kaddish*).
- After the service is officially over, people line up to greet each of the chief mourners (and, traditionally, to wish them 'Long Life').
- Many of these rituals are designed to help the bereaved accept the reality of the death (see Chapter 4).

(Based on Gordon, 1975; Katz, 1993.)

The mourners then return to a designated home (usually that of the deceased) to begin the *shiva*. Awaiting them will be a meal of 'recovery' or 'recuperation', a visible sign of communal solidarity and support, and a symbolic reminder that life must still go on.

> Until now, the mourner was allowed to withdraw into his own pain and loss and identification with the deceased, but now the community reaches out to redirect him back towards the path of complete living.
>
> (Gordon, 1975, p. 50)

This can be understood in terms of the oscillation between the loss- and restoration-orientations identified by the Dual-Process Model (DPM) (see Chapter 3).

Throughout the *shiva*, people come to pay their respects, bringing food or other gifts; formal prayers are recited each evening, including the *Kaddish*.

Reflecting Judaism's recognition that there are levels and stages of grief, there are five graduated periods of mourning: (i) between death and the funeral; (ii) immediate post-burial; (iii) the *shiva* week; (iv) 30 days from the burial (marking the official end of mourning, unless the deceased is a parent, in which case it continues for 12 months); (v) between 30 days and 12 months, when the memorial headstone is erected (Katz, 1993). The underlying aim is to help the bereaved gradually become reintegrated into the community, having accepted – but not forgotten – their loss. This represents an affirmation of life in the face of death (Gordon, 1975). (Again, this can be seen in terms of the DPM.)

Summary and conclusions

* Anthropologists have shown how a community's rituals and beliefs facilitating the transition from life to death help us understand how culture works.
* Culture is a major part of our assumptive world, helping to reassure us that a community's life survives the death of its individual members.
* However, in culturally diverse societies, as well as traditional societies subject to Western influence, the relationship between culturally-sanctioned death and grief rituals and an individual or family's experience may be *discordant*.
* Major beliefs and expectations cut across the diversity of human cultures, including grieving for a lost loved one, belief in some continued relationship with the deceased (as in the building of an altar by Japanese widows), the expectation that the bereaved should feel angry with those responsible for the death, and prescribing a time when mourning should end (as illustrated by the double-funeral of the Kota)
* Klass and Chow believe that the distinction between (subjective) grief and (culturally required) mourning is false, since grief can only be expressed – and experienced – within a particular cultural context.
* How culture *polices* grief is another crucial feature of their relationship: this may be seen in terms of *dominant grief narratives*, the distinction between normal and *complicated grief*, beliefs regarding how grief is *expressed*, and management of *continuing bonds* with the dead.
* Policing grief's emotions is related to gender differences, and the distinction between intuitive and instrumental grieving.
* Another aspect of policing concerns how grief is *handled*: in terms of Stroebe and Schut's Dual-Process Model, this may take the form of an emphasis on the restoration orientation (as in China in recent years).
* In culturally diverse societies (such as the US and UK), differences between different ethnic groups' beliefs and practices regarding death and grief may be underestimated; this may lead to intolerance and a failure to offer them appropriate forms of support.
* All religions offer guidelines regarding how to dispose of dead bodies and possible meanings for both physical and emotional suffering.
* In traditional societies with one dominant religion, the mourner's inner experience was largely prescribed. But in modern societies, people are exposed to many religious beliefs and practices: their grief narratives are no longer prewritten.

- An important distinction, with implications for helping the bereaved, is that between *official* and *lived* religion. This is illustrated by Wikan's study of Muslims in Egypt and Bali, and differences in official versions of Buddhism.
- According to Klass, all religions share three elements: encounter or merger with *transcendent reality*, a *worldview*, and a *community* to which we belong.
- Official versions of Christianity (including Church of England, Roman Catholicism, and Jehovah's Witnesses), Rastafarianism, Islam, Hinduism, Sikhism, Buddhism, and Judaism all prescribe ways of managing the dying, treating the dead body, and the nature of funerals (such as whether cremation is permitted – or obligatory). Each also provides rules regarding blood transfusion and organ donation. Some, notably Judaism, also dictate levels/stages of mourning.
- While there may be different official forms of each major religion, knowing a bereaved person's religious background and beliefs is a crucial requirement for being able to offer them effective support.

Chapter 6

Grief and relationship with the deceased

Kinship

The chapter addresses the following questions:

- What is meant by 'kinship' in the context of 'relationship with the deceased'?
- Why has spousal bereavement (loss of a spouse) become the norm for grief research?
- Why might young widow(er)s find it more difficult to cope?
- What is the difference between spousal bereavement and widow(er)hood?
- What is the impact of spousal bereavement in later life?
- What is the impact of loss of a parent in (particularly, young) adulthood?
- What is meant by '*adaptation anxiety*' in relation to loss of elderly parents?
- What is the impact of loss of a sibling in (i) childhood and (ii) adulthood?
- What is meant by the 'adult-sibling tie'?
- How does evolutionary theory account for the claim that loss of an adult child produces more intense and persistent grief than loss of a spouse, parent, or sibling?
- What is the impact of (i) miscarriage, (ii) termination, (iii) stillbirth, and (iv) sudden infant death syndrome (SIDS)?
- How do mothers and fathers typically react to different kinds of child death?
- How might a couple's relationship be affected by loss of a child?
- What parenting challenges are presented by the loss of a child?

Parkes and Prigerson (2010) identify three broad categories of influences on the outcome of bereavement:

(i) *Antecedent* (i.e. those which exist in some way *prior to* a particular bereavement), including relationship with the deceased, childhood experiences, later experiences, previous mental illness, prior life crises, and mode of death (see Chapter 7);

(ii) *Concurrent* (i.e. those which exist *alongside* or simultaneously with the bereavement), including gender, age, personality, socioeconomic status/ social class, nationality, religion, cultural and familial factors influencing the expression of grief (see Chapter 5).

(iii) *Subsequent* (i.e. those that occur *after* the bereavement), including social support/isolation, secondary stressors, and emergent life opportunities (see Chapter 8).

'Relationship with the deceased' is further broken down into (a) kinship (e.g. spouse, child, parent); (b) strength and security of attachment (see Chapter 2); (c) degree of reliance; (d) involvement; and (e) intensity of ambivalence (love/hate).

These all represent 'risk factors' for complicated grief, which is discussed in detail in Chapter 7. In the present chapter, we look in detail at *kinship*.

Spousal bereavement: The loss of a husband, wife, or partner

Not only is there no shortage of research into the psychological consequences of losing a partner (married or otherwise), but most of the research into the prediction of risk after bereavement has been conducted with widows and widowers in the English-speaking world: 'in that setting the reaction to the loss of a spouse has come to be seen as the norm for grief' (Parkes, 2006, p. 177).

As we noted in Chapter 1, a number of the earlier studies of bereavement involved widows (and sometimes widowers as well), including the London Study (Parkes, 1970, 1972), the Harvard (Boston) Study (Glick et al., 1974; Parkes and Weiss, 1983), Marris (1958), and Hobson (1964). It's also important to point out that Stroebe and Schut's (1999, 2010) Dual-Process Model (DPM), arguably the most influential and oft-cited of all major theories/models of grief, was developed with widowhood in mind – although it is potentially applicable to other forms of bereavement (Bennett and Soulsby, 2012).

This focus on widow(er)s is partly a reflection of its frequency and inevitability (it's 'on-time': Lopata, 1996). Especially in later life, spousal bereavement is a high probability event for women (Smith et al., 2005), who are likely to outlive their husbands/male partners and who tend to marry or partner men older than themselves in the first place. Age at widowhood has increased by almost seven years since the 1970s, from a median age of around 65 to 72 (Hirst and Corden, 2010); this, of course, reflects the increase in average life expectancy for both men and women (80 for women and 74 for men: Westendorp and Kirkwood, 2007).

Thirty-one per cent of women aged 65–74 are widowed, rising to 80 per cent of women aged 85 and over. Amongst men, 9 per cent of those aged 65–74 are widowed, and 47 per cent aged 85 and over (Smith et al., 2005). The differences in these figures for women and men are accounted for not only by the fact that women are more likely to marry men older than themselves, but also by the finding that widowed men are more likely to remarry than women (Bennett et al., 2003; Stroebe et al., 2001). Men do not expect to be widowers as much as women expect to be widows (Martin-Matthews, 1991). Widows are less likely to remarry because there is a dearth of potential partners: in the US, the ratio of 65–85-year-old women to men is 1.5:1, and for those of 85 and over it is more than 3:1. Also, cultural norms encourage men to marry women younger than themselves, so widowed men may opt to remarry younger women; older widows do not typically have access to a similarly expanded pool of potential spouses (Carr and Jeffreys, 2011).

Spousal bereavement versus widow(er) hood

As a general rule:

> The loss of a spouse affects almost every domain of life, and as a consequence has a significant impact on wellbeing: psychological, social, physical, practical, and economic.
>
> (Bennett and Soulsby, 2012, p. 322)

What Bennett and Soulsby are identifying here are the *secondary* losses that are part of the fall-out of the bereavement (the *primary* loss) (see Chapters 1 and 3). They observe that the terms 'spousal bereavement' and 'widowhood' are often used interchangeably, both in everyday conversation and by researchers and practitioners; this is a mistake. *Spousal bereavement* is the state of having experienced the death of one's spouse (the primary loss); its consequences (grief) are usually (though not always) short-term and have personal meanings. *Widowhood*, by contrast, is a long-term, ongoing state which not only has personal consequences but carries with it *social* consequences and meanings (see Chapter 4).

One reason for distinguishing between spousal bereavement and widow(er) hood is that the effects of each may well be different. Bennett and Soulsby (2012) give the example of short-term disruptions to sleeping and eating patterns as a consequence of bereavement (see Chapter 1), which don't often continue into long-term widowed life; two years is often regarded as an appropriate cut-off point for 'normal' grieving (see Chapter 7) or these 'symptoms' may not be seen as related to the bereavement at all. Longer-term consequences are more likely to be associated with the state of widowhood, both (a) *personal* (*intra*individual) such as continuing to miss the deceased, loneliness, and continuing restorative activities; (b) continuing changes in *identity*, which demonstrate the interaction between the *intra-* and *interpersonal* (Bennett, 2010a); and (c) *social*, such as changes in friendships, social support, and status, which continue long after the spouse has died. Widowed women, in particular, talk about changes in their friendships, how they are dropped by their married friends and make new friendships with other widows. They also speak of how little social support (formal and informal) they receive compared with their widower friends (Bennett et al., 2003); this was confirmed by Bennett (2009). Men also face a reduced social network when their wife dies, and remarrying is one solution to this problem (see above).

Consistent with this distinction between spousal bereavement and widowhood, Carr and Jeffreys (2011) distinguish between widowhood as (a) an *event* (how it's been characterised historically) and (b) as a *process*. Most older adults today die from chronic disease or long-term incurable illnesses. Heart disease, cancer, cerebrovascular disease, and chronic obstructive pulmonary disorder account for almost two-thirds of modern late-life widowhood; thus most become widowed following at least one spell of caregiving for an ailing spouse, and this may have lasted for months or even years prior to death.

Another illustration of the *normative* nature of spousal bereavement (i.e. both common and expected) is the history of Cruse Bereavement Care, the UK's largest provider of bereavement support.

Box 6.1   A brief history of Cruse Bereavement Care

- It began life in 1959 in the home of Margaret Torrie, a Quaker with a social work background, as a pilot scheme: a small group of widows in Richmond, Surrey, met to discuss the needs and problems created by widowhood – and society's attitude to bereavement.
- It was subsequently launched as a National Charity, with branches being set up where local committees could be formed.
- In 1970, Torrie published *Begin Again: A Book for Women Alone*, which became the 'bible' for widows (especially the young and middle-aged), social workers, relatives, and so on.
- Parkes's *Bereavement: Studies of Grief in Adult life* was published in 1972 by Tavistock (then by Penguin in 1975); Parkes was then, and continues to be, one of the world's leading experts in the field, and the book gave bereavement a much higher profile. He is Cruse's first Life President (since 1992) and was awarded the OBE for his services to bereaved people in 1996.
- In 1974, Cruse received its first government grant as recognition of its valuable community work and in the field of preventative healthcare.
- In 1980, *widowers* were formally included within Cruse's provision of help and changed its name to 'Cruse: The National Organisation for the Widowed and their Children'. The formal decision to extend provision to *all* bereaved people was taken in 1986.
- It changed its name to 'Cruse Bereavement Care' in 1987.

Spousal loss is the most frequent type of bereavement leading to psychiatric referral (Parkes, 2006). In one study, Parkes (1964) found that six times as many patients admitted to two London psychiatric units (1949–1951) showed symptoms of illness within six months of loss of a spouse as would have been expected given the death rate in the population. Death of parents was much less often recorded in these patients.

Among the factors which have been shown to predict problematic reactions to the death of a partner in several studies are an ambivalent or dependent relationship. For example, in the Harvard Bereavement Study (Parkes and Weiss, 1983), high levels of marital conflict were associated with little distress during the first few week of bereavement; after that, however, these widows and widowers' grief became severe and prolonged (even two to four years later). While dependent relationships were also associated with long-term grief, it was intense from the start.

Waskowic and Chartier (2003) found that widows and widowers classified as 'insecurely attached' to their spouse (using Griffin and Bartholomew's 1994 RSQ) suffered more anger, guilt, death anxiety (see Chapter 8), somatic symptoms, despair, depersonalisation, rumination, and social isolation compared with more securely attached people. These assessments were made an average of over eight years following bereavement.

In Parkes's (2006) Love and Loss Study, people who were referred for psychiatric help following the death of a partner were, on average, older and more often left to live alone than those referred following other kinds of loss. Although they were no more or less insecurely attached to their parents, they were rather more likely than others to report having had an unusually close relationship with their fathers. Both men and women reported significantly higher rates of unusual closeness to, and dependence on, their partners, less aggression and assertiveness, and greater loneliness after the partner's death; this loneliness was not reduced either by living with others or having a confidant(e). As a group, these widowed individuals were intensely bound up with their partner in a passive and mutually dependent way; either as a child or adult, they only ever displayed this clinging to their partner. The attachment to the deceased partner was *exclusive* and no substitute for a lost partner was acceptable.

Spousal bereavement as normative and non-normative

As noted above, for the majority of older widowed people widowhood is a common experience, with common and familiar effects (Bennett and Soulsby, 2012). For example, the widowed experience lower levels of psychological well-being (Hughes and Waite, 2009), and Bennett reported higher levels of depressive symptoms, lower morale, and reduced social engagement four to eight years following bereavement (Bennett, 1997, 1998; Bennett and Morgan, 1992). However, other studies suggest the effects are more short-lived (e.g. Zisook et al., 1994). The negative impact of becoming widowed on psychological health may recover over time (e.g. Lapota, 1996; Stroebe et al., 1993).

As far as physical health is concerned, the picture is less straightforward. A number of researchers have suggested that it is health *behaviours* and health *maintenance* behaviours which are challenged by bereavement. For example, widows may eat less well, sleep patterns may be disrupted, and consulting the GP may increase or decrease; these changes may depend on who was the health 'gatekeeper' – traditionally, the wife – and whether s/he is the one who has died (Williams and Umberson, 2004). Men, in particular, are more likely to die themselves, from a wide range of causes, but particularly from accidents; there is also evidence of people dying from a broken heart (Parkes et al., 1969).

Jagger and Sutton (1991) confirmed the findings of earlier studies regarding a significantly increased risk of mortality among elderly widows; this risk was greatest immediately after the husband's death, then returns to more normal levels over the next six months. This was true even after controlling for mental and physical health problems that pre-dated the bereavement and are associated with mortality.

For younger widowed people, bereavement is a *non-normative* event, and, therefore, its effects are less familiar. At younger ages, widowhood is associated with a greater decline in physical and psychological health (Prigerson et al., 1999; Stroebe and Stroebe, 1987). Off-time widowhood is seen as the most disruptive because younger adults are generally less prepared emotionally and practically than older adults to cope with spousal loss (Scannell-Desch, 2003; Stroebe and Stroebe, 1987). Parkes and Weiss (1983) and Lopata (1979) found that young widows present more psychological problems and have fewer friendships that those widowed later in life, and Parkes (1964) reported higher consultation rates for psychiatric symptoms for widows under 65. This difference is exaggerated when she becomes widowed suddenly (Ball, 1977): symptoms are both more severe and pronounced. A longitudinal study by Sanders (1980–1981) found that although initially younger adults had poorer psychological health, it improved significantly after two years; for older widows, the opposite pattern was found. Spousal bereavement at a young age may involve substantial restrictions of social life and may result in single-parenthood (Lopata, 1979).

Spousal bereavement in later life

While spousal loss can, of course, occur at any age, almost 75 per cent of widows in the US today (and other Western countries) experience this transition at age 65 or over (Carr and Jeffreys, 2011). Among people aged 65–74, 26.3 per cent of women and 7.3 per cent of men are widowed; these proportions jump to 58.2 (women) and 20.5 (men) for the over-75s.

Older bereaved spouses vary widely in their psychological adjustment to loss (see above). Some may have minor symptoms of depression and anxiety during the first three to six months following the bereavement, while others may experience severe, debilitating, and persistent symptoms, including complicated grief (Prigerson et al., 2008: see Chapter 7). While acknowledging that adjustment to bereavement may be affected by a wide range of biological, psychological, social, and economic factors, Carr and Jeffreys (2011) focus on four influences that recent research has identified as particularly important: (i) the nature of the relationship; (ii) circumstances surrounding the death; (iii) social support and integration; and (iv) other co-occurring losses and stressors.

(i) ***Nature of the relationship:*** Those writing from a psychoanalytic perspective predicted that bereaved people with the most troubled marriages would suffer heightened and pathological grief (Parkes and Weiss, 1983): they would find it hard to let go of their spouse, but at the same time feel angry at the deceased for having abandoned them. However, longitudinal studies that track married couples over time and into the widowhood transition have found the *opposite* to be true: older people whose marriages were warm and mutually dependent, with little conflict, experience heightened levels of grief within the first six months post-loss (Carr et al., 2000).

However, the strong emotional ties to the deceased spouse may prove *protective* in the longer term; this relates to the Continuing Bonds research discussed in Chapter 3. Maintaining a psychological tie to is an integral part of adaptation (Field, 2008), as when the bereaved partner wonders what the late spouse would have done in a challenging situation that s/he has to face (Rando, 1993). Others may keep the late spouse's legacy alive by recognising the continuing positive influence the deceased has on one's current life (Carr and Jeffreys, 2011).

(ii) *Circumstances surrounding the death:* Adjustment to spousal loss is affected by the timing and nature of the late spouse's death. In general, anticipated deaths tend to be less distressing than unanticipated ones: knowing that one's partner is going to die imminently gives the couple time to address unresolved emotional, financial, and practical issues before the actual death. This preparation for death makes the transition to widowhood smoother. However, for older people, 'anticipated' deaths are often accompanied by long-term illness, painful images of the loved-one's suffering, intensive caregiving, and neglect of one's own health; this can all take a toll on the survivor's physical health and emotional well-being (Carr et al., 2001).

Yet some research suggests that caregivers' psychological health may actually *improve* following the loss because they are relieved of the burden of their stressful caregiving duties: they no longer have to witness their loved one suffer, or they experience a sense of satisfaction, meaning, and achievement from caring for their partner in his/her final days (Schulz et al., 2008). However, like all carers, these elderly people may need practical and emotional support both before and after the loss.

Older adults who believe that their loved one was in pain and/or received less than satisfactory medical care at the end of life report greater anxiety and anger post-loss than those whose loved ones had a 'good death' (Carr, 2003). Use of hospice/palliative care services is associated with better bereavement outcomes (Christakis and Iwashyna, 2003). Similarly, deceased spouses who'd received hospice-at-home care, as compared with hospital or nursing home, were considered by their relatives to have received high-quality care, to have been treated with dignity and respect, and to have been given adequate emotional support (Teno et al., 2004). However, as we saw in Chapter 4, most people in Western countries will die in a hospital.

(iii) *Social support and integration:* Women's emotionally intimate social relationships during their lifetime are an important resource as they adjust to widowhood. Older widows typically receive more practical and emotional support from their children than do widowers, reflecting mothers' closer relationships with their children. Women are also more likely to have larger and more varied friendship networks than men, and these represent an important source of support as women cope with their loss (Ha, 2008). As we noted earlier, men are more likely to seek social support through new romantic relationships (whether dating or remarriage).

However, for both men and women social isolation and limited social contact – for whatever reasons – can impede adjustment to loss. The deaths of siblings and friends may also leave older bereaved spouses feeling isolated, as they have no one with whom to reminisce or share their private thoughts and feelings. This makes recreational, mealtime, educational, spiritual, and support groups hugely important community resources (Carr and Jeffreys, 2011).

(iv) *Other losses and stressors:* For older bereaved persons, the death of a spouse is almost always accompanied by other losses and stressors which may compromise their well-being, including financial difficulties, the loss of work and community roles (including retirement and relocation), compromised mobility (whether walking or driving), health deterioration, worsening of sight and vision, and even the loss of daily routines that gave life order and meaning (Carr, 2008)

These losses and stressors are *additional* to the *secondary* losses resulting from the bereavement itself; these may also compromise emotional and physical well-being. For widowers, the loss of a confidante, help-mate, and caregiver may be particularly harmful, while for widows, financial and practical difficulties are often a major source of distress (Stroebe et al., 2006). For widowers, it may be these secondary losses that account for their own increased mortality soon after their wife's death, rather than her death itself. Wives monitor their husband's diet, remind them to take daily medications, and urge them to reduce or stop smoking and/or drinking and other vices (Umberson et al., 1992). Widowers are more likely than married men to die of accidents, alcohol-related deaths, lung cancer, and chronic ischemic heart disease during the first six months post-loss, but not from causes that are less closely linked to health behaviours (Martikainen and Valkonen, 1996).

For elderly widows, more than half in poverty were not poor before their husband's death. Because the current generation of older women typically have had fewer years of paid work, they will have smaller pensions (state or private) compared with older widowers; this means they are more likely to live more frugally and rely on state benefits. These financial strains may compound the emotional pain and cognitive disruption triggered by spousal loss (Carr and Jeffreys, 2011).

Loss of a parent in adult life

As Parkes (2006) observes, 'most people who reach the age of 50 are orphans; they will have lost one or both parents' (p. 158). Despite spousal bereavement being the normative loss as far as the major theories/models of grief are concerned, the largest group of people going to Cruse Bereavement Care (see Box 6.1) in 2013–2014 were those who had experienced the death of a parent (Debbie Kerslake, Cruse Chief Executive, personal communication). This is consistent with statistics for previous years.

Although there have been many studies of the psychological effects of the loss of a parent, most of these have involved children of school or pre-school age, when the death of a parent is relatively uncommon. In general, it appears that in this age group long-term problems are more likely to arise from inadequate subsequent parental care than from the loss itself (Harris et al., 1986) (yet another example of the impact of *secondary* losses).

Although understanding a child's grief when a parent dies is beyond the scope of this book, we will consider the effects of losing a sibling in childhood. The flip-side of this childhood loss of a sibling is the parents' response to the loss of a (young) child: surviving siblings can become the victims of their parents' grief for the deceased child. We shall also see that loss of a young child may put a strain on the marital relationship to the point of separation/divorce and a large number of studies have investigated the effects of divorce on children (e.g. Hetherington and Stanley-Hagan, 1999), including its effects on the security of the child's attachments (see Feeney and Monin, 2008; see Chapter 2).

Loss of parents in young adulthood

Because loss of one's parents as an adult is *normative* and timely, studies of its effects are few compared with the number of child studies (Parkes, 2006). However, according to Abrams (1992), there has, traditionally, been an even greater dearth of studies of the effects of parental loss when children are in their teens and early-mid 20s; clearly, losing a parent at this age is *not* normative and timely.

In the Introduction to *When Parents Die*, a personal account of the loss of her biological father when she was 18 and her step-father two years later, Abrams (1992) says that she wrote the book for people whose parents have died long before the acceptable age of 70 or 80:

> long before you are up and running with your own life; long before you are ready to live without them; whose death makes you different from everyone else of your age . . . whose death, in short, interferes at every level with the business of being young and growing up.
>
> (Abrams, 1992, p. xiii)

Before she wrote her book, Abrams says that there was no published material that addressed these issues and concerns. She quotes a student counsellor from Kent University whose ideas about bereavement had changed totally as a result of his work with young adults: having assumed that the grief resulting from the loss of a parent at this age was similar to that of older adults, he wondered whether students had to bear the *additional* burden of pain and guilt related to their separation – physical and intellectual – from their families. Abrams agrees: such death is untimely and unexpected, is not 'in the scheme of things' at this time of your life. If the death is also sudden (her father died of a heart attack), there is no opportunity to prepare, which 'leaves you feeling that the whole world has become an unsafe and unreliable place in which nothing can be trusted or valued any longer' (p. xiv). She believes that perhaps the hardest aspect of a parent's death for young people – and the most consistently overlooked and misunderstood – is that grief involves feelings of helplessness and lack of control that are exceptionally difficult to cope with when you are at precisely the stage of your life when you need to feel powerful and in control:

> at a time when everyone expects you to be taking charge of your life – yourself included. Immense pressures on people in their teens and early twenties often make it *impossible* to grieve Often the only solution, the only effective strategy for survival, is to put it off and deal with grieving later.
>
> (Abrams, 1992, p. xvi; emphasis in original)

She goes on to acknowledge that grief avoided for 5, 10, 20 years becomes more difficult to feel: delayed grief often becomes denied grief, which can cause untold anguish later in life (see Chapter 7). One implication of this is that, in order to understand a person's grief and to be able to support them through it, it is necessary to *contextualise* it within their life at the time the bereavement occurred. In Abrams's account, the context is provided by the intra- and inter-personal expectations relating to teenage-hood and young adulthood (see Chapter 4). This, in turn, begs the question as to when we become adults.

Box 6.2   When do we become adults?

- According to Apter (2001), in *The Myth of Maturity*, it's taking young people far longer to achieve adult status than in previous generations. She refers to 18–24-year-olds as 'thresholders', because they are only *on the brink* of achieving self-sufficiency and autonomy (commonly cited adult qualities); they are like 'apprentices to adulthood'.
- A total of 58 per cent of 22–24-year-olds and 30 per cent of 24–30-year-olds (still) live with their parents.
- Leaving home isn't a single event but a prolonged *process*: 40 per cent of female and 50 per cent of male thresholders who leave home will subsequently return.

Apter's findings, as described in Box 6.2, imply that, compared with previous generations, many more young people will still be living at home (either never having left or having returned) when one of their parents dies. Also, with *blended* families fast becoming the norm (see Chapter 4), young people are much more likely than in previous generations to experience the deaths of both biological and step-parents (as well as step-siblings and other step-relatives).

Death of an elderly parent

While adult children begin to prepare for the deaths of elderly parents and to see these as normative occurrences, there is no consensus as to whether such antici- pation mitigates the impact of the loss (Balk, 2013). In the case of Alzheimer's disease, or other forms of dementia, the loss seems to occur *before* death itself and has appropriately been called *ambiguous* (Boss, 1999: see Chapter 1). Adult children who have been caring for their sick parent may experience a range of responses to his/her death: sorrow, clinical depression, numbness, relief, and guilt, and emotional distress increases for those who were already distressed prior to the death (Aneshensel et al., 2004). Dementia only serves to highlight a more general phenomenon: old people often become physically and emotionally dependent on their children, which can re-arouse earlier attachment problems and spoil the final years together.

As parents become old, their adult children begin to display signs of *adapta- tion anxiety* (Moss et al., 2001), such as worrying about how to provide for parents at the very end of life, how to cope with their actual dying, and how to manage their life without them. The evidence is mixed regarding the benefits of anticipa- tory grieving:

(a) some research has concluded that following an elderly parent's death, adult children who reported anticipatory grief were better adjusted than persons who did not (Smith, 2005);
(b) other research indicates that adaptation anxiety did not make coping any less difficult (Lund, 1989; Moss et al., 2001).

The reality of anticipatory grief/mourning has been disputed (Fulton, 2003), and Balk (2013) cites research evidence showing that (i) over time spousal bereave- ment outcomes may be indistinguishable between sudden and anticipated deaths (see earlier discussion in this chapter) and (ii) an anticipated death that is difficult and drawn out over a protracted period of time may have severe psychological costs – especially if the parent experienced significant suffering.

Moss et al.'s (2001) review of research concluded that complicated or patho- logical grief tends to be rare for surviving adult children. However, some studies have shown increased rates of depression (Birtchnell, 1975; Cleiren, 1991) and suicide (Bunch et al., 1971) following the death of parents. This increase in sui- cides was largely confined to men who had never married and continued to live with their mother; this suggests longstanding clinging or other insecure attachments (Parkes, 2006), such as intense 'partnership' relations with the dead parent (Horowitz et al., 1981).

Parkes's (2006) Love and Loss Study suggested that there is a minority of adult children who may not have fully achieved the autonomy (usually during adolescence) which allows us to survive without our parents' nurture. Unusually close attachments may persist, reducing the chance of making new relationships and spoiling those that are made. Parkes found a large proportion of orphans who were either unmarried or in conflict with their partner. When the parent finally dies, this may threaten mental health; on the other hand, it may also provide the orphans with opportunities to discover their true worth, strength, and potential.

Because women marry men who, on average, are older than themselves, and because men, on average, die earlier than women (see above), most people lose their father before their mother. It could be that the greater distress expressed following a mother's death reflects the fact that she will have been the remaining parent and so the adult child is now parent-less (a 'true' orphan); the child has now moved to the 'head of the queue' (Parkes, 2006) (unless there is an older sibling or siblings: see later discussion). As Parkes (2006) says, 'There is nothing like the death of a parent to bring home the prospect of one's own mortality' (p. 160).

Loss of a sibling in children and adults

According to Dunn (2000):

> our relationships with our siblings are the longest-lasting we'll probably have – longer than those with our parents or partners, or with our children. Indeed, towards the end of the lifespan, relationships between siblings take on particular importance for many people as sources of support.
>
> (p. 244)

Similarly, Gill White (2006) observes that these relationships are unique in their duration and intimacy and are potentially the longest ones we will ever have. Consequently, the death of a brother or sister can be traumatic for siblings at any age; indeed, siblings' stories reveal that the impact of such a death lasts a lifetime, influencing their surviving siblings' ways of being in the world. While the impact of sibling death in childhood is well documented, this is not the case in adulthood (Marshall and Davies, 2011).

Childhood sibling loss

Children are affected in varying degrees by a sibling's death. Many factors affect children's grief responses, including the child's age and gender, health status, temperament or coping style, previous experience with loss, cause and location of death, duration of the sibling's illness, and the degree to which they were involved in the sibling's illness and events surrounding the death (such as the funeral or memorial service) (Marshall and Davies, 2011). Bereaved children who are actively involved in the care of their sibling or in planning the funeral or related events display fewer behavioural problems than those who are excluded (Davies, 1988a, 1999). Giving children a clearly informed choice about whether or not they want to be involved is of key importance.

Also critical is the nature of the pre-death relationship. When siblings have shared many aspects of their lives, the loss of one of them leaves a large empty space in the surviving sibling(s); this empty space is even larger when they were especially close (Davies, 1988a, 1999). Again, where the family freely expresses feelings and thoughts, this fosters a sense of cohesion and closeness and bereaved children display fewer behavioural problems (Davies, 1988b, 1999: see Chapter 4).

Based on her research with bereaved children and adolescents, and with adults who lost a sibling in their childhood, Davies (1999) characterised bereavement responses using the siblings' own words. These are described in Box 6.3.

Box 6.3   Sibling bereavement responses (Davies, 1999; Marshall and Davies, 2011)

- *'I hurt inside'*: This includes all the physical responses and emotions typically associated with grief that arise from the vulnerability of being human, from loving others and missing them when they are no longer with us. Unlike adults, children are often unable or inexperienced at identifying what they are feeling; instead, they express emotions through *behaviour*. This can take many forms, both positive and negative, some of which are quite clearly signs of grief (such as eating and sleeping disturbances), while others may not be (such as decline in school performance).

- *'I don't understand'*: How children begin to make sense of death depends on their level of cognitive development; once they have personal experience of death, their worlds are changed forever. As they develop new ways of understanding and approaching the world, they will have new questions about the death and will want to hear the story of the death afresh.

- *'I don't belong'*: A death in the family tears apart the normal day-to-day patterns of family life. Parents are overwhelmed by their grief (see text below) and siblings don't know what to do or how to help (or if they should try); they may begin to feel as if they are not part of what is happening. Over time, as roles and responsibilities realign within the family, siblings may feel as if there's no longer a place for them. Adolescents may feel very different from their peers and that they don't belong here either.

(Continued)

Box 6.3   Continued

- *'I'm not enough'*: Siblings typically want to help reduce their parents' despair, but nothing they do seems to help and they may begin to feel that they are 'not enough' to make their parents happy. Moreover, some may feel that the deceased sibling was the parents' favourite: *they* should have been the one to die. While these feelings of inferiority may have been present before the death, they are compounded when parents direct intense emotion and longing towards the deceased child. These feelings can be exacerbated if the mother subsequently has another child. (As Abrams (1992) observed when discussing loss of a parent, the bereaved children – in this case siblings – are often overlooked: the focus is on the bereaved spouse or – in this case – the bereaved parents.)

Adult sibling loss

Echoing many aspects of Davies's descriptions of the sibling's grief responses, Rowe (2007) observes that:

> There are the efforts, often lifelong, to preserve the dead sibling in some way, and the efforts to save others in the way the living sibling should have saved the dead sibling. For many children the only solution is to become especially good.
>
> (p. 196)

Rowe gives the example of J. M. Barrie, who immortalised his brother, David, in *Peter Pan*, the boy who would never grow up. David was killed in a skating accident, aged 13, when Barrie was aged 6. This immortalisation through literature is an extreme example of trying to keep the deceased alive through our memories of them (see discussion of Continuing Bonds in Chapter 3).

What Connidis (1992) calls the *adult sibling tie*, helps to connect this discussion of sibling loss with the earlier discussion of loss of one's parents in adulthood. When elderly parents die, many adult children find that, despite believing they were prepared for this normative death, they are shocked by the discovery that they are now facing the world 'on their own'. Some people stay close to their siblings, even though they may not particularly like them, because they feel that the connection to their siblings maintains the connection to their deceased parents who, somehow, continue to act as a buffer between themselves and the infinite (Rowe, 2007: see Chapter 8).

Sibling loss has been described as a *disenfranchised loss* (Doka, 2002; Wray, 2003; Zampitella, 2006). As discussed in Chapter 4, some people's grief isn't typically recognised as being as significant or justified as others'. As we saw above, amongst relatively young adults, concern is first directed towards the surviving spouse, then probably the parents of the deceased, then the children; siblings will be relatively overlooked. (Abrams, 1992, observed that teenage or young adult children can also be overlooked.) In the case of a child's death, the focus will be on the parents, with the sibling(s) again often being overlooked (often by the grieving parents themselves).

Marshall and Davies (2011) use Davies's (1999) four-part model (see Box 6.3) as a framework for considering sibling loss in adults:

- *'I hurt inside'*: Adults, like children, experience tremendous pain and suffering following the death of a sibling. But as a disenfranchised loss, friends, work colleagues, and even relatives are often ill-prepared to offer support: they simply do not understand the pain. This lack of support may inhibit the ability to integrate the loss into their lives.
- *'I don't understand'*: Losing a sibling is not seen as normative or part of the 'natural order' in the way that loss of elderly parents is. At the same time, they may have to support their elderly grieving parents who have lost a child; they suddenly seem fragile and unable to cope, characteristics which the adult child may not have witnessed or acknowledged previously.
- *'I do not belong'*: The absence of a sibling permeates all aspects of an adult's life, as if one does not belong to the 'new order'. The changed structure of the family of origin is also painful and the relationship with the deceased sibling's family (sister-or-brother-in-law and nieces and nephews) is also changed.
- *'I am not enough'*: Adults are able to understand their elderly parents' grief at the loss of a child, and this recognition is painful. As with children, individual, situational, and environmental factors interact and impact on how the adult responds to the death of a sibling. Coping style, temperament, previous experiences of loss, the circumstances of the death, and the prior relationship with the deceased sibling are all contributory influences. Death of a sibling in adulthood 'ripples across multiple levels. We are changed as parents, as children of ageing parents, and as aunts and uncles to the children of our deceased siblings' (Marshall and Davies, 2011, p. 114).

The loss of a child

According to Raphael (1984):

> The loss of a child will always be painful, for it is in some way a loss of part of the self. . . . In any society, the death of a young child seems to represent some failure of family or society and some loss of hope.
>
> (p. 227)

From a purely practical perspective (such as the degree of disruption to one's life), we might expect that the death of a post-adolescent child would be less stressful to the surviving parents than spousal bereavement is to the surviving husband or wife (Parkes, 2006). However:

intuition and the evidence from both clinical and comparative research tell a different story. To most people in the west, the death of a child is the most agonising and distressing source of grief.

(p. 166)

While we might expect the loss of a baby or young child to be the most painful of all, Stroebe and Schut (2001) claim that the loss of an adult child results in more intense, or more persistent, grief and depression than loss of a spouse, parent, or sibling. This can be accounted for by *evolutionary theory* (e.g. Archer, 1999).

Box 6.4   The evolutionary account of the intensity of grief for a child (Archer, 1999)

- The strength of an attachment – and the intensity and duration of the grief resulting from its loss – is proportionate to the *genetic value* of the lost person.
- Since a child is the major means of perpetuating our genes, we should expect that the death of a child would produce severe and lasting grief: we are losing our *genetic immortality*.
- Despite a lack of systematic evidence, the evidence there is indicates a steady overall *increase* in the intensity of grief from early pregnancy through to loss of an adult child; in other words, the older the child, the more intense and long-lasting the grief.
- This conclusion is consistent with the increase in reproductive value of the child as it gets older, which is also correlated with the *decline* in parental reproductive capacity.
- Evidence consistently supports the further predictions that (a) *mothers'* grief would be greater than fathers' early in the child's life; and (b) this difference would largely disappear as the child gets older.
- Based on studies of miscarriage, abortion, and loss of child, it seems that grief is more pronounced among *older* mothers; this is consistent with their (relative) loss of reproductive value (as indicated by going through the menopause).
- Women with no other children have been shown to react more strongly to both miscarriage and even more so to child deaths at later ages.
- Giving birth to a subsequent child is strongly correlated with reduced grief and depression, and improved family outcome (Kissane and Bloch, 2002). While this is consistent with the evolutionary approach, it's possible that the subsequent pregnancy could be a *consequence*, rather than a cause, of emotional recovery (Parkes, 2006).

Parkes (2006) notes that in Third World countries, women continue to have large families because they expect many of their children to die; here the death of a child, especially in infancy, is *less* psychologically devastating than it is in Western countries (Scheper-Hughes, 1992). In the Western 'medically privileged world', a child's death is untimely and non-normative, and is often traumatic, sudden, and sometimes inexplicable (as in sudden infant death syndrome/SIDS: see below) (Parkes, 2006). However, Miles (1985) found no difference in the grief of parents whose child died from chronic disease and those who lost a child in an accident. Parkes cites a similar study in Turkey which found higher rates of chronic grief and persisting 'traumatic stress' in parents of sons who'd been killed in armed conflicts compared with those whose sons had died from leukaemia.

Parkes (2006) suggests that *social support* is crucial in determining how parents, and especially the mother, cope with the loss of a child, and, to a greater extent than with other types of loss, *gender differences* in how parents grieve can cause problems between the parents. Both these issues are discussed in more detail below.

Inevitably, when a child dies, and however it dies, parents will feel cheated of the child's life and future. Their relationship with their child begins long before birth. For each parent there is the fantasy child s/he will have, which builds on the pre-conception images of what a baby – this baby – will be. Of course, many pregnancies are unplanned or unwanted (initially or even throughout), which makes the relationship with the unborn baby highly ambivalent (Raphael, 1984). But, in all cases the loss of a baby will need to be grieved for, at whatever stage of pregnancy this might occur. (Recall that in Chapter 4 miscarriage, termination, and stillbirth are all given as examples of *disenfranchised grief*, making the grief potentially more complicated: see Chapter 7.)

Miscarriage (spontaneous abortion)

According to Raphael (1984), the level of the mother's grief will be affected by whether or not the baby was wanted; this can be true even with an early miscarriage (i.e. before the baby is viable). But after the baby's movements have been felt, it is more likely to be seen as the loss of a 'person'. The loss is not 'nothing' or 'just a scrape' (dilatation or curetage) or 'not a life', but the beginning of a baby. The use of technical terms to describe the baby – products of conception, conceptus, embryo, foetus – might be perceived as an attempt to *deny* the existence of a baby the woman already loved, and thus to deny the reality of the grief she experiences for that baby (Buggins, 1995).

The sadness of the loss is often compounded by fear and panic, as in any emergency situation. There is rarely time to deal with these emotions, and many women report feelings of total helplessness (Sherr, 1989). Even if the mother does not have a very clear concept of her lost baby, as with other losses it can never be replaced (by another pregnancy).

Termination (therapeutic or induced abortion)

In the UK, the 1967 Abortion Act defined therapeutic termination as one undertaken before the gestational age of 28 weeks. But due to advances in technology, the chances of survival for pre-term babies have greatly increased, and a reduction to 24 weeks was approved by Parliament in 1990. The Abortion Act made it possible for a woman to have an abortion legally, provided two doctors independently agreed that the termination was necessary to prevent:

- The likelihood of the woman's death
- Permanent illness (physical or psychological)
- Damage to a woman's existing children
- Abnormality in the baby

The Act stopped far short of endorsing the idea that a woman has an absolute right to control her body. Practically, the law relies on individual doctors exercising discretion as to who is eligible for an abortion.

Despite its legality, abortion is still a very 'live' moral issue. But the debate has also involved empirical concerns about the links between unwanted pregnancy, abortion, and long-term mental health. Specifically, many authors have proposed that abortion may have adverse mental health effects owing to guilt, unresolved loss, and lowered self-esteem (Fergusson et al., 2006). According to Raphael (1984), the pattern of grief is similar to that for miscarriage, but suppression or inhibition of grief is much more likely.

Stillbirth

A stillbirth occurs when a baby born after 24 weeks' gestation fails to breathe (Murphy, 2012). Knowledge of the fact that there is no live baby at the end of the labour can magnify the experience of pain. The increased use of drugs may reflect the feeling that the labour is futile, but it is unclear whether parents want greater control and perceive the birth as a purely medical event to protect them from the reality.

Despite being a relatively rare event in the UK, 4,100 babies were stillborn in 2010 (Sands, 2012). The unusual nature of this type of death marks parents out as 'different': in Goffman's (1963) terms, it is 'stigmatising'. While this term tends to be perceived as wholly negative (Shih, 2004), Goffman himself suggested that some positives could be found in stigmatised identities. Murphy (2012) suggests that, while bereavement by stillbirth is, overall, a negative experience, for some parents there may be positives to be found in their loss. (See the discussion of *posttraumatic growth* (PTG) in Chapter 8.) Over the past 40 years, understanding of stillbirth and its affect on parents have changed markedly (as described in Box 6.5).

Box 6.5   Changes in the medical management of stillbirths

- Up until the 1970s, parents would not see the baby and they would normally be advised to go home and try again (Kohner and Henley, 2001). Stillbirth was not considered by medical staff to be a 'proper bereavement' (Lovell, 1983), and this belief was often reinforced by the parents' friends, families, and colleagues (despite the parents' 'obvious' grief).
- Sands (The Stillbirth and Neonatal Death Society), formed in 1978 by bereaved parents angry at the lack of recognition of their loss (Allsopp et al., 2004), has made important progress working with health professionals and publication of guidelines.
- Sands recommends that parents should be offered the chance to see, hold, and spend time with their baby (Schott et al., 2007), and many hospitals now have a bereavement midwife who will oversee the management of care following loss, as well as trained staff to support parents.
- Even if the baby has a physical abnormality, it is much worse to fear an imaginary baby than to view the real one: parents seem to see the baby as beautiful no matter what (Sherr, 1989). If there is a congenital abnormality or intrauterine event that makes the baby obviously not viable – or that it has already died – it may be possible for the parents to engage in some anticipatory grieving (Raphael, 1984).

Gender differences in grieving styles

While general social attitudes may not have 'caught up' with those among health professionals, the grief experienced by parents following stillbirth is now well documented in academic literature (Murphy, 2012). Often the focus is on *gender differences* in grieving styles. Peppers and Knapp (1980) reported that men tend to suppress their grief after a pregnancy loss or infant death, while women are more expressive. (This corresponds to what Doka and Martin (2010) call *instrumental* and *intuitive* grieving, respectively: see Chapter 1). This led to couple conflict, as mothers tended to think that a failure to express grief meant that their partners weren't as attached to the unborn child as they should have been. Similarly, McCreight (2008) found that fathers said their experience of grief had been marginalised by medical professionals, as well as family and friends, who directed their support to their partners; indeed, it was *expected* of them that they should put aside their own feelings in order to support their partner.

In terms of the DPM, we could conclude that men's suppression of grief reflects a *restoration orientation*, as they seek to distract themselves from their loss; women, by contrast, in the early aftermath of the loss, are *loss-oriented*. These differences reflect the more general gender roles, whereby women are expected to be the primary caregiver and may well have decided to take maternity leave from work in order to perform that role. The lost role of mother impacts to a greater extent on women than the lost role of father does on men, who are expected to return to work shortly after the baby is born (Murphy, 2009). These 'male' economic considerations serve as a distraction from their loss and aid their 'restoration'.

Overcoming the stigma of stillbirth

Based on in-depth interviews with 10 couples and 12 mothers, Murphy (2012) identified three main ways in which participants would specifically call on their identity as 'bereaved parents' as a form of *empowerment*:

1 *Challenging the medical professions*: Seeking to change medical practice with the ultimate aim of trying to prevent what happened to them (i.e. medical negligence or actual errors) happening to other parents.
2 *Improving bereavement care*: Telling the story of the loss of the baby to health professionals – describing the *lived experience* of stillbirth.
3 *Raising awareness of stillbirth*: Educating family, colleagues, friends, and neighbours about the reality of stillbirth.

In terms of the DPM, Murphy (2012) believes that parental empowerment following stillbirth is a manifestation of *both* the loss and restoration orientations:

> On the one hand such behaviour exhibits a loss-orientation as such actions necessarily focus around their own grief. But it is also restoration-orientation as a new identity is taken on that, in some senses, can distract them from grief in order to evoke change for the future.
>
> (p. 102)

Sudden infant death syndrome (SIDS)

SIDS refers to the unexpected and abrupt death of an infant under 12 months old (also called *cot death* in the UK and *crib death* in the US) (Balk, 2013). It accounts for more deaths of infants between 1 and 12 months than any other cause, with a peak between 2 and 4 months.

Apart from violation of the general 'rule' that parents should not outlive their children (of whatever age), three prevalent emotional responses to a SIDS death are extreme guilt, anger, and blame; also, communication between spouses and mutual emotional support decline (Schiffman, 2004: see Box 6.6).

According to Raphael (1984), mothers and fathers display discrepant coping responses and dyssynchronous patterns of recovery. Consistent with the earlier discussion regarding gender differences in response to stillbirth, Raphael (1984) notes that 'the mother tends to be more depressed, withdrawn, more disrupted by her loss. The [father] takes over protective, management functions, suppresses his feelings, deals with his distress more quickly and cannot understand his wife's continuing preoccupation with [the death]' (p. 260). Fathers' responses are also angrier and more aggressive than the mothers'.

Cook (1988) suggests that fathers may be caught in a double-bind: men have been raised to understand that expressing strong negative emotions is to be kept in check, as well as being expected to comfort their wives. But if 'healthy grieving' requires disclosing the distress associated with grief, what are they to do with their anger?

Given that the cause of SIDS is still unknown, parents' dread that they are powerless to prevent such a tragedy occurring again is increased. It is as though caring for their infant was futile, which does nothing to assuage their overwhelming guilt and self-blame (Raphael, 1984). No wonder SIDS constitutes a risk for complicated grief (Prigerson and Jacobs, 2001: see Chapter 7).

Changes in the couple relationship following loss of a child

As we saw above, gender differences in grieving styles can be a source of conflict between bereaved couples. Bereaved couples are left to negotiate the challenge of fostering mutually supportive relationships while dealing with their own grief. While supportive families can serve to buffer or protect the bereaved couple (Oliva et al., 2009), we have seen, at least with regard to stillbirth, that this is not always forthcoming. Without such support, the death of a child can have a profoundly negative effect on the quality of the couple's relationship (Lohan and Murphy, 2006).

Understanding how bereaved parents *describe* their perceptions and experiences regarding the relationship with their partner can help us better understand 'the lens through which they conceptualise their relationships' (Umphrey and Cacciatore, 2014). Umphrey and Cacciatore looked specifically at the *metaphors*, which can help the bereaved to describe and express their grief, the negotiation of the grief process with their partner, as well as the nature of the relationships left behind. Previous research has identified several useful metaphors for the grieving process, notably 'grief as a journey' (Graves, 2009) and 'the bereaved as an amputee' (Schwartz-Borden, 1992).

Box 6.6   Relational metaphors following the death of a child

- Umphrey and Cacciatore (2014) conducted an online study of 420 bereaved parents, mainly white, well-educated females, on average just over four years since their bereavement.
- They were asked, 'In your own words, please tell us how your loss affected your relationship with your spouse or partner'.

- Three major themes emerged from the metaphors used by the participants:
  - (i) *relational adjustment/trajectory*: 71.5 per cent said that the child's death had brought them closer together, 20.8 per cent said that it had pushed them apart, and 7.7 per cent said that their relationship had periods of strain and coming together. Some example include 'Strain', 'tear us apart or make us stronger', 'drifted apart', 'it nearly destroyed us', 'it tore us apart', 'it strengthened our marriage', 'brought us together'.
  - (ii) *Grieving styles*: Grief in relation to a partner was commonly described in terms of enduring a difficult journey (see previous discussion). Understanding and adapting to a partner's different grieving style proved challenging for many, as reflected in being on different paths or having to negotiate grief with the partner in terms of a process. While some were able to adjust to these differences and accept them for what they were, for others the difference was too great, as illustrated by 'He could not take that I cried and he eventually left'.
  - (iii) *Communication skills*: The decision about whether or not to discuss the topic of the death was metaphorically reflected by several participants as 'the elephant in the room' or 'We tiptoed around the issue'. For most, effective communication between couples was metaphorically described as 'open'.

Parenting challenges after the death of a child

As we noted when discussing children's response to the loss of a sibling, they are also often experiencing a significant change in their relationship with their grieving parents. Turning that around:

> In the midst of the pervasive sense of loss at the death of a child, many bereaved parents must also contend with the challenges of parenting their surviving, bereft children.
>
> (Buckle and Fleming, 2011, p. 93)

Surviving siblings suffer many secondary losses in the form of their parents' functional incapacity and the demise of the comforting safety, security, and predictability their family previously provided. Bereaved parents are confronted with the

> delicate, complicated task of simultaneously relinquishing their parental role with their deceased child while continuing to function in this capacity with surviving children.
>
> (Buckle and Fleming, 2011, p. 93)

Buckle and Fleming refer to this phenomenon as *bereaved parenting*. Based on an in-depth, qualitative study of 10 bereaved parents, Buckle and Fleming (2010) found bereaved parenting to be a complex and intimidating task that involves a number of themes, namely:

(i) responding to loss-induced personality and behaviour changes in their surviving children;

(ii) revisiting the loss over time: the death was reviewed as bereaved siblings matured and could accommodate a deeper understanding of the loss and its profound impact;

(iii) appreciating and adjusting to their children's differing grieving styles: where there is more than one surviving child, parents face the daunting task of differentially responding to each child's reaction to multiple levels of loss (e.g. loss of a friend, rival, confidant, playmate, and/or role model; the 'loss' of their parents in a functional sense; and the loss of their family as they knew it).

(iv) grappling with the task of parenting a sole, bereaved child;

(v) enduring the powerlessness of being incapable of shielding their surviving children from such horrendous life experiences and the unavoidable pain of grief;

(vi) trying to make sense of a meaningless and incomprehensible event: the excruciating, senseless tragedy that is the death of a child left parents reflecting on the importance of providing their surviving children with wisdom, a sense of hope, or otherwise the ability to derive meaning from the death. This was a particularly daunting task, because the parents themselves were grappling with these same issues; when this proved to be beyond them, they were left feeling guilty and sad.

Summary and conclusions

- *Kinship* constitutes a major feature of the relationship with the deceased, which represents a major risk factor for complicated grief.

- Many of the early major studies of grief-involved widows (and sometimes widowers too) and the influential Dual-Process Model (DPM) was originally developed with these groups in mind. This reflects the frequency and inevitability of spousal bereavement, with women more likely to be widowed than men.

- Bennett and Soulsby distinguish between *spousal bereavement* and *widowhood*, only the latter carrying *social* consequences and meanings.

- An illustration of the *normative* nature of spousal bereavement is the history of Cruse Bereavement Care.

- Spousal bereavement is the most frequent type of bereavement leading to psychiatric referral, and several studies have shown that an ambivalent or dependent relationship with the deceased predicts complicated grief reactions.

- Highly dependent, clinging, relationships are also likely to result in extreme loneliness following the spouse's death.
- Rather than physical health itself being challenged by bereavement, it is *health behaviours* and *maintenance* that suffer, especially among widowers.
- For younger people, spousal bereavement is *non-normative*, and sudden death is especially distressing and disruptive.
- The adjustment of older bereaved spouses is highly variable, reflecting a wide range of biological, psychological, social, and economic factors. But factors other than the nature of the relationship seem to be especially important: (i) circumstances surrounding the death; (ii) social support and integration; and (iii) other concurrent losses and stressors.
- Loss of one's parents in adulthood is *normative*, which helps explain why it has been little studied compared with studies involving childhood loss. This applies especially to the effects of parental loss in one's teens and early-mid-twenties (which is *non-normative*). The loss of control that, especially, sudden deaths involve is happening just when the young person needs to feel powerful and in control. This, in turn, is related to the questions as to when we attain psychological adulthood.
- The death of an elderly parent may be anticipated, but caring for a sick parent, especially perhaps who suffered from Alzheimer's disease (or other forms of dementia), can produce *ambiguous/ambivalent* grief responses.
- While *adaptation anxiety* may be quite normative, the benefits – and indeed the reality – of anticipatory grieving have been disputed.
- Some adults may become depressed following the death of their elderly parents, especially single men who still lived 'at home' and others who were unusually dependent on them.
- Those with our siblings are (potentially) the longest-lasting of all our relationships. As with parental bereavement, the impact of sibling loss in adulthood is under-researched compared with childhood sibling loss.
- Factors influencing children's response to a sibling's death include circumstances surrounding the death, the relationship with the sibling, how they make sense of the loss, and their parent's grief and ability to support the surviving sibling(s).
- The *adult sibling tie* links sibling loss with loss of parents in adulthood.
- Sibling loss has been identified as an example of *disenfranchised* and *non-normative* bereavement.
- While it is widely agreed that loss of a child is the most painful of all bereavements, *evolutionary theory* maintains that losing an *adult* child produces more intense and persistent grief than either a younger child, spouse, parent, or sibling.
- Evidence supports the further predictions that (a) loss as a result of miscarriage, abortion, and loss of a child causes more pronounced grief among *older* mothers; (b) women with no other children react more strongly to both miscarriage and even more so to later child deaths.

- At whatever stage of pregnancy a baby dies, a relationship with it would have begun and so needs to be grieved for. The disenfranchised nature of miscarriage, termination, and stillbirth potentially make the grief more complicated.
- Sudden infant death syndrome (SIDS) is likely to induce extreme guilt, anger, and blame in the parents, although mothers and fathers are likely to display discrepant coping responses and *dyssynchronous* recovery patterns.
- These gender differences in grieving styles may put a strain on the couple's relationship and how they construe it may determine whether they can support each other or find they can no longer live together.
- *Bereaved parenting* refers to the difficult task of relinquishing their parental role with their deceased child while continuing to function as parents for their surviving children.

Chapter 7

Complicated grief

The chapter addresses the following questions:

- How do the major theories/models describe the course of normal/healthy grieving?
- What is the relationship between grief work and complicated grief (CG)?
- How are the Dual-Process Model (DPM), attachment theory, and Continuing Bonds (CB) related?
- How does the *meaning reconstruction* (e.g. Neimeyer) approach help explain CG?
- To what extent are the differences between CG and uncomplicated grief (UCG) *quantitative* or *qualitative*?
- What are the major features of *prolonged grief disorder* (PGD)?
- Can CG be equated with PGD, or are there different kinds of CG syndromes?
- What functions are performed by CG?
- What are the major risk factors for CG?
- Can CG be understood outside of its cultural context?
- What evidence exists showing that sudden and traumatic death is a major risk factor for CG?
- What makes suicide a distinctive risk factor for CG?
- How are suicide and gender related?

Theories and models of 'normal' grief

Probably the most logical – and convenient – place to begin trying to understand complicated (problematic, abnormal, or pathological) grief is to remind ourselves of what major theories and models of grief tell us about *normal* (uncomplicated) grief. As we saw in Chapters 1 and 3, these models and theories present views regarding what normal or healthy grieving *should* look like, be it:

(i) withdrawing emotional energy from the deceased (*decathexis*: Freud, 1917);
(ii) *stages* that need to be gone through (though not necessarily in a fixed, rigid, order) (Bowlby, 1980; Kübler-Ross, 1969);

(iii) *tasks* that need to be accomplished and completed (Worden, e.g. 1982);
(iv) *oscillating* between *loss*-orientation and *restoration*-orientation (Stroebe
      and Schut, 1999);
 (v) experiencing the six 'Rs' (Rando, 1993); adapting to change and creating a
      new assumptive world (Parkes, 1993);
(vi) functioning satisfactorily at the biopsychosocial level and in terms of rela-
      tionship to the deceased (Rubin, 1981);
(vii) maintaining emotional bonds with the deceased (Klass et al., 1996).

Grief work and complicated grief

In most of the accounts summarised above, the focus is on healthy grieving, with
the nature of abnormal or complicated grief being *implicit*. However, Freud's
account of *grief work* states very clearly that pathological grief involves a failure
to psychologically let go of the deceased.

Grief work assumes that all mourning entails experiencing and expressing the
difficult thoughts, emotions, and memories that have been triggered by the loss.
Seen from this broad psychodynamic perspective, grieving has been viewed as
a process of painfully reviewing or working through, and then letting go, of the
attachment to the deceased by way of confrontation with the reality of the death
and emotional *catharsis* (release) of the resulting emotions. From this perspective, assessment of the grieving process involves judging the extent to which this
grief work has been accomplished (or avoided); interventions are designed to
facilitate the necessary detachment from the deceased. Failure to confront the
reality of the loss, as well as failure to go through the process of psychologically letting go, have been viewed as the core of a pathological grief response
(Neimeyer and Jordan, 2013). Neimeyer and Jordan point out that this viewpoint
emphasises 'the largely intrapsychic nature of grieving, with pathological grief
residing within the psychological skin of the mourner' (Neimeyer and Jordan,
2013, p. 220).

As we noted in Chapter 3, many of the more recent models and theories of grief
(notably the Dual-Process Model/DPM and Continuing Bonds) represent direct
challenges to the grief work concept (best seen in stage theories and Worden's task
approach). Longitudinal studies of bereavement adaptation largely fail to support
the idea of stages of grief (Maciejewski et al., 2007).

Holland and Neimeyer (2010) found that, for a large cohort of bereaved individuals whose loved ones had all died from natural causes, acceptance of the death –
presumably the final stage of adaptation – was the predominant response from the
earliest weeks of loss; yearning and depression were the strongest of the negative
indicators of grief-related distress across two years of bereavement, while denial
and anger occurred at consistently low levels. By contrast, among those whose
loved ones had died as a result of an accident, murder, or suicide, disbelief did
predominate in the early weeks, with anger and depression proving stronger than
yearning for the loved one across much of the two-years of follow-up.

Such findings argue against the relevance of one-size-fits-all models of mourning, as well as for the importance of evaluating popular models against actual data on adaptation to loss.

(Neimeyer and Jordan, 2013, p. 221)

Research has also questioned whether it is necessary for every mourner to confront and work through the loss. For example, at least after spousal loss, not everyone appears to go through a painful process of depression and mourning; some spouses seem to begin coping well within a matter of weeks, and some even experience apparent relief following their partner's lengthy illness or a long but conflict-ridden marriage (Bonnano, 2004; Bonnano et al., 2004; Wortman and Silver, 1987: see Chapters 3 and 6). Such findings suggest that traditional models of grief have underestimated people's resilience in the face of loss. More recent empirical studies indicate that many normal grievers will adapt well to bereavement over the course of several months, with or without formal grief counselling – especially following more normative losses such as the death of a partner/spouse in later life (Currier et al., 2008).

Similarly, the Continuing Bonds perspective claims that establishing ongoing emotional ties with the deceased is both healthier and more normative across human cultures than the notion of detachment from the deceased (Klass et al., 1996; Rubin, 1999). Evidence suggests that maintaining an emotional tie with the loved one may be comforting or distressing, depending on such factors as how far along survivors are in their bereavement (Field and Friedrichs, 2004), whether they have been able to make sense of the loss (Neimeyer et al., 2006), and perhaps their level of security in important current attachments (Stroebe and Schut, 2005).

The DPM, attachment theory, and complicated grief

The DPM depicts grieving as a *cyclical* rather than linear and stage-like process, with the mourner repeatedly revisiting the loss and its associated emotions, striving to reorganise the relationship to the deceased, and taking on new roles and responsibilities necessitated by a changed world. According to Neimeyer and Jordan (2013), this view of normal grieving also extends our understanding of pathological grieving, by suggesting that the inability to distract oneself from or avoid grief may be as much a sign of abnormality as the inability to confront it. However, we still cannot say exactly what constitutes the optimal balance and timing of focusing on the loss- and restoration-orientations (Carr, 2010).

As we saw in Chapter 3, Stroebe and Schut (1999, 2010) argue that the model provides a framework for understanding complicated or pathological forms of grief (such as *chronic, absent* or inhibited: Parkes, 1996; Parkes and Weiss, 1983). In earlier models, these forms of grief were not nearly so differentiated or explicit, with chronic grievers focusing on loss, absent grievers on restoration-oriented activities; those who suffer a complicated form of traumatic bereavement might be expected to have trouble alternating smoothly between the two orientations, and manifesting extreme symptoms of intrusion and avoidance. However, in both loss-oriented (e.g. chronic) and restoration-oriented (e.g. absent) types of complicated grief, *reactions are extreme*, focusing excessively on one orientation and avoiding the other. Stroebe and Schut (2010) point out that these patterns are *very different* from the confrontation-avoidance oscillation that the DPM sees as characteristic of 'normal' coping with bereavement. Such pathological forms of grieving can be regarded as disturbances of oscillation (Stroebe and Schut, 1999).

We also noted in Chapter 3 that the relationship between complicated grief and patterns of attachment have recently been discussed within the context of the DPM (e.g. Mikulincer and Shaver, 2008; Parkes, 2006; Stroebe et al., 2005). For example, the DPM predicts that the extent to which bereaved individuals will engage in either loss-oriented or restoration-oriented processes depends on various factors, in particular their attachment styles (see Chapter 2):

- *Securely-attached* individuals would be expected to display healthy oscillation between loss- and restoration-related activities.
- *Anxious-avoidant* individuals would suppress and avoid attachment-related emotions and present absent or inhibited grief reactions, behaving as if nothing had happened and focusing on restoration-related activities. The bond with the deceased would be too *loose* (Zech and Arnold, 2011).
- *Anxious-ambivalent* individuals would focus on the loss-orientation to the exclusion of restoration-related activities (i.e. chronic grief). The bond with the deceased would be too *strong* (Zech and Arnold, 2011).
- *Disorganised* individuals would be unable to think and talk coherently about attachment-related memories and would show *traumatic grief* reactions (Stroebe et al., 2005).

Anxiously-attached individuals have been described as *hyperaroused*, and avoidantly-attached individuals as *hypoaraoused* (Ogden et al., 2006). This would subsequently impact on bereavement outcomes, specifically, the ability to meet the challenges in an integrated way (i.e. oscillating between loss- and restoration-orientations).

A meaning reconstruction approach to grief

Another important and recent theoretical development (not previously discussed in this book) is the *meaning reconstruction* approach to grief (Neimeyer, 2011; Neimeyer et al., 2010). From this perspective, bereavement challenges the survivor's self-narrative, the basic organisation of life events and themes that allows us to interpret the past, invest in the present, and anticipate the future. Although the meaning systems people rely on to negotiate life transitions are often resilient, providing resources that help them to adapt, a painful search for meaning in the near aftermath of loss predicts more intense grief months and years later; by contrast, the capacity to find significance in the loss predicts greater long-term well-being and resilience (Coleman and Neimeyer, 2010).

This quest for meaning may be especially critical in cases of traumatic loss, such as suicide (see below), murder/homicide, and fatal accidents. An inability to make sense of these violent as opposed to natural deaths, appears to mediate their impact on the survivor's subsequent adaptation (Currier et al., 2006), perhaps especially in the case of suicide bereavement (Jordan, 2008; Jordan and McIntosh, 2011). Similarly, studies of parents who have lost a child report that a struggle to make sense of the loss accounts for considerably more of the intensity of their grief compared with such objective factors as the passage of time, cause of death, or parents' gender (Keesee et al., 2008: see Chapter 6).

While spiritual meaning-making can help to reduce the intensity of grief after tragic loss (Lichtenthal et al., 2010), spiritual coping is no panacea for profound grief: longitudinal study of people bereaved by the homicide of loved ones indicates that high levels of complicated grief symptomatology earlier in bereavement predicted later spiritual struggles, whereas neither positive nor negative religious coping predicted subsequent grief (Burke et al., 2011; Neimeyer and Burke, 2011).

As we noted earlier, grieving – whether healthy or unhealthy, uncomplicated or complicated – has traditionally been seen as something that takes place *within the individual*. However, recent approaches have begun to focus on the *transactional* nature of mourning at levels ranging from family processes (Walsh and McGoldrick, 2004) to cultural discourses about bereavement (Dennis, 2011). As we discussed in Chapters 4 and 5, the meaning of the loss for an individual cannot be separated from the family, community, and societal meanings ascribed to death and loss and the resulting social responses to the mourner.

> This more systemic approach recognises that the bereaved must adapt not only to a world where the deceased is no longer physically available, but also where many other altered aspects of the postloss interpersonal landscape must be confronted.
>
> (Neimeyer and Jordan, 2013, p. 223)

These changes clearly have internal, subjective components, but they also intimately involve interactions between the mourner and other people: the latter approve or disapprove, support or don't support the mourner, acknowledge or don't the mourner's right to grieve (as in disenfranchised grief: see Chapter 4).

All these developments in bereavement theory are beginning to change our understanding of what constitutes a normal, expectable response to loss, and with it, our view of what constitutes pathological grief. This shift towards a more complex and refined understanding of the heterogeneity of the grief response is particularly important for assessment and intervention (Neimeyer and Jordan, 2013).

Complicated grief: Symptomatology and diagnosis

Differences between complicated and uncomplicated grief: quantitative or qualitative?

According to Stroebe et al. (2013),

> In general terms, complicated grief (CG) can be understood as something like a 'derailing' of the normal, usually painful process of adapting to the loss of a significant person.
>
> (p. 3)

Similarly, Parkes and Prigerson (2010) claim that there is no sharp dichotomy between CG and uncomplicated grief (UCG): it is largely a matter of degree (i.e. there's only a *quantitative* difference between them). For example, Holland et al. (2009) reported evidence for the view that Prolonged Grief Disorder (PGD) lies at one extreme end of a continuum, with 'normal', UCG at the other.

However, different definitions and criteria have been adopted to try to describe the concept more precisely, for both scientific and clinical purposes (Stroebe et al., 2013). For example, Stroebe et al. (2008) defined CG as:

> a clinically-significant deviation from the (cultural) norm in either (a) the time course or intensity of specific or general symptoms of grief and/or (b) the level of impairment in social, occupational, or other important areas of functioning.
>
> (p. 7)

While this could be read as being consistent with a view of the CG-UCG difference being merely quantitative, the use of 'clinically-significant' raises many important questions; for example, at what point does a difference of degree become a difference of kind (i.e. a *qualitative* difference)? The reference to PGD above underlines this question: much heated debate in recent years has focused on whether or not CG (specifically PGD) should be regarded – and treated – as a distinct mental disorder, that is, different from major depressive disorder (MDD), or post-traumatic stress disorder (PTSD). (CG is often described in terms that overlap with the symptoms of these 'well-established' mental disorders.)

Prolonged grief disorder (PGD)

In the Bethlem study (Parkes, 1965 a and b: see Chapter 1), 15 of the 21 bereaved patients (4 male, 17 female) displayed grief that seemed more prolonged than expected; 6 had been bereaved for two years or more and their grief was relentless (what Anderson, 1949, called *chronic grief*: see below). Years after the bereavement, many were still preoccupied with memories of the dead loved one, pining intensely and severely distressed by any reminder. Eight cried uncontrollably, several others said they felt 'too hurt to cry', and agitated and aggressive out-bursts occurred in four cases; four admitted to having suicidal preoccupations. The intensity of their grief impaired ability to work in eight cases and caused most to stay at home, withdrawing from contact with family and friends.

As Parkes and Prigerson (2010) observe, there's more to PGD than just severe and prolonged grief. In addition, there is a cluster of other phenomena that are commonly reported by people diagnosed with PGD. Before 2013, the mental health community, as represented by the *Diagnostic and Statistical Manual of Mental Disorders* (DSM-IV-R, 2000) (the 'bible' of American psychiatry and used throughout the world) did not officially recognise any pattern of grief as pathological. Rather, bereavement was viewed as a life problem that, while it may sometimes need clinical attention, is not – in and of itself – a mental disorder. Any difficulties adjusting to a loss must be diagnosed in terms of depression, anxiety, or other disorders (such as PTSD).

However, a great deal of evidence has accumulated over the last 15 years or so that supports the diagnosis of CG (Shear et al., 2011) or PGD (Prigerson et al., 2009). While these two terms are functionally equivalent, the former emphasises the disruption of a normal course of grief, while the latter stresses a chronic state of intense grieving that disturbs the functioning over a period of months or years (Neimeyer and Jordan, 2013). Again, 'CG' is often used to highlight some grief response that differs from 'UCG' (or 'normal' grief), while PGD denotes a par-ticular form that CG can take. From this point on, 'PGD' will be used. The major diagnostic features of PGD are shown in Box 7.1.

Box 7.1 Diagnostic features of PGD

1   The features described below have continued for at least six months.
2   Marked and persistent separation distress, reflected in intense feelings of loneliness, yearning for, or preoccupation with, the deceased.
3   At least five of the following nine symptoms experienced almost daily to a disabling degree:
   •   Diminished sense of self (e.g. self as empty or confused, or as if part of oneself has died).
   •   Difficulty accepting the loss as real, both emotionally and intellectually.
   •   Avoidance of reminders of the loss.
   •   Inability to trust others or to feel that they understand.
   •   Extreme bitterness or anger over the death.
   •   Extreme difficulty moving on with life (e.g. making new friends, pursu-ing new interests).

(Continued)

Box 7.1 Continued

- Pervasive numbness (absence of emotion/inability to feel) or detachment (social withdrawal).
- Belief that life is empty and seeing the future as meaningless or without purpose.
- Feeling stunned, dazed, or shocked by the death.
4 Significant impairment in social, occupational, or family functioning (e.g. domestic responsibilities).

Based on Neimeyer and Jordan, 2013; Parkes and Prigerson, 2010.

The criteria for PGD essentially describe a combination of intense and prolonged separation distress/anxiety regarding the deceased, plus signs that the mourner's social and psychological adaptation has been compromised by the death (Neimeyer and Jordan, 2013); Neimeyer and Jordan point out that the diagnosis refers to symptoms experienced by the bereaved person, regardless of the circumstances of the death (sudden/violent or not). A considerable amount of research has demonstrated that the PGD is associated with increased rates of psychological distress, physical illness, and social dysfunction (e.g. Prigerson et al., 2008).

Parkes and Prigerson (2010) describe several cases from the Bethlem study – and subsequently – that involved an apparent relationship between bodily symptoms experienced by the bereaved person and those experienced by the dying spouse (or other loved one). These usually involved aches and pains at the site of a pain that had been prominent during the illness, such as chest pains resembling the pain of coronary thrombosis, the apparent effects of a stroke, and recurrent (actual) vomiting. These are all examples of *identification symptoms*. In a few cases, the identification symptom was an exaggeration of symptoms that are common in 'normal' grief reactions; these included palpitations and gasping (that often accompany anxiety but which 'mimic' a heart attack), and loss of sensation or movement (*dissociative* symptoms) (see Chapter 1).

The features described in Box 7.1 have been shown to constitute a distinct symptom cluster, differing sufficiently from major depression (MDD) and post-traumatic disorder (PTSD) to be legitimately considered a separate diagnostic category (i.e. mental disorder) (Prigerson and Maciejewski, 2006); they also predict harmful health outcomes even after depression and anxiety symptoms have been taken into account (Bonnano et al., 2007).

Is there more to CG than PGD?

According to Rando (2013), while there is impressive research that documents the usefulness of PGD, we simply *cannot* equate CG with PGD. She identified *four* forms of CG, that is, four different types of presentation for CG, namely, *symptoms, syndromes, diagnosable mental* or *physical disorders*, and *death* (Rando, 1993).

1   *Complicated grief symptoms*: The bereaved person experiences some psychological, behavioural, social, or physical symptoms of distress, disability, dysfunction, pathology, or loss of freedom. Although inadequate in terms of number, intensity, duration, or type to meet criteria for any of the other three forms of CG, these symptoms accompany a *compromise, distortion*, or *failure* in one/more of the normal grief processes (Rando, 2013).
2   *Complicated grief syndromes*: CG symptoms can combine to form one of eight CG syndromes; these are listed in Box 7.2.

Box 7.2   Complicated grief syndromes

*   *Absent (or minimal) grief* (Deutsch, 1937; Bowlby, 1980).
*   *Delayed grief* (e.g. Raphael, 1984).
*   *Inhibited grief* (e.g. Raphael, 1984).
*   *Distorted grief* (of the extremely angry and guilty types: Raphael, 1984).
*   *Conflicted grief* (Parkes and Weiss, 1983).
*   *Unanticipated grief* (Parkes and Weiss, 1983).
*   *Chronic grief* (Bowlby, 1980).
*   PGD (see text above) is a type of *chronic grief*.

Only some of these syndromes have been investigated (Rando, 2013). According to Bonnano et al. (2008), minimal or absent grief reactions are very common, while delayed grief reactions are quite rare; chronic grief/PGD has been generally well accepted as a pathological category; delayed, inhibited, and absent remain the subject of much debate (Stroebe et al., 2008). Despite this, chronic and absent grief have been well explained by the DPM (Rando, 2013: see above). To the extent that unanticipated grief is associated with traumatic bereavement, it has been more extensively studied (see discussion of suicide below).

The functions of CG

According to Rando (1993), CG serves two major functions: *avoidance* and *connection*. Given the variability among grievers and their situations, these may be the only elements that are common to all types of CG (Rando, 2013).

> In all forms of complicated [grief], the mourner attempts to do two things: (a) deny, repress, or avoid aspects of the loss, its pain, and the full realisation of its implications for the mourner and (b) hold on to and avoid relinquishing the lost loved one.
>
> (Rando, 1993, p. 149)

Parkes and Prigerson (2010) point out that the diagnostic criteria for PGD allow for the fact that some bereaved people do not develop PGD *immediately* after the bereavement; only after a delay do they become severely and lastingly disturbed. However, this failure to express grief cannot be taken to mean that something has necessarily gone wrong: people vary greatly in their resilience, capacity for emotional control, and the intensity of their attachments. Also, the greater the delay in expressing grief, the more difficult it becomes to prove that subsequent symptoms are actually the result of the bereavement: other traumatic life events may have occurred and so it is difficult to establish clear cause and effect. Alternatively, CG may be linked to earlier attachment problems – rather than to the bereavement itself. For example, in Parkes's (2006) Love and Loss study, he reports on 25 bereaved participants who, prior to the bereavement, displayed an *avoidant attachment disorder*: all had been emotionally inhibited, distrustful of others, and controlling of others by aggression or assertion rather than by affection. They had reacted to the loss in a variety of ways, which had prevented them from leading functionally effective lives and had caused them to seek psychiatric help.

- Some appeared to cope well at first: their lack of overt grief – and reluctance to ask for help – led others to assume that they did not need any support. Only later did it become clear that their compulsive independence was a cover-up.
- At this point, some experienced a break-through of delayed grief or turned it on themselves and became depressed.
- Some developed psychosomatic symptoms reflecting chronic anxiety and tension.
- Some became irritable and prone to outbursts of anger or rage.
- Some reacted immediately to the bereavement but found the break-through of emotions extremely distressing and tried very hard to inhibit or conceal them.
- Some experienced severe anxiety and panic but were quite unable to cry; they feared that if they 'broke down' and showed their true feelings, they would indeed have a 'nervous breakdown'.

While some cases of delayed grief go on to meet the criteria for PGD, inhibition of grief can produce different patterns of response (Parkes and Prigerson, 2010).

The second function of CG identified by Rando, *connection*, relates to the Continuing Bonds approach (see above and Chapter 3). There have been enough research findings confirming associations with CG to justify further investigations to identify under which conditions continuing bonds is adaptive and under which conditions it is not (Rando, 2013).

3   *Diagnosable mental or physical disorder*: Research consistently shows that bereavement can cause great suffering, associated with serious consequences for health and well-being (Stroebe et al., 2007). Bereaved individuals in general are at increased risk of physical and mental illness (see Chapter 1); in terms of CG specifically, PGD is associated with increased risk of both mental and physical impairments (Prigerson et al., 2008). The psychiatric disorders most commonly associated with CG are depression and anxiety (e.g. Stroebe et al., 2007).

4   *Death*: CG can be manifested in death that is consciously chosen (i.e. suicide). Research shows that CG is a risk factor for *completed* suicide (Luoma and Pearson, 2002) and *suicidality* (Latham and Prigerson, 2004). Also, death resulting from complicated grief-related behaviour can be 'subintended' or unintended (Rando, 1993), such as a car crash from drunk driving, or self-neglect.

Risk factors for CG

According to Parkes and Prigerson (2010), there are six broad categories of risk for CG:

1   *Kinship, gender and age*: Much of the relevant research is discussed in Chapter 6 (also see Chapter 1). Burke and Neimeyer (2013) found the loss of a spouse or child (especially to a violent, sudden death) to be the most salient. Other important *potential* risk factors they point to include being female and young; they also identify other *circumstantial* or *demographic* conditions/variables, such as being a member of a minority group, having low levels of education, little income, and prior losses.

2   *Personal vulnerability*: Relevant here are different attachment styles (Burke and Neimeyer, 2013: see Chapters 2 and 3) and related attachment disorders (see above), high levels of pre-death marital dependency, pre-existing psychological problems (such as disposition toward depression or anxiety) (Burke and Neimeyer, 2013). Also relevant here is the concept of *resilience*.

According to Burke and Neimeyer (2013), grief-specific distress can be placed on a continuum that runs from 'resilience' at one extreme, through 'moderate distress', to CG at the other extreme.

- *Resilient* individuals regain their psychological equilibrium quite quickly following bereavement (Bonanno and Kaltman, 2001).
- People experiencing *moderate distress* adapt to the loss over time.

- *CG* refers to a state of protracted grieving (i.e. PGD), reflected in profound separation distress, emotionally disturbing and invasive memories, emptiness, meaninglessness, an inability to accept the loss, and considerable difficulty in continuing to love without the deceased (Holland et al., 2009).

3　*Social and cultural influences*: Notable examples as reported by Burke and Neimeyer (2013) are lack of social support, and low family cohesion (see Chapters 4 and 5).
4　*Mode of death*: Both these last two categories are discussed below and comprise the last two major sections of the chapter.
5　*Multiple losses*.
6　*Disenfranchised grief*: This is discussed in Chapter 4.

CG as a cultural phenomenon

As we saw in Chapters 4 and 5, we cannot properly understand UCG or 'normal' grief unless we examine it within the socio-cultural context in which it occurs. The same applies to CG. According to Rosenblatt (2013a), typically when CG is being discussed, authors do not make it explicit that what they say applies to all people in all cultures; however, the implication is that it *does*. However:

> the concept of [CG] and research on [CG] are grounded in a particular culture, and so we should be cautious about applying the work on [CG] to people of other cultures.
>
> (Rosenblatt, 2013a, p. 27)

He also argues that, to the extent that we all live in *pluralistic* (i.e. diverse, multicultural) societies, we should also be careful about applying the concept and clinical implications of CG to *all* people (or sub-cultural groups) within our own society.

Rosenblatt cites the work of Wikan (1988), who reported that in Cairo, Egypt, a bereaved mother whose grieving went on for years, with obvious suffering, muted depression, withdrawal, inactivity, and self-absorption, was seen as sane and making cultural sense. Similarly, the parents of Israeli soldiers who died in action may grieve for decades, and in Israel that grief is honoured and understood (Malkinson and Bar-Tur, 2000). Charmaz and Milligan (2006) claimed that historically in the US and Europe, what is now seen as a problem (i.e. extreme, prolonged, intense grief), was at one time considered normal. In other words, norms regarding what is UCG or CG differ between different cultures and change over time within the same culture.

Rosenblatt (2013a) identifies four major assumptions commonly made in discussion of CG (in the main, by Western researchers), which he believes should be made explicit. These are described in Box 7.3.

Box 7.3   Assumptions regarding CG

1   Grief that goes on too long and too intensely is a problem that needs to be treated. (This is implicit in much of the chapter's preceding discussion about the nature of CG.)

2   When it's judged that the grief has gone on for too long, it is assumed that there is a discrete point in time at which the loss can be said to occur; this point of time serves as a *marker* from which the duration of grieving can be measured. However, from a cross-cultural perspective, thinking of grief as arising at a discrete point in time is challenged by the experiences of people for whom a specific loss goes on continuously, occurs repeatedly, or is part of an ongoing series of losses. For example, there are several Native American cultures that have experienced severe historical traumas, including near-genocide, mass sexual abuse, and the destruction of culture and the social and physical environment, and these losses have been spread over many years and continue (Brave Heart and DeBruyn, 1998; Tafoya and Del Vecchio, 2005). In these cases, it would be a mistake to assume that grief can be assessed based on a discrete starting point.

3   Much of what's written about CG could be understood to imply that grieving in all cultures is essentially the same. However, there is considerable evidence that people deal with and talk about losses quite differently from one culture to another (Charmaz and Milligan, 2006; Currer, 2001; Rosenblatt, 2001; Wierzbicka, 2003) (see Chapter 5). Related to this is the concept of *recovery*, which is a concept of Western culture; in some cultures there may be no sense that something like recovery from grief is normal or desirable (Rosenblatt, 2008b).

4   Looking at PGD, for example, as a *psychological* problem may lead us to ignore or discount what grieving people would say about their economic, political, or environmental challenges. Rosenblatt (2013a) gives the example of a Guatemalan widow whose husband has been assassinated by the military because he spoke out against injustices. Imagine that she continues to show symptoms of CG many years after his death and explains her pain largely in terms of the ongoing economic, political, and environmental oppression suffered by poor Guatemalans. If we suggest that she receives help to reduce the intensity of her grief, she may see this as a betrayal of crucial values. Her grief is being taken out of its context and so is being misunderstood.

The mode of death: CG and traumatic bereavement

According to Parkes and Prigerson (2010), almost all those bereaved people who seek psychiatric help are found to have suffered unusually traumatic forms of bereavement and/or show evidence of prior vulnerability (see above).

> Sudden unexpected deaths, multiple deaths, violent deaths and deaths involving human agency (murders, suicides, etc.) represent a special risk to mental health even in the absence of other vulnerability.
>
> (Parkes and Prigerson, 2010, p. 152)

In most cases, deaths by natural causes are relatively untraumatic (Weinberg, 1994), although sudden/unexpected deaths can, of course, be natural. 'Sudden/unexpected' often implies *untimely*, as in any child death and those of teenagers and young adults (although these needn't be sudden/unexpected: see below and Chapter 6).

Sudden/unexpected deaths

The young widows and widowers in the Harvard Study (Parkes and Weiss, 1983) were quite clearly more emotionally disturbed following deaths which they had little or no time to prepare for; their disturbance persisted throughout the first year of bereavement. 'Short duration of terminal illness' came first among 55 antecedent variables as a predictor of poor outcome 13 months after bereavement. Parkes and Prigerson (2010) cite other American, as well as British and Swedish studies, that have reported similar findings.

In young widows and widowers, the increased mortality that follows bereavement was greater after a sudden and unexpected death than if it was expected. While this was also found among older widowers – although to a lesser extent – there was no evidence of sudden death increasing mortality amongst older widows (Smith, 1990, in Parkes and Prigerson, 2010). The death of a spouse in old age may be sudden, but this doesn't mean that it is untimely; studies that involve a substantial proportion of older widows show no significant association between sudden death and poor outcome (Clayton et al., 1972; Fulton and Gottesman, 1980). In Gerber et al.'s (1975) study of older men and women, it was those whose spouse had suffered a prolonged illness who had the *poorest* outcome after bereavement.

Almost by definition, *sudden infant death syndrome* (SIDS) is likely to produce CG. Misunderstandings commonly arise in the course of police enquiries; parents may blame each other, and some engage in a relentless search for a cause (Raphael, 1984). 'Shadow grief' may continue to plague some mothers every so often for the rest of their lives (Peppers and Knapp, 1980: see Chapter 6).

Shanfield and colleagues (e.g. Shanfield et al., 1985) found that deaths of adult children in *road traffic accidents* were associated with more intense grief in the bereaved parents (especially the mothers), more physical health problems, greater depression and guilt compared with parents who had lost older adult children to cancer and who had died in a hospice. The deaths of younger, unmarried children still living at home and of children killed in single-car, single-driver accidents, or who had alcohol or relationship problems, also predicted poor outcome in the parents.

However, as Parkes and Prigerson (2010) point out, even if we know that someone is dying, we may suppress our own anticipatory grief for fear of upsetting the dying person. Experience in hospices suggests that if a husband and wife can share their anticipatory grief, they may achieve a degree of contentment and calm that persist until the death occurs; the bereaved spouse can then look back on this time together with satisfaction.

In the Harvard Study, unexpected and untimely deaths initially provoked a prolonged period of numbness and disbelief, combined with social withdrawal and a continuing sense of the presence of the deceased. Despite this sense of the loved one being close, the bereaved spouse became lonely, anxious, and depressed; these feelings sometimes lasted up to four years following the bereavement. They may also become preoccupied with memories of the deceased, and if the death was particularly painful and was witnessed by the bereaved person, the memories themselves will be painful and meet the criteria for PTSD (Parkes and Prigerson, 2010).

Violent deaths

These include murder and manslaughter, suicide, civil disaster, and military action, all of which have been shown to increase the risk of mental health problems. Where the violent death is due to human agency (as in murder/manslaughter, and suicide), anger and guilt are likely to predominate.

> the combination of sudden, unexpected, horrific, and untimely death, with all the rage and suspicions that followed, and the long, drawn-out legal proceedings . . . can be expected to overwhelm the family as a support for its members and lead to lasting psychological problems.
>
> (Parkes and Prigerson, 2010, p. 157)

These problems can take the form of PTSD, intense rage, undermining trust in others (including the police and legal system, especially perhaps when the perpetrator receives a sentence that seems trivial relative to the magnitude of the loss), and guilt (at failing to protect the deceased). These reactions easily set up vicious circles, which perpetuate the problem; for example, lack of trust may mean that offers of help are refused, angry outbursts may further alienate those who might have provided support, and guilt may lead to self-punitive/destructive behaviour (Parkes and Prigerson, 2010).

Is suicide a special case?

Whether, and in what ways, grief reactions to suicide are similar to or different from those produced by other causes of death, has important implications for both research and clinical practice (Jordan and McIntosh, 2011). For example, Jordan and McIntosh say that if the bereavement experience of the suicide-bereaved is reliably different from that of other bereaved 'groups', then the former may benefit more from support groups dedicated to such bereavement; alternatively, they may require specialised types of interventions that target their unique problems.

Based on a large number of empirical studies, clinical experience, and personal experience of the suicide-bereaved, Jordan and McIntosh (2011) summarise the findings as shown in Table 7.1.

Jordan and McIntosh (2011) then go onto propose a framework for conceptualising differences between bereavement from suicide and other causes of death within a broader context. As shown in Figure 7.1., this framework looks at the response to bereavement by suicide as incorporating:

(i) *Universal* or *normative* aspects (i.e. grief responses that apply to all bereavements, regardless of the cause of death).
(ii) *Non-normative* aspects (i.e. responses associated with all forms of *unexpected* and *sudden* death, as well as sudden, *violent* death).
(iii) Responses that apply to all *traumatic* deaths.

While (i) describes very *general* aspects of grief, (ii) and (iii) describe increasingly *specific* aspects: the suicide-bereaved experience all those responses shared by *all* bereaved people (as described in Chapter 1), but *in addition* experience responses that are only associated with particular causes of death (sudden and violent, i.e. traumatic). As Jordan and McIntosh put it:

> suicide bereavement is most different from mourning after death from natural causes; is somewhat different from other sudden, unexpected deaths; and is most similar to loss after other types of sudden and violent causes.
>
> (Jordan and McIntosh, 2011, p. 227)

Table 7.1 Common features of suicide bereavement (based on Jordan and McIntosh, 2011)

Increased levels of:
• Abandonment and rejection
• Shame and stigma
• Concealment of the cause of death as suicide
• Blaming
• Self-destructiveness or suicidality
• Guilt
• Anger
• Searching for an explanation/need to understand 'why' ('make meaning')
• Relief
• Shock and disbelief
• Family system effects, social support issues, and/or social isolation
• Activism, obsession with the phenomenon of suicide, and involvement with prevention efforts

- Feelings of sorrow
- Yearning for the deceased loved one

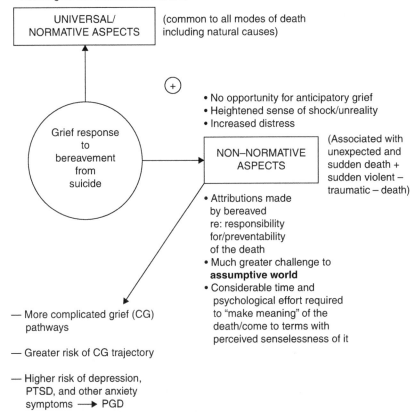

Figure 7.1 Jordan and McIntosh's (2011) framework for conceptualising difference between bereavement from suicide and other modes of death.

They also point out that suicides are not all the same; hence, the impact on the bereaved is not always the same. Consistent with Parkes and Prigerson's (2010) (and others') identification of four broad categories of risk factors for CG, Jordan and McIntosh (2011) conclude by stating that:

> the individual course and intensity of grief and bereavement experiences are complex and are affected by many potential variables, only one of which is the mode of death.

> (p. 227)

Suicide and gender

While more women worldwide attempt suicide (*parasuicide*) each year, more men actually die from suicide; for example, in the Western hemisphere, twice as many men complete suicide compared with women. While this gender gap has existed for at least 120 years, it has widened in recent times: men now represent a large majority of all suicides across the world (WHO, 2011).

While the death of young men in car accidents, or from knife and gun crimes, attract intense media scrutiny – as well as attention from politicians – it is suicide that is the biggest killer of young men in the UK. In 2010, there were 4,532 suicides recorded in England and Wales alone, of which 3,421 (75 per cent) were males. For males aged 15–34, there were 868 deaths by suicide, more than three times the number of women in the same age group (O'Hara, 2012).

Until quite recently, the relationship between suicidal behaviour and men's gender (or *masculinities*) has largely been taken for granted or marginalised. But emerging evidence suggests that a more detailed examination of gender provides a powerful means of explaining the gender gap. More specifically, the construction of masculinities is believed to one of the most important factors influencing how men discuss, contemplate, and enact suicide (Swami et al., 2008).

Box 7.4   Suicide and masculinities

- In the West, men experience considerable social pressure to aspire to dominant (*hegemonic*) gendered identities, such as being independent, strong, and competitive, while also denying anxieties and insecurities (Golombok and Fivush, 1994). If all behaviours are an expression of gender, then perhaps 'doing masculinity' puts men at higher risk for suicidal behaviours compared with women's 'doing femininity'.

- Payne et al. (2008) have documented the many ways in which the construction of masculinities impacts on men's greater rates of completed suicide. These include:

  (a) In general, men are more likely to die through the use of violent methods, such as firearms and hanging. Such violent methods are consistent with the 'macho' construction of masculinity, as is men's greater familiarity with and ownership of shotguns and pistols etc. It may also explain why women are so much more likely to survive suicide attempts.

  (b) While most societies tend to stigmatise suicidal behaviours (see text above), surviving a suicidal act is more likely to be perceived as 'inappropriate' for men.

  (c) Male suicides are less likely than female suicides to have had contact with health services or to have been known to psychiatric services. This reflects the fact that men are less likely than women to consult for most conditions, especially mental health and emotional problems:

(Continued)

Box 7.4 Continued

men are supposed to deny pain, emotional sensitivity, and anxiety. Asking for help, even in the face of possible suicide, may be viewed as feminine behaviour.

(d) Men's response to depression often involves social withdrawal (including hiding symptoms from others), unwillingness to consult healthcare professionals, and a denial of symptoms. Not surprisingly, alcohol and substance misuse more often precede suicide among men than among women.

(e) While the widowed, divorced/separated, and single have higher suicide rates than married adults, non-married men are at higher risk than non-married women.

(f) Because men experience pressure to be successful and ambitious, being made redundant or their business going bust is likely to have a detrimental effect on men's well-being; they're more sensitive to negative changes in their employment or socioeconomic status than women.

Consistent with these 'masculinities' is the gender difference in how depression is *experienced*: while for women, the primary emotion is usually sadness, for men it's more typically anger or irritability, often coupled with recklessness. Hormones are a major candidate for explaining this male-female difference (Westly, 2012). Given the widely-accepted finding that men significantly under-report health problems (including mental health), relying only on men's disclosure of traditional symptoms could lead to an *under*-diagnosis of depression in men. Indeed, when this is allowed for, the prevalence of depression between men and women disappears (Martin et al., 2013) This is consistent with the typical instrumental and intuitive grieving styles of men and women, respectively (see Chapter 1).

Summary and conclusions

- All the major theories/models of grief tell us what normal/healthy grieving *should* be; by implication, they inform us about the nature of abnormal or *complicated grief* (CG).
- From the *grief work* perspective, interventions are designed to facilitate the necessary detachment from the deceased. Failure to confront the reality of loss and let go are at the core of CG.
- Criticisms of the grief work approach include the claim that everyone should grieve in the same way. Research evidence is often inconsistent with this claim and suggests that people are much more resilient than assumed by traditional theories/models.

- The *Dual-Process Model* (DPM) suggests that the inability to distract oneself from, or avoid, grief (*chronic grief*) may be as much a sign of abnormality as the inability to confront it (*absent grief*).
- Chronic and absent correspond to the loss- and restoration-orientations, respectively, but in both cases *reactions are extreme*; they can be regarded as *disturbances of oscillation*.
- The DPM also predicts that the extent to which bereaved individuals will engage in either loss- or restoration-oriented processes depends on their *attachment styles*.
- According to the *meaning reconstruction approach*, the difficulty that bereaved people have in making sense of traumatic loss, such as suicide or murder, or fatal accidents, may impact on the intensity of their grief and their ability to adjust to the loss.
- The meaning of the loss for an individual cannot be divorced from its family, community, and societal meanings, which, in turn, affect social responses to the bereaved. This, in turn, contributes to a view of grief as a much more complex and heterogeneous phenomenon than described by traditional theories/models.
- A key controversy regarding CG is whether it represents one end of a contin-uum, with uncomplicated grief (UCG) at the other (a *quantitative* difference), or a *qualitatively* different, clinically-significant, mental disorder (specifi-cally, *prolonged grief disorder*/PGD).
- The criteria for PGD basically describe a combination of intense and prolonged separation anxiety and compromised psychological adaptation. Also, evidence shows that it is associated with increased physical illness and social dysfunction.
- Another controversy relates to whether or not there is more to CG than PGD. Rando identifies four different manifestations of CG: *symptoms, syndromes, diagnosable mental* or *physical disorders*, and *death*.
- Regarding *syndromes*, CG symptoms can combine to form one of eight grief syndromes, including *delayed, inhibited, distorted*, and *conflicted*. PGD is a type of *chronic grief.*
- According to Rando, CG performs two function: *avoidance* and *connection*; the latter relates to the *Continuing Bonds* approach.
- *Risk factors* for CG include *kinship, gender, age, personal vulnerability* (attachment styles and resilience), *social/cultural influences, mode of death* (sudden, untimely, and traumatic deaths are especially relevant), *multiple losses*, and *disenfranchised grief.*
- The concept of CG implicitly applies to all people in all cultures, but this may not be valid: as with UCG, we must examine CG in its socio-cultural context.
- According to Jordan and McIntosh, the response to bereavement by *suicide* is the most different from bereavement from natural causes, but it shares ele-ments of bereavement from other unexpected, sudden, and violent deaths.
- There is an important relationship between suicide and *gender*, with more men than women actually dying (as opposed to *parasuicide*). This has been explained in terms of '*masculinities*', which are consistent with the gender difference in the experience of depression.

Chapter 8

The wider context of grief

Loss of pets and loss of self

The chapter addresses the following questions:

- Is it valid to apply 'bereavement' to the loss of (non-human) pets?
- What evidence is there showing that grief responses to pet loss are comparable to the loss of human loved ones?
- Can responses to pet loss be explained in terms of Continuing Bonds (CBs)?
- Is pet loss a form of disenfranchised grief?
- Is fear of our own death part of the human condition?
- How can fear of our own death be seen as a form of anticipatory grieving?
- How can attachment theory help explain our fear of death?
- According to Becker, how do we manage to keep our own death terror in check?
- Do men and women differ in their death anxiety?
- Is death anxiety related to age?
- What are the major features of *terror management theory* (TMT)?
- How does the *meaning reconstruction approach* explain the way that people deal with major bereavements?
- What is the relationship between meaning, traumatic loss, and complicated grief?
- What are the three phases of the *tripartite model of suicide bereavement* (TMSB)?
- What is meant by *post-traumatic growth* (PTG)?
- What evidence is there for PTG and how does it come about?

We have noted at several points in the preceding chapters that the traditional view of grief work as the only healthy way to deal with bereavement has been challenged from many directions, one of which is the Continuing Bonds (CBs) approach (e.g. Klass et al., 1996). Also, in Chapter 1 (and elsewhere), 'bereavement' has been defined as the death of a loved one; implicitly, this refers to another human being. However, just as 'loss' is commonly used to refer to 'bereavement', so 'bereavement' is no longer used exclusively to denote the loss, through death, of a spouse, parent, child, other relative, or friend. While the concept of CBs has not been used explicitly in the pet bereavement literature, similar phenomena have been described in this context (Carmack and Packman, 2011).

As we saw in Chapter 1, Kübler-Ross's (1969) stage theory was originally proposed to describe the *process of dying*, that is, how the terminally ill individual comes to terms with his/her imminent and inevitable death through a process of *anticipatory grieving*. While her five stages have since been applied to the process of grieving for *others*, and while the sample of patients her stage theory was originally based on are clearly not representative of people in general (most of us are *not* terminally ill at any single point in time), her work raises a fundamental question relevant to everyone: is anticipatory grieving (in some form or another) something that we *all* do, perhaps throughout our (adult) lives, by virtue of our certain knowledge that we are going to die? Are we all afraid of *death* (*not* dying), that is, not existing any more, and could that fear be explained in terms of *attachment theory* (see Chapter 2)? Also, if this fear is part of the human condition (one of the 'givens of existence': Yalom, 1980), how do we deal with it in a way that enables us to lead a reasonably positive and constructive life?

Finally, and related to the question regarding how we deal with our fear of death, is it possible – and is there any evidence to suggest – that people can find strength from the depths of despair and emerge from their grief as stronger and more effective human beings?

Pet loss

People often describe being *more* emotionally attached to their pets than to people in their lives (Carmack, 1985). Animal companions provide a sense of security and well-being, unconditional love, and acceptance, that are difficult to attain or sustain in relationships with people (Sharkin and Knox, 2003). Many pet owners – of all ages – describe their pets as family members or consider pets as children (e.g. Toray, 2004).

Not surprisingly in view of these observations, the loss of a pet induces grief responses that are just as severe as those associated with the loss of another human being (Archer, 1997; Carmack, 2003; Field et al., 2009). Similarities of grief responses include sleep loss, days missed from work, and other social and psychological difficulties (Quackenbush, 1985). Archer and Winchester (1994) also found parallels between the grief responses of pet-bereaved and person-bereaved individuals: over half of the former reported that their initial reactions were numbness and/or disbelief, and over half became preoccupied with thoughts of the deceased pet and felt that 'a part of them had gone'. About a quarter of the pet-bereaved reported feeling angry, depressed, and anxious (see Chapter 1).

Gerwolls and Labott (1994) found that at two and eight weeks post-loss, the grief scores for those who had been pet- and person-bereaved were similar; at eight weeks and six months, there were no statistically significant differences in grief scores between the two groups. This comparable grief severity was confirmed by Field et al. (2009).

Pet loss and continuing bonds

Individuals report hearing or in some other way sensing the presence of their deceased pet (Carmack, 2003). Bereaved pet owners also experience an ongoing attachment with their deceased pet in two major ways: (i) remembering the pet is initially painful, but eventually the memories of 'special times' become a source of comfort; (ii) keeping physical reminders of the pet (such as dog collars, food dishes, and favourite toys) (Cowles, 1985). A dog's ashes may be kept in an urn inside the family home and photographs may be on display, just as they are with lost human loved-ones.

Research by Packman et al. (2011) examined and quantified *continuing bond expressions* (CBEs) displayed by 33 people (27 females and 6 males, aged 25–79) who had lost a cat or dog within the previous 12 months, together with their *psychosocial adjustment* (grief, symptoms, and growth). The measures used by the researchers included the Inventory of Complicated Grief (ICG) (Prigerson et al., 1995b) and the Continuing Bonds Interview (CBI) (Field et al., 2007). The CBI is designed to explore the different features of CBs and goes well beyond simply assessing extent of CBs to determine whether the CBEs are indicative of poor versus successful adaptation to the loss (Field, 2008).

The most frequently endorsed CBEs relating to the pet were:

- recalling fond memories (85 per cent)
- holding onto or using special belongings of the pet in order to feel close (79 per cent)
- reminiscing with others (79 per cent)
- learning lessons from the pet (i.e. its positive lasting influence) (76 per cent).

Also, 58 per cent reported thoughts of being reunited with their pet, 52 per cent had dreams involving their pet, 48 per cent endorsed a sense of the pet's presence, and 48 per cent reported being drawn to places associated with the deceased pet. Each of the following was reported by 39 per cent: living up to the ideals or wishes of the deceased, creating memorials, and intrusive sights or sounds of the deceased. The *least* endorsed was the pet's influence in making everyday decisions and choices (18 per cent).

In a separate but related study, Field (2010) compared this sample of pet-bereaved people with a sample of widows whose husbands had died one to two years previously. Both groups were similar in terms of relative frequency of endorsement of each CBE (such as high endorsement of reminiscing with others, focusing on fond memories, and using the deceased's belongings).

Drawing on previous research which had highlighted the importance of the comforting and distressing dimensions of CBEs (Field, 2010; Hsu, 2008; Ronen et al., 2009), an average score was derived for the extent of comfort and distress for each CBE. Both the pet-loss and spousal-loss groups showed an overall tendency to experience a CB as *more comforting* than distressing. This is important, because whether or not CBEs are associated with better adjustment may depend on the extent to which they are experienced as comforting or distressing. The relationships between (a) CBEs and grief, and (b) CBEs and symptoms, both appear to depend on comfort: individuals who use *more* CBEs and derive comfort from them experience *less* grief and fewer symptoms. In addition, those who use CBEs and derive comfort from them experience *growth* (see below). However, individuals who report using many CBEs accompanied by distress do *not* experience more grief and symptoms (Packman et al., 2011).

Pet loss and disenfranchised grief

Pet loss was given as an example of disenfranchised grief (DG) in Chapter 4. Carmack and Packman (2011) observe that those grieving the loss of a pet often feel invalidated and unsupported: they are reluctant to speak of the intensity of their grief or any experiences of CBE, either because of previous rejection or fear of their grief being disenfranchised. Comments such as 'It was just a dog' or 'What's the big deal – there are lots of cats who need homes', which are often directed to the bereaved, reinforce feelings of disenfranchisement and invalidation (Carmack and Packman, 2011, p. 281).

Fear of death

As has been argued by many philosophers, psychologists, psychotherapists, and others (e.g. Jones, 2008; May, 1969; Yalom, 1980), part of what makes us unique as a species is awareness of our mortality. These writers (and others, notably Becker, 1973) acknowledge that this awareness inevitably produces fear of death (or 'death terror') within each and every human being. According to Yalom (1980), for example, the realisation that we all die and the resulting death terror is one of four 'givens of existence' (or 'facts of life') (the others being *freedom, existential isolation*, and *meaninglessness*: see Gross, 2012). The awareness of death's inevitability in an animal that desperately wants to live produces a conflict that cannot easily be brushed aside.

Fear of death and anticipatory grief

In a very powerful poem, 'Aubade', Philip Larkin (1977/1993) describes a form of *anticipatory grief*, namely, fear of one's own death – of 'being dead' as opposed to *how* one is going to die. 'Aubade' concerns the inevitability of death and expresses the terror that we, as individuals, experience when realising that inevitability: it is the certainty of our death that makes it terrifying, the 'extinction' of our self, the prospect of being 'lost in that extinction forever, not to be 'here' or 'anywhere' '.

Larkin also conveys a sense of helplessness/powerlessness in the face of inevitable death, as well as anger with the attempts of religion to trick us into believing that we never (really) die – the ultimate deception.

As we have seen in Chapter 1, while Kübler-Ross's stages were originally intended to describe the process of dying in terminally-ill patients, they have since been applied to describe the experience of grieving for loved-ones who have died. However, there is a fundamental difference between these two 'populations':

> the difference is that such patients are both the soon-to-be-bereaved *and* the soon-to-be-deceased. So, in one case the loss has already happened, while in the other it is imminent.
>
> (Gross, 2014b, p. 17; emphasis added)

But how might this apply to loss of self that might seem quite remote, or, at least, which (albeit certain) is seen as occurring at some indeterminate point in the future? Is it appropriate to describe thoughts of our own death as anticipatory grief when we are not actually dying (i.e. we don't have a known terminal illness)? This is precisely what 'Aubade' does.

Fear of death and attachment theory

In terms of Bowlby's (e.g. 1969) attachment theory (see Chapter 2), the affectional bond with our partner serves precisely the same functions as the child's tie to its mother (-figure), namely:

- to provide a *safe base* (from which to explore and master the environment);
- to provide a *safe haven* (a source of comfort and support at times of distress and threat either to the self, the attachment figure, or to their relationship);
- *proximity maintenance* (a desire to stay close);
- *separation protest* (resisting separations).

In the case of the baby and young child. attachment behaviour serves to ensure its survival; the attachment itself (if secure) enables the child to separate from the attachment figure and achieve independence/autonomy (i.e. *detachment*). But in the adult, could it be that attachment to our partner helps us to deny – or, at least, feel less terrorised by – our fear of death?

> Perhaps in the desperate searching and pining for the lost spouse, the widow(er) is seeking protection against what has now become closer ('It's my turn next').
>
> (Gross, 2014b, p. 17)

As noted in Chapter 1, the anger that is a common component of normal grief often takes the form of blaming the deceased for abandoning the survivor ('Why have you left me on my own?'). Could this be 'translated' as 'Why have you left me on my own to face my extinction all by myself?' 'Why did you have to go before me?'. The anger is really *fear*, not of the process of dying, but of becoming lost in that 'extinction' forever. While our partner lives, we can pretend that the inevitable might not actually happen (Gross, 2014b).

Explaining our fear of death

While acknowledging human beings' fear of death, Freud (1913/1953) interpreted it as a kind of cover story used to disguise the true, underlying problem, namely, some unresolved, unconscious, conflict. Indeed,

> Our own death is indeed quite unimaginable, and whenever we make the attempt to imagine it we can perceive that we really survive as spectators. Hence at bottom nobody believes in his own death, or to put the same thing in a different way, in the unconscious every one of us is convinced of his own immortality.
>
> (Freud, 1913/1953, pp. 305–306)

Freud also argued that we cannot be said to fear death because we haven't experienced it. What we call fear of death is, in fact, a projection of (unconscious) anxieties based on actual experience (such as an adult male's unresolved castration anxiety, originating as part of the male child's Oedipus complex: see Gross, 2015).

Only the most devoted psychoanalytic thinkers would agree with Freud's explanation. As Kastenbaum (2000) puts it:

> The fear of death is not to be explained away as a superficial and disguised representation of a 'deeper' conflict. Quite the opposite! Anxiety – *all* anxiety – is rooted in the awareness of our mortality.
>
> (Kastenbaum, 2000, p. 104)

The consequences of this are enormous and manifest themselves in virtually every aspect of individual and cultural life. Becker (1973) was a leading proponent of this view. In *The Denial of Death*, he argued that it is death terror that has broken through the 'normal' defences that underlies psychosis (as in schizophrenia and major depressive disorder). Most ('normal') people buffer themselves through everyday activities and relationships from the full realisation of helplessness, hopelessness, and death. By contrast, people with schizophrenia are poorly integrated into the supportive cultural structure and so must face death alone.

According to Becker, in ordinary, everyday life, at least in Western countries, there is heavy repression of death-related anxiety (and, hence, of *all* anxiety). One form this takes is conformity with social norms, values, and roles; this provides us with a sense of security by tying into a system that will meet our dependency needs and help us deny our intrinsic vulnerability. This represents a collusion between individuals and society.

An illustration of this collusion is the way that death has become medicalised and sanitised, and generally removed from family and community involvement (see Chapter 4). Similarly, we typically try to keep a distance from the living who have been touched by death: neighbours and colleagues often avoid substantive contact with people who have been recently bereaved (Kastenbaum, 2000). Kastenbaum also observes that the stimulus for the provision of hospice care, and the death-awareness movement, was the social isolation of people with life-threatening or terminal illness.

> Paradoxically perhaps, those who excel in not dying have also been shunned: the aged remind us too much of our own mortal limits.
>
> (Kastenbaum, 2000, p. 99)

But what happens when we experience some traumatic event, which can disrupt this 'let's pretend' system? We are faced with the challenge of either restoring the tenuous collusion or confronting death as an aware and vulnerable individual (Kastenbaum, 2000). If too many people become preoccupied and crippled by death anxiety, society itself may be threatened. On the other hand, how can we function as mature adults unless we live with the full realisation of our mortality? Becker's (1973) proposed solution to this fundamental dilemma is that we must retain a keen sense of death-threat in order to protect ourselves from threats to our lives; we should also work this realisation into our philosophy of life in order to promote our individual development. The trick is to keep the awareness of mortality from overwhelming us with anxiety and despair (Kastenbaum, 2000).

Are there gender differences in death anxiety?

As measured by the Death Anxiety Scale (DAS) (originally constructed by Templer and Ruff (1971, then later revised by Thorson and Powell, 1994; Kelly and Corriveau, 1995), women, in general, indicate more death anxiety than men. While these measures, and most of the research studies using them, have been American, the limited data from other countries and cultures confirm the American pattern (Kastenbaum, 2000).

As Kastenbaum (2000) points out, women are more likely to be the ones who provide care for the dying, whether in a family/community or professional context. This suggests that their higher level of self-reported death anxiety is somehow associated with sensitivity to others' needs and a willingness to provide care and comfort. Also, while Dattel and Neimeyer (1990) found *no* gender differences in the experience and expression of death concern, Holcomb et al. (1993) found that men tended to think about death in more abstract and distanced terms (consistent with relatively lower death-anxiety scores).

Is death anxiety related to age?

According to Kastenbaum (2000), there are two *opposing* hypotheses that we could test regarding the relationship between death anxiety and age:

1   People become *more anxious* as they get older because they get closer to death.

2   People become *less anxious* as they get older because (a) death does not threaten as many of our values, and/or (b) there is a continued developmental process through which we 'come to terms' with our mortality.

While the first is 'reductionist' (i.e. advancing age is all that matters, with the individual's life history and personality being irrelevant), the second is consistent with *life-span developmental theories* such as those of Erikson, (e.g. 1963) and Butler's (1963) concept of *life review*. Life's final task is to accept the life we have led, including the death that is its conclusion; in Erikson's terms, the aim is to achieve a greater sense of *ego-integrity* than *despair*, the latter being characterised by fear of death.

> The 'successful maturer' might be expected to experience less death anxiety as the turbulence of youth and identity-seeking gives way to a mature sense of fulfilment and acceptance death is not the same catastrophic threat that it was when so much of what one valued existed only in the realm of expectation and hope.
>
> (Kastenbaum, 2000, p. 122)

Reviewing the evidence, Kastenbaum (2000) draws the following conclusions:

*   Older people in general do not report higher levels of death anxiety. Virtually no evidence exists to support the view that elderly adults live with a heightened sense of fear, anxiety, or distress regarding their mortality. Again, fear of death is not an automatic or natural correlate of growing old.
*   However, while simply knowing a person's age doesn't provide a satisfactory basis for predicting his/her self-reported level of death anxiety, age *may* be a useful variable as part of a more complex and realistic approach to understanding how and why people contemplate death.
*   For example, a study by Stricherz and Cunnington (1981–1982) found that high school students were most apprehensive about the possible loss of a loved one, death as a punishment, and the finality of death. By contrast, employed adults (average age 42) were most concerned about experiencing a painful and a premature death; compared with the students and a group of older, retired people, they showed the least concern about the possible impact of their deaths on other people. The retirees' concerns centred around the fear of becoming helpless and dependent on others – the *process* of dying, rather than the outcome. A particular concern was of being kept alive in an undignified, semi-vegetative state; they preferred a quick death at the right time to a long, lingering decline. The elderly participants were also the most concerned of all three groups about the impact of their dying and death on their loved ones.
*   One interesting research finding, reported by Munnichs (1966) in the Netherlands, concerned differences between the 'young old' (people in their 70s)

and the 'old old' (people in their 80s and over). The former were often still confronting the prospect of their death, as if asking themselves, 'What should death mean to me at this time in my life?'. By contrast, the latter seemed to have passed this stage, standing by the answers they had previously given to this question; the prospect of their death was by now a well-known, familiar phenomenon.

• Individual personality seems to be much more important than age as a long life approaches its end.

Terror management theory

Drawing on Becker's writings, *terror management theory* (TMT) (e.g. Solomon et al., 2004) maintains that human beings are potentially exposed to a paralysing terror and sense of pointlessness through awareness of our mortality. To combat these, we embrace a conception of reality as meaningful (a *cultural worldview*); this enables us to achieve a sense of purpose or self-esteem by adhering to the norms and values prescribed by that worldview. In turn, self-esteem can serve as a buffer against the anxiety aroused by reminders of death (see the discussion of conformity and collusion between the individual and society above).

According to Solomon et al. (2004):

> Meaning is derived from cultural worldviews that offer an account of the origin of the universe, prescriptions of appropriate conduct, and guarantees of safety and security to those who adhere to such instructions – in this life and beyond, in the form of symbolic and/or literal immortality.
>
> (p. 16)

Symbolic immortality can be achieved by perceiving oneself as part of a culture that endures beyond one's lifetime, or by creating tangible testaments to one's existence in the form of works of art or literature, scientific discovery, impressive buildings or monuments, amassing vast fortunes or properties, and producing offspring. *Literal immortality* is achieved by the various afterlives promised by almost all organised religions (see Chapter 5). (See Gross, 2014a.)

Meaning reconstruction in bereavement

While TMT focuses on the role of cultural worldviews in providing meaning, other theoretical approaches have concentrated more on the need of the individual to make sense of bereavement. Despite being complementary ways of looking at the need for meaning-making, TMT adopts a broader, more abstract approach than the *constructivist* theory of Neimeyer and his colleagues (e.g. Neimeyer et al., 2010), which we discuss below.

Just as we are the only species that is aware of its mortality (as far as we can tell), so

> To a far greater extent than other animals, we as human beings are distin-
> guished by living not only in a present, physical world, but also in a world
> populated by long-term memories, long-range anticipations, reflections,
> goals, interpretations, hopes, regrets, beliefs, and metaphors – in a word,
> *meanings*.
>
> (Neimeyer and Sands, 2011, p. 9; emphasis in original)

In 'acts of meaning' (Bruner, 1990), we seek an order, a foundation, a plan, a significance in human existence, especially our own. However, there are occasions
when the 'stubborn physicality of the present moment' threatens to, or actually
destroys our all-too-vulnerable *assumptive worlds* (Neimeyer and Sands, 2011,
p. 9: see Chapter 3); such occasions include the diagnosis of our own serious illness, betrayal by an intimate partner, or news of a loved one's sudden death.

> At such moments, we can feel cast into a world that is alien, unimaginable,
> and uninhabitable, one that radically shakes or severs those taken-for-granted
> 'realities' in which we are rooted, and on which we rely for a sense of secure
> purpose and connection.
>
> (Neimeyer and Sands, 2011, p. 10)

Neimeyer and Sands describe these moments as *crises of meaning*.

Neimeyer (2000, 2009) has focused on how people construct meaningful
episodes from the constant bombardment of stimulation and information that
surround them. From within this constant flow of events, we are able to detect
recurrent themes that give them personal significance; we then test out the validity
of these themes through our relationships with others. We ultimately construct a
life story (or *self-narrative*) that is uniquely our own, though it inevitably draws
on the social discourses of our place and time (Neimeyer et al., 2010) (see above
and Chapter 4). A self-narrative can be defined as:

> an overarching cognitive-affective-behavioural structure that organises the
> 'micro-narratives' of everyday life into a 'macro-narrative' that consoli-
> dates our self-understanding, establishes our characteristic range of emo-
> tions and goals, and guides our performance on the stage of the social
> world.
>
> (Neimeyer, 2004, pp. 53–54)

From this perspective, our self-identity is achieved through the stories that
we tell about ourselves and significant others. Importantly, it's precisely this
self-narrative that is threatened and disturbed by 'seismic' life events such as the
death of a loved one; they force us to reaffirm, repair, or replace the basic plot and
theme of our life story (Calhoun and Tedeschi, 2006; Neimeyer, 2006).

Box 8.1   Different levels of the search for meaning

In the aftermath of life-changing loss, the bereaved are commonly thrown into a *search for meaning*; this can take place at different levels:

- a *practical* level (*How* did my loved-one die?);
- a *relational* level (*Who* am I, now that I'm no longer a spouse?);
- a *spiritual* or *existential* level (*Why* did God allow this to happen?)

(Based on Neimeyer and Sands, 2011)

How – and whether – we address these questions and resolve or simply stop asking them shapes how we accommodate the loss itself and who we become in the light of it (Neimeyer and Sands, 2011). However, loss does not inevitably destroy survivors' self-narratives: many people find consolation in systems of secular and spiritual beliefs and practices that have served them well in the past (Attig, 2000). Especially when the death is relatively normative and anticipated, only a minority of bereaved people report searching for meaning, and the absence of such a search is one predictor of a positive outcome (Davis et al., 2000). Yet even in the case of normative, timely, losses (such as late-life widowhood), a significant minority of spouses struggle to find meaning in their loss over an extended period of time (Bonnano et al., 2004). In this same prospective longitudinal study of widows and widowers, those who reported a more intense search for meaning at six and 18 months following the loss showed a more painful and prolonged grief reaction up to *four years* post-bereavement (Coleman and Neimeyer, 2010).

Meaning, traumatic loss, and complicated grief

With regard to complicated grief, a struggle with meaninglessness is a critical marker of debilitating grief reactions such as PGD (Prigerson et al., 2009: see Chapter 7). In a study of a large group of bereaved young adults who had suffered a variety of losses, Holland et al. (2006) found that inability to 'make sense' of the death was associated with marked and preoccupying separation distress across the first two years of bereavement.

In the case of losses that are objectively more traumatic, trying to make sense of the loss is more common. Evidence shows that a crisis of meaning is especially acute for those bereaved by suicide, homicide, or fatal accident, compared with those whose loved-ones died from natural causes. According to Currier et al., (2006), it is this need to make sense of the loss which accounts for almost all the difference between the complicated grief of those suffering a traumatic bereavement and the uncomplicated grief of those bereaved by natural causes.

Keesee et al. (2008) studied a large group of parents who had lost a child between a few months and several years previously. The passage of time, the parent's gender, and even whether the child died a natural or violent death accounted for little of their subsequent adaptation; this was true regardless of whether this was assessed in terms of normative grief symptoms (such as sadness and missing the child) or complicated grief (such as an ongoing inability to care about others, and long-term disruption of functioning in work and family contexts). In contrast, their degree of sense-making accounted for *15 times more* of these parents' distress than any of these objective factors.

A further analysis of these parents' qualitative responses to questions regarding sense-making (Lichtenthal et al., 2010) reported that 45 per cent could still not make sense of their child's death even (on average) six years later, and over 20 per cent could identify no unsought benefits (such as greater personal strength) to mitigate the great pain of the tragedy. The most common sense-making themes involved religious beliefs (e.g. their child's death was part of a divine plan, or a belief in reunion in the afterlife); the most common benefit-finding themes involved an increased desire to help and show compassion for others' suffering. Those parents who invoked specific sense-making themes, as well as those who reported benefits, experienced fewer maladaptive grief symptoms.

Evidence from longitudinal studies of normative bereavement, such as spousal-loss, demonstrates that sense-making in the first six months of loss predicts higher levels of positive affect and well-being a full four years post-loss (Coleman and Neimeyer, 2010).

> Fostering reconstruction of a world of meaning would therefore seem to be a therapeutic priority for many bereaved clients, one that could carry benefits not only in alleviating complicated grief symptomatology, but also in renewing a sense of hope and self-efficacy in their changed lives.
>
> (Neimeyer and Sands, 2011, p. 13)

The special case of suicide

From a meaning reconstruction perspective, the death of a loved-one through suicide poses an especially severe challenge to survivors' attempts to make sense of it. According to Sands et al. (2010);

- suicide violates cherished assumptions about the safety and predictability of the world and the continued presence of the loved-one;
- the volitional nature of the act challenges core beliefs regarding the inherent value of life and the seemingly inscrutable explanation for the deceased's fatal decision.

Consequently, the question *Why?* reverberates in the survivor's self-narrative more forcefully than almost any other triggering event.

The *tripartite model of suicide bereavement* (TMSB) (Sands, 2008, 2009) is a meaning-making model that focuses on the distinctive themes facing the suicide-bereaved. The model identifies three phases of the grief process, and within each one, considers how the relationships with the deceased, the self, and others change as the bereaved struggle with challenges to their assumptive world. The three phases are described in Box 8.2.

Box 8.2 The three phases of grief as identified in the tripartite model of suicide bereavement (TMSB) (Sands, 2008, 2009)

Phase 1: Understanding Relationship (*Trying on the Shoes*): focuses on the difficulties of decoding and understanding the self-volition of a suicide death. These issues are explored through a range of 'why' questions.

Phase 2: Reconstructing Relationship (*Walking in the Shoes*): focuses on making sense of the pain of the life and death of the deceased. This entails trying to understand the deceased's experience, in particular the pain and trauma, known or imagined, of his/her life and death. Significantly, the struggle to reconstruct meaning can place the bereaved in a similar position to the deceased of experiencing hopelessness and being vulnerable to suicidal ideation.

Phase 3: Repositioning Relationships (*Taking off the Shoes*): this makes way for more subtle layers of grief, and it validates the suffering of the deceased but rarely the manner of the death.

A more detailed account of the TMSB is given in Figure 8.1.

Post-traumatic growth

When describing the findings from Lichtenthal et al.'s (2010) study of bereaved parents, we noted that those who reported benefits (such as an increased desire to help others) were less likely to experience maladaptive symptoms. An outcome such as an increased desire to help others is an example of *post-traumatic growth* (PTG).

According to Linley and Joseph (2003), various philosophies, literatures, and religions throughout history have claimed that personal gain can be found in suffering. The concept of PTG was coined by Tedeschi and Calhoun in 1996 to denote how trauma can serve as a catalyst for positive changes. It stimulated considerable research interest and the study of PTG has become one of the flagship topics for Positive Psychology (PP) (Seligman, 2011).

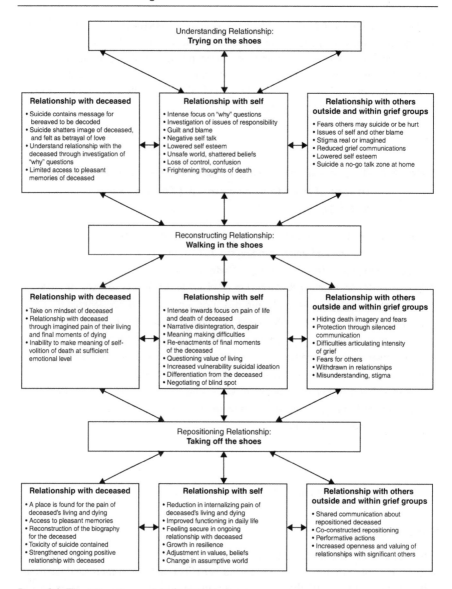

Figure 8.1 The tripartite model of suicide bereavement

Evidence for PTG

Calhoun and Tedeschi (1999) found that 30–90 per cent of people who experience some form of traumatic event report at least some positive changes following the trauma (the figure varies according to the type of event and other factors). These positive changes can underpin a whole new way of living that embraces the central tenets of PP (Linley, 2000).

Several self-report psychometric tools were published during the 1990s to assess positive changes following trauma, including the Posttraumatic Growth Inventory/PTGI (Taku et al., 2008; Tedeschi and Calhoun, 1996). Respondents are asked to think about how they've changed since an event and to rate the extent of this change on a series of items.

Using such measures of perceived growth, combined with open-ended interviews, a large number of studies have shown that growth is common for survivors of various traumatic events, including transportation accidents (shipping disasters, plane crashes, car accidents), natural disasters (hurricanes, earthquakes), interpersonal experiences (combat, rape, sexual assault, child abuse), medical problems (cancer, heart attack, brain injury, spinal cord injury, HIV/AIDS, leukaemia, rheumatoid arthritis, multiple sclerosis), and other life experiences (relationship breakdown, parental divorce, bereavement, emigration). Typically, 30–70 per cent of survivors report positive change of one form or another (Linley and Joseph, 2004).

What happens during PTG?

According to Calhoun et al. (2010), an interplay of several classes of variables is potentially central in the likelihood of PTG developing following trauma.

These variables include, among others:

(a) cognitive processing, engagement, or rumination;
(b) expression or disclosure of concerns surrounding traumatic events;
(c) reactions of others to self-disclosures;
(d) sociocultural context in which traumas occur and attempts to process, disclose, and resolve take place;
(e) survivors' personal dispositions and the degree of resilience; and
(f) degree to which events allow for the above processes to occur, or the degree to which events suppress them.

According to Joseph (2012), following experience of a traumatic event, people often report three ways in which their psychological functioning increases:

1   Relationships are enhanced in some way. For example, people say that they come to value their friends and family more, feel an increased sense of compassion for others and a longing for more intimate relationships.
2   People change their view of themselves. For example, they develop wisdom, personal strength, and gratitude, possibly combined with a greater acceptance of their vulnerabilities and limitations.
3   People describe changes in their philosophy of life. For example, they might find a fresh appreciation for each new day and re-evaluate their understanding

of what really matters in life; this may manifest as becoming less material-
istic and better able to live in the present. This re-setting of priorities is what
Tedeschi and Calhoun (2012) refer to as identifying *core values*.

Trauma survivors who have been provoked to growth by their experience often
report that previous views of life seem shallow to them. So, in our growth toward
meaningful, wise living, traumas can help crystallise discontent, what Baumeister
(1991) describes as provoking changes in meaning.

PTG involves the re-building of the shattered *assumptive world* (Parkes, 1993).
According to Joseph (2012):

> When adversity strikes, people often feel that at least some part of them – be
> it their views of the world, their sense of themselves, their relationships – has
> been smashed. Those who try to put their lives back together exactly as they
> were remain fractured and vulnerable. But those who accept the breakage
> and build themselves anew become more resilient and open to new ways of
> living.
>
> (p. 817)

**Box 8.3   The relationship between degree of post-traumatic
stress and degree of PTG (based on Joseph, 2012)**

- While there exists some evidence to support this claim that post-traumatic
  stress acts as the 'engine' of PTG (e.g. Dekel et al.'s 2012 study of Israeli
  combat veterans), other research indicates that there might be an
  inverted-U relationship between post-traumatic stress and PTG.
- For example, Butler et al. (2005) found that, following 9/11, greater
  post-traumatic stress was associated with greater PTG – but only up to a
  point.
- At *low* levels of post-traumatic stress, the person has been minimally
  affected, so we'd expect minimal PTG.
- At *moderate* levels, the individual's assumptive world has been challenged, triggering the intrusive and avoidant symptoms. But s/he remains
  able to cope, think clearly, and engage sufficiently in the necessary
  affective-cognitive processing needed to work through.
- At *high* levels, a diagnosis of PTSD might be considered; here, the abilities
  shown at moderate levels break down.

Summary and conclusions

- Despite being an example of *disenfranchised grief*, the loss of a *pet* induces grief responses that are just as severe as those associated with the loss of another human being. The nature of the grief is also strikingly similar.
- Research by Packman et al. examined pet loss grief in terms of *continuing bond expressions* (CBEs), including recalling fond memories, keeping special possessions, and reminiscing with others.
- Awareness of our mortality inevitably produces *fear of death* (or *death terror*). This represents one of Yalom's 'givens of existence' and is captured in Larkin's poem 'Aubade'.
- Fear of our own death can be understood as a form of *anticipatory grief*. In terms of attachment theory, attachment to our partner/spouse may help protect us from that fear – either through denial or reducing its threat.
- Freud regarded fear of death as a superficial and disguised representation of some 'deeper' conflict. But Becker regarded all anxiety as stemming from our death terror, which in everyday life, at least in Western countries, is heavily repressed.
- Individuals and society collude through the *medicalisation* and *sanitisation* of death, removed from family and community involvement.
- As measured by the *Death Anxiety Scale* (DAS), women in general indicate more death anxiety than men. Men are also more likely to think about death in more abstract and distanced terms than women.
- Older people in general do not report higher levels of death anxiety: it is not an inevitable or natural correlate of growing old as some have claimed. All age-groups may contemplate death, but for different reasons and in different ways. There are also important individual differences.
- According to *terror management theory* (TMT), in order to combat our potentially paralysing terror and sense of pointlessness related to the awareness of our mortality, we adopt a *cultural worldview*; this enables us to achieve a sense of purpose/self-esteem by adhering to the norms and values that it prescribes.
- *Religion* forms a major part of our cultural worldview, offering *literal immortality*. Perceiving oneself as belonging to a culture that endures beyond one's lifetime, or by leaving behind some kind of legacy affords us *symbolic immortality*.
- According to Neimeyer's *meaning reconstruction approach*, major bereavements create *crises of meaning*: our *self-narratives* are threatened and disturbed, forcing us to reaffirm, repair, or replace the basic plot and theme of our life story.
- The *search for meaning* can take place at a practical, relational, or spiritual/existential level. With regard to *complicated grief* (CG), a struggle with meaninglessness is a critical marker of debilitating grief reactions such as prolonged grief disorder (PGD).

- Death of a loved one through *suicide* poses an especially severe challenge to survivors' attempts to make sense of it.
- The *tripartite model of suicide bereavement* (TMSB) identifies three phases of grief, within each of which changes to the relationship with the deceased, the self, and others are considered as the bereaved struggle with challenges to their assumptive world.
- Research evidence shows that a large proportion of people who experience some form of traumatic event report at least some degree of *post-traumatic growth* (PTG)
- Trauma survivors often report that their experience has revealed the shallowness of their previous life, provoking changes in meaning and the re-building of their shattered assumptive world.
- There may be an *inverted-U relationship* between PTG and *post-traumatic stress*.

Recommended reading and websites

Recommended reading

Academic texts on grief and bereavement

Archer, J. (1999) *The Nature of Grief: The Evolution and Psychology of Reactions to Loss.* London: Routledge.

Bonnano, G. A. (2009) *The Other Side of Sadness: What the New Science of Bereavement Tells Us About Life After Loss.* New York: Basic Books.

Doka, K. J. & Martin, T. L. (2010) *Grieving Beyond Gender: Understanding the Ways Men and Women Mourn* (revised edition). New York: Routledge.

Meagher, D. K. & Balk, D. E. (eds.) (2013) *Handbook of Thanatology: The Essential Body of Knowledge for the Study of Death, Dying, and Bereavement* (2nd edition). New York: Routledge.

Neimeyer, R. A., Harris, D. L., Winokuer, H. R. & Thornton, G. F. (eds.) (2011) *Grief and Bereavement in Contemporary Society: Bridging Research and Practice.* New York: Routledge.

Parkes, C. M. (1993) Bereavement as a psychosocial transition: Processes of adaptation to change. In M. S. Stroebe, W. Stroebe & R. O. Hansson (eds.), *Handbook of Bereavement: Theory, Research and Intervention.* New York: Cambridge University Press.

Parkes, C. M. (2006) *Love and Loss: The Roots of Grief and Its Complications.* London: Routledge.

Rubin, S., Malkinson, R. & Witztum, A. E. (2012) *Working With the Bereaved: Multiple Lenses on Loss and Mourning.* New York: Routledge.

Stroebe, M. & Schut, H. (2010) The Dual Process Model of coping with bereavement: Rationale and description. *Omega, 61*(4), 273–289.

Stroebe, M., Hansson, R. O., Schut, H. & Stroebe, W. (eds.) (2008) *Handbook of Bereavement Research and Practice: Advances in Theory and Intervention.* Washington, DC: American Psychological Association.

Stroebe, M., Schut, H. & van den Bout, J. (eds.) (2013) *Complicated Grief: Scientific Foundations for Health Care Professionals.* London: Routledge.

Personal accounts of grief

Abrams, R. (1992) *When Parents Die.* London: Charles Letts & Co.

Abse, D. (2007) *The Presence.* London: Hutchinson.

Barnes, J. (2013) *Levels of Life*. London: Jonathan Cape.
Cockburn, A.-M. (2013) *5,742 Days: A Mother's Journey Through Loss*. Oxford: Infinite Ideas Limited.
Dinnage, R. (1990) *The Ruffian on the Stair: Reflections on Death*. London: Penguin.
Downey, A. (1987) *Dear Stephen: A Letter Written to Stephen by His Mother*. London: Arthur James.
Keizer, B. (1997) *Dancing with Mister D: Notes on Life and Death*. London: Black Swan.
Lewis, C.S. (1961) *A Grief Observed*. London: Faber & Faber.
McCarthy, S. (2001) *A Voice for those bereaved by suicide*. Dublin: Veritas.

Anthologies and poetry

Astley, N. (ed.) (2003) *Do Not Go Gentle: Poems for Funerals*. Tarset: Bloodaxe Books.
Benson, J. & Falk, A. (eds.) (1996) *The Long Pale Corridor: Contemporary Poems of Bereavement*. Newcastle-upon-Tyne: Bloodaxe Books.
Paterson, D. (ed.) (2012) *The Picador Book of Funeral Poems*. London: Picador.
Whitaker, A. (ed.) (1996) *All in The End Is Harvest: An Anthology for Those Who Grieve*. London: Darton, Longman and Todd.

Useful websites (mainly UK)

General

Cruse Bereavement Care http://www.crusebereavementcare.org.uk
A related site (for young people) is: RD4U ('The road for you') http://www.hopeagain.org.uk
The WAY Foundation http://www.wayfoundation.org.uk
Merry Widow http://www.merrywidow.me.uk
Childhood Bereavement Network http://www.childhoodbereavementnetwork.org.uk
Bereavement UK http://www.bereavement.co.uk
National Association of Bereavement Services http://www.self-help.org.uk
Macmillan Cancer Support http://www.macmillan.org.uk
Cancer Help UK http://cancerhelp.cancer-researchuk.org/
BACUP (British Association for Cancer United Patients and their Family and Friends) http://www.aim25.ac.uk
Samaritans http://www.samaritans.org.uk
MIND (The National Mental Health Charity) http://www.mind.org.uk
Westminster Pastoral Foundation http://www.wpf.org.uk
Women's Therapy Centre (WTC) http://www.womenstherapycentre.co.uk
Dying Matters http://www.dyingmatters.org/
British Association for Counselling and Psychotherapy (BACP) http://www.bacp.co.uk
Healthtalkonline http://www.healthtalkonline.org
Age UK http://www.ageuk.org.uk/

Loss of a child

The Compassionate Friends http://www.tcf.org.uk
Related helpline: Support in Bereavement for Brothers and Sisters (SIBBS).

Tel: 08451 232304
SANDS (Stillbirth and Neonatal Death Society) http://www.uk-sands.org
Child Bereavement Charity (CBC) http://www.childbereavment.org.uk
Foundation for the Study of Infant Deaths (FSID) http://www.fsid.org.uk
Miscarriage Association http://www.miscarriageassociation.org.uk
Grief Encounter http://www.griefencounter.com
Much Loved (online Tribute charity) http://www.muchloved.com
The Child Bereavement Trust http://www.childbereavement.org.uk
Together for Short Lives http://www.togetherforshortlives.org.uk/

Children and teenagers

Winston's Wish http://www.winstonswish.org.uk
Teenage Cancer Trust http://www.teenagecancertrust.org/
Siblinks http://www.siblinks.org/
Childline http://www.childline.org.uk

Sudden, violent, and traumatic bereavement

SCARD (Support and Care After Road Death) http://www.scard.org.uk
Roadpeace http://www.roadpeace.org
BRAKE (The Road Safety Charity) http://www.brake.org.uk
Royal Society for the Prevention of Accidents (ROSPA) http://www.rospa.com
SAMM (Support after Murder and Manslaughter) https://www.samm.org.uk
SAMMA (Support after Murder and Manslaughter Abroad) http://www.sammabroad.org
MAMAA (Mothers Against Murder and Aggression) http://www.mamaa.org
The Compassionate Friends: Shadow of Suicide Group (SOS) http://www.tcf.org.uk
SOBS (Survivors of Bereavement by Suicide) http://www.uk-sobs.org.uk/
PAPYRUS http://www.papyrus-uk.org
American Association of Suicidology (AAS) http://www.suicidology.org
American Foundation for Suicide Prevention (AFSD) http://www.afsp.org
Centre for Suicide Research (University of Oxford) http://www.psychiatry.ox.ac.uk/csr
Suicide Prevention Information New Zealand (SPINZ) http://www.spinz.org.nz
International Association for Suicide Prevention (IASP) http://www.iasp.info/index.php
SAVE (Suicide Awareness Voices of Education) – Coping with Loss http://www.save.org/
    coping
National Association of Victim Support Schemes http://www.counselling-directory.org.uk
European Directory of Survivor Services http://lasso.uio.no/ssff/iasp
Homicide Victims' Support Group (Australia) hvsgnsw.org.au
Inquest http://www.inquest.org.uk

Faith and other minority groups

Interfaith Seminary http://www.theinterfaithseminary.com
In truth One Spirit: Tel. Helpline 01483 898969
Asian Family Counselling Service: Tel. Helpline 020 8571 3933
Islamic Cultural Centre http://www.iccuk.org
Muslim Women's Helpline: 020 8904 8193/020 8908 6715
Jewish Bereavement Counselling Service http://www.jvisit.org.uk/jbcs (London-based)

Foundation for Black Bereaved Families southwarkfsd.openobjects.com
London Lesbian and Gay Switchboard http://www.llgs.org.uk
Lesbian and Gay Bereavement Project Tel. Helpline 0207 7403 5969

Funerals

British Humanist Association http://www.humanism.org.uk
Cremation Society of GB http://www.cremation.org.uk
National Association of Funeral Directors (NAFD) http://www.nafd.org.uk
Natural Death Centre http://www.naturaldeath.org.uk

References

Abrams, R. (1992) *When Parents Die*. London: Charles Letts & Co.

Abse, D. (2007) *The Presence*. London: Hutchinson.

Ainsworth, M.D.S. (1967) *Infancy in Uganda: Infant Care and the Growth of Love*. Baltimore, MD: Johns Hopkins University Press.

Ainsworth, M.D.S., Bell, S.M.V. & Stayton, D.J. (1971) Individual differences in Strange Situation behaviour of one-year-olds. In H.R. Schaffer (ed.) *The Origins of Human Social Relations*. New York: Academic Press.

Ainsworth, M.D.S., Blehar, M.C., Waters, E. & Wall, S. (1978) *Patterns of Attachment: A Psychological Study of the Strange Situation*. Hillsdale, NJ: Lawrence Erlbaum Associates.

Ainsworth, M.D.S. & Wittig, B.A. (1969) Attachment and exploratory behaviour of 1-year-olds in a strange situation. In B.M. Foss (ed.), *Determinants of Infant Behaviour, Volume 4*. London: Methuen.

Allsopp, J., Jones, K. & Baggott, R. (2004) Health consumer groups in the UK: A new social movement? *Sociology of Health and Illness, 26*(60), 737–756.

American Psychiatric Association (2000) *Diagnostic and Statistical Manual of Mental Disorders* (4th edition revised). Washington, DC: American Psychiatric Association

American Psychiatric Association (2013) *Diagnostic and Statistical Manual of Mental Disorders* (5th edition). Washington, DC: American Psychiatric Association

Anderson, C. (1949) Aspects of pathological grief and mourning. *International Journal of Psychoanalysis, 30*, 48–55.

Aneshensel, C.S., Botticello, A.L. & Yamamoto-Mitani, N. (2004) When caregiving ends: The course of depressive symptoms after bereavement. *Journal of Health & Social Behaviour, 45*, 422–440.

Apter, T. (2001) *The Myth of Maturity*. New York: Norton.

Archer, J. (1997) Why do people love their pets? *Evolution and Human Behaviour, 18*, 237–259.

Archer, J. (1999) *The Nature of Grief: The Evolution and Psychology of Reactions to Loss*. London: Routledge.

Archer, J. & Winchester, G. (1994) Bereavement following death of a pet. *British Journal of Psychology, 85*, 259–271.

Aries, P. (1974) *Western Attitudes Towards Death: From the Middle Ages to the Present*. Baltimore, MD: Johns Hopkins University Press.

Aries, P. (1981) *The Hour of Our Death*. London: Allen Lane.

Aries, P. (1993) Death Denied. In D. Dickenson & M. Johnson (eds.), *Death, Dying & Bereavement*. London: Sage Publications and the Open University. (Extract from *The Hour of Our Death* (1981), London: Allen Lane.)

Arkowitz, H. & Lilienfeld, S.O. (2011) Grief without tears. *Scientific American Mind, 22*(5), 68–69.

Attig, T. (2000) *The Heart of Grief*. New York: Oxford University Press.

Attig, T. (2004) Disenfranchised grief revisited: Discounting hope and love. *Omega, 49*(3), 197–215.

Balk, D.E. (2013) Life span issues and loss, grief, and mourning: Adulthood. In D.K. Meagher & D.E. Balk (eds.), *Handbook of Thanatology: The Essential Body of Knowledge for the Study of Death, Dying, and Bereavement* (2nd edition). New York: Routledge.

Ball, J.F. (1977) Widow's grief: The impact of age and mode of death. *Omega: Journal of Death & Dying, 7*, 307–333.

Barnes, J. (2013) *Levels of Life*. London: Jonathan Cape.

Bartholomew, K. & Horowitz, L.M. (1991) Attachment styles among young adults: A test of a four-category model. *Journal of Personality & Social Psychology, 61*, 226–244.

Baumeister, R.F. (1991) *Meanings of Life*. New York: Guilford Press.

Becker, E. (1973) *The Denial of Death*. New York: Free Press.

Belsky, J., Rovine, M. & Taylor, D.G. (1984) The Pennsylvania Infant and Family Development Project: III. The origins of individual differences in infant-mother attachment: Maternal and infant contributions. *Child Development, 55*, 718–728.

Bennett, K.M. (1997) Widowhood in elderly women: The medium- and long-term effects on mental and physical health. *Mortality, 2*(2), 137–148.

Bennett, K.M. (1998) Longitudinal changes in mental and physical health among recently widowed men. *Mortality, 3*, 265–274.

Bennett, K.M. (2009) 'Can't do enough for you.' Why do older men get more social support than women following bereavement? *Bereavement Care, 28*(3), 5–9.

Bennett, K.M. (2010a) 'You can't spend years with someone and just cast them aside': Augmented identity in older British widows. *Journal of Women & Ageing, 22*(3), 204–217.

Bennett, K.M., Hughes, G.M. & Smith, P.T. (2003) 'I think a woman can take it': Widowed men's views and experiences of gender differences in bereavement. *Ageing International, 28*(4), 408–424.

Bennett, K.M., and Morgan, K. (1992) Health, social functioning, and marital status: Stability and change among elderly recently widowed women. *International Journal of Geriatric Psychiatry, 7*(11), 813–817.

Bennett, K.M. & Soulsby, L.K. (2012) Wellbeing in bereavement and widowhood. *Illness, Crisis & Loss, 20*(4), 321–337.

Benoit, D. & Parker, K. (1994) Stability and transmission of attachment across Three Generations. *Child Development, 65*(5), 1444–1456.

Benore, E.R. & Park, C.L. (2004) Religiousness and beliefs in continued attachment after death. *International Journal of the Psychology of Religion, 14*, 1–22.

Biddle, L. & Walter, T. (1998) The emotional English and their queen of hearts. *Folklore, 109*, 96–111.

Birtchnell, J. (1975) Psychiatric breakdown following recent parent death. *British Journal of Medical Psychology, 10*, 699–713.

Black, J. (1987) Death and Bereavement: The Customs of Hindus, Sikhs, and Moslems. *British Medical Journal, 295*, 536–539.

Blauner, R. (1966) Death and social structure. *Psychiatry, 29*, 378–394.

Boerner, K. & Heckhausen, J. (2003) To have and have not: Adaptive bereavement by transforming mental ties to the deceased. *Death Studies, 27*, 199–226.

Boerner, K., Mancini, A. D. & Bonnano, G. (2013) On the nature and prevalence of uncomplicated and complicated patterns of grief. In M. Stroebe, H. Schut & J. van den Bout (eds.), *Complicated Grief: Scientific Foundations for Health Care Professionals*. London: Routledge.

Bonnano, G. A. (2004) Loss, trauma, and human resilience: Have we underestimated the human capacity to thrive after extremely adverse events? *American Psychologist, 59*, 20–28.

Bonnano, G. A. (2009) *The Other Side of Sadness: What the New Science of Bereavement Tells Us About Life After Loss*. New York: Basic Books.

Bonnano, G. A., Boerner, K. & Wortman, C. (2008) Trajectories of grieving. In M. Stroebe, R. O. Hansson, H. Schut & W. Stroebe (eds.), *Handbook of Bereavement Research and Practice: Advances in Theory and Intervention*. Washington, DC: American Psychological Association.

Bonnano, G. A. & Field, N. P. (2001) Evaluating the delayed grief hypothesis across 5 years of bereavement. *American Behavioural Scientist, 44*, 798–816.

Bonnano, G. A. & Kaltman, S. (2001) The varieties of grief experience. *Clinical Psychology Review, 21*, 705–734.

Bonnano, G. A. & Keltner, D. (1997) Facial expressions of emotion and the course of conjugal bereavement. *Journal of Abnormal Psychology, 106*, 126–137.

Bonnano, G. A., Neria, Y., Mancini, A. et al. (2007) Is there more to complicated grief than depression and post-traumatic stress disorder? A test of incremental validity. *Journal of Abnormal Psychology, 116*, 342–351.

Bonnano, G. A., Wortman, C. B., Lehman, D. R. et al. (2002) Resilience to loss and chronic grief: A prospective study from pre-loss to 18 months post-loss. *Journal of Personality & Social Psychology, 83*, 1150–1164.

Bonnano, G. A., Wortman, C. B. & Nesse, R. M. (2004) Prospective patterns of resilience and maladjustment during widowhood. *Psychology & Ageing, 19*, 260–271.

Boss, P. (1999) *Ambiguous Loss: Learning to Live With Unresolved Grief*. Cambridge, MA: Harvard University Press.

Bowlby, J. (1951) *Maternal Care and Mental Health*. Geneva: WHO.

Bowlby, J. (1969) *Attachment and Loss, Vol.1: Attachment*. Harmondsworth: Penguin.

Bowlby, J. (1973) *Attachment and Loss, Vol.2: Separation*. Harmondsworth: Penguin.

Bowlby, J. (1979) The making and breaking of affectional bonds. In J. Bowlby (ed.) *The Making and Breaking of Affectional Bonds*. London: Tavistock.

Bowlby, J. (1980) *Attachment and Loss, Vol. 3: Loss, Sadness, and Depression*. London: Hogarth Press.

Bowlby, J. (1988) *A Secure Base: Clinical Applications of Attachment Theory*. London: Tavistock/Routledge.

Bowlby, J. & Parkes, C. M. (1970) Separation and loss within the family. In E. J. Anthony (ed.), *The Child in His Family*. New York: Wiley.

Bowman, L. (1975) *The American Funeral*. Westport, CT: Greenwood.

Brabant, S., Forsyth, C. J. & McFarlain, G. (1997) The impact of the death of a child on meaning and purpose in life. *Journal of Personal & Interpersonal Loss, 2*, 255–266.

Brave Heart, M.Y.H. & DeBruyn, L. M. (1998) The American Indian holocaust: Healing historical unresolved grief. *American Indian & Alaska Native Mental Health Research, 8*(2), 60–82.

Breuer, J. & Freud, S. (1895/1955) *Studies on Hysteria*. Standard Edition of the Complete Psychological Works of Sigmund Freud, Vol. 2. London: Hogarth Press.

Bruner, J.S. (1990) *Acts of Meaning*. Cambridge, MA: Harvard University Press.

Buckle, J.L. & Fleming, S.J. (2010) *Parenting After the Death of a Child: A Practitioner's Guide*. New York: Routledge.

Buckle, J.L. & Fleming, S.J. (2011) Parenting challenges after the death of a child. In R. A. Neimeyer, D.L. Harris, H.R. Winokuer & G.F. Thornton (eds.), *Grief and Bereavement in Contemporary Society: Bridging Research and Practice*. New York: Routledge.

Buggins, E. (1995) Mind your language. *Nursing Standard, 10*(1), 21–22.

Bunch, J., Barraclough, B.M., Nelson, B. et al. (1971) Suicide following death of parents. *Social Psychiatry, 6*, 193–199.

Burke, L.A. & Neimeyer, R.A. (2013) Prospective risk factors for complicated grief: A review of the empirical literature. In M. Stroebe, H. Schut & J. van den Bout (eds.), *Complicated Grief: Scientific Foundations for Health Care Professionals*. London: Routledge.

Burke, L.A. Neimeyer, R.A., McDevitt-Murphy, M.E., Ippolito, M.R. & Roberts, J.M. (2011) Faith in the wake of homicide: Religious coping and bereavement distress in an African American sample. *International Journal for the Psychology of Religion, 21*, 289–307.

Butler, L.D., Blasey, C.M., Garlan, R.W. et al. (2005) Posttraumatic growth following the terrorist attacks of September 11, 2001: Cognitive, coping and trauma symptom predictors in an internet convenience sample. *Traumatology, 11*, 247–267.

Butler, R.N. (1963) The life review: An interpretation of reminiscence in the aged. *Psychiatry, 26*, 65–76.

Calhoun, L.G. & Tedeschi, R.G. (1990) Positive aspects of critical life problems: Recollections of grief. *Omega: Journal of Death & Dying, 20*, 265–272.

Calhoun, L.G. & Tedeschi, R.G. (1999) *Facilitating Posttraumatic Growth: A Clinician's Guide*. Mahwah, NJ: Lawrence Erlbaum.

Calhoun, L.G. & Tedeschi, R.G. (2006) (Eds.) *Handbook of Posttraumatic Growth*. Mahwah, NJ: Lawrence Erlbaum.

Calhoun, L.G., Cann, A. & Tedeschi, R.G. (2010) The posttraumatic growth model: Socio-cultural considerations. In T. Weiss & R. Berger (eds.), *Posttraumatic Growth and Culturally Competent Practice: Lessons Learned From Around the Globe*. New York: Wiley.

Carlson, V., Cicchetti, D., Barnett, D. & Braunwald, K. (1989) Disorganised/disoriented attachment relationships in maltreated infants. *Developmental Psychology, 25*, 525–531.

Carmack, B.J. (1985) The effects on family members and functioning after the death of a pet. *Marriage & Family Review, 8*(3–4), 149–161.

Carmack, B.J. (2003) *Grieving the Death of a Pet*. Minneapolis, MN: Augsburg.

Carmack, B.J. & Packman, W. (2011) Pet loss: The interface of continuing bonds research and practice. In R.A. Neimeyer, D.L. Harris, H.R. Winokuer & G.F. Thornton (eds.), *Grief and Bereavement in Contemporary Society: Bridging Research and Practice*. New York: Routledge.

Carr, D. (2003) A good death for whom? Quality of spouse's death and psychological distress among older widowed persons. *Journal of Health & Social Behaviour, 44*, 215–232.

Carr, D. (2008) Late-life bereavement: The changing lives of older couples study. In M. Stroebe, R. O. Hansson, H. Schut & W. Stroebe (eds.), *Handbook of Bereavement Research and Practice: 21st Century Perspectives*. Washington, DC: American Psychological Association.

Carr, D. (2010) New perspectives on the Dual Process Model (DPM): What have we learned? What questions remain? *Omega: Journal of Death & Dying, 63*, 371–380.

Carr, D., House, J. S., Kessler, R. C. et al. (2000) Marital quality and psychosocial adjustment to widowhood among older adults: A longitudinal analysis. *Journal of Gerontology: Social Sciences, 55B*, S197–S207.

Carr, D., House, J. S., Wortman, C. B., Nesse, R. M. & Kessler, R. C. (2001) Psychological adjustment to sudden and anticipated spousal death among the older widowed. *Journal of Gerontology Series B: Psychological Sciences & Social Sciences, 56*, S237–S248.

Carr, D. & Jeffreys, J. S. (2011) Spousal bereavement in later life. In R. A. Neimeyer, D. L. Harris, H. R. Winokuer & G. F. Thornton (eds.), *Grief and Bereavement in Contemporary Society: Bridging Research and Practice*. New York: Routledge.

Charmaz, K. & Milligan, M. J. (2006) Grief. In J. E. Stets & J. H. Turner (eds.), *Handbook of the Sociology of Emotion*. New York: Springer.

Christakis, N. A. & Iwashyna, T. J. (2003) The health impact on families of health care: A matched cohort study of hospice use by decedents and mortality outcomes in surviving, widowed spouses. *Social Science & Medicine, 57*, 465–475.

Clark, D. (1993) Death in Staithes. In D. Dickenson & M. Johnson (eds.), *Death, Dying & Bereavement*. London: Sage Publications and the Open University. (Abridged extract from *Between Pulpit and Pew* (1982) Cambridge: Cambridge University Press.)

Clarke, A. & Clarke, A. (2000) *Early Experience and the Life Path*. London: Jessica Kingsley.

Clayton, P. J., Halikas, J. A. & Maurice, W. L. (1972) The depression of widowhood. *British Journal of Psychiatry, 120*, 71–78.

Cleiren, M.P.H.D. (1991) *Adaptation After Bereavement*. Leiden: DSWO.

Cockburn, A.-M. (2013) *5,742 Days: A Mother's Journey Through Loss*. Oxford: Infinite Ideas Limited.

Coleman, R. A. & Neimeyer, R. A. (2010) Measuring meaning: Searching for and making sense of spousal loss in later life. *Death Studies, 34*, 804–834.

Collins, N. L. & Read, S. J. (1990) Adult attachment, working models, and relationship quality in dating couples. *Journal of Personality & Social Psychology, 58*, 644–663.

Collins, W.L. & Doolittle, A. (2006) Personal reflections of funeral rituals and spirituality in a Kentucky African American family. *Death Studies, 30*, 957–969.

Connidis, I. A. (1992) Life transitions and the adult sibling tie: A qualitative study. *Journal of Marriage & The Family, 54*(4), 972–982.

Cook, A. S. (2013) The family, larger systems, and loss, grief, and mourning. In D. K. Meagher & D. E. Balk (eds.), *Handbook of Thanatology: The Essential Body of Knowledge for the Study of Death, Dying, and Bereavement* (2nd edition). New York: Routledge.

Cook, A. S. & Dworkin, D. S. (1992) *Helping the Bereaved: Therapeutic Interventions for Children, Adolescents, and Adults*. New York: Basic Books.

Cook, A. S. & Oltjenbruns, K. A. (1998) *Dying and Grieving: Lifespan and Family Perspectives* (2nd edition). Dallas, TX: Harcourt Brace.

Cook, J. (1988) Dad's double binds: Rethinking father's bereavement from a men's studies perspective. *Journal of Contemporary Ethnography, 17*, 285–308.

Corr, C. A. (2002) Revisiting the concept of disenfranchised grief. In K. J. Doka (ed.), *Disenfranchised Grief: New Directions, Strategies, and Challenges for Practice*. Champaign, IL: Research Press.

Corr, C. A. & Corr, D. M. (2013) Culture, socialisation, and dying. In D. K. Meagher & D. E. Balk (eds.), *Handbook of Thanatology: The Essential Body of Knowledge for the Study of Death, Dying, and Bereavement* (2nd edition). New York: Routledge.

Coward, R. (2002) The problem with grieving. *Guardian*, 10 April,

Cowles, K. V. (1985) The death of a pet: Human responses to the breaking of the bond. *Marriage & Family Review, 8*(3–4), 135–148.

Currer, C. (2001) Is grief an illness? Issues of theory in relation to cultural diversity and the grieving process. In J. Hockey, J. Katz & N. Small (eds.), *Grief, Mourning, and Death Ritual*. Philadelphia, PA: Open University Press.

Currier, J. M., Holland, J. & Neimeyer, R. A. (2006) Sense making, grief, and the experience of violent loss: Toward a meditational model. *Death Studies, 30*, 403–428.

Currier, J. M., Neimeyer, R. A. & Berman, J. S. (2008) The effectiveness of psychotherapeutic interventions for the bereaved: A comprehensive quantitative review. *Psychological Bulletin, 134*, 648–661.

Dattell, A. R. & Neimeyer, R. A. (1990) Sex differences in death anxiety: Testing the emotional expressiveness hypothesis. *Death Studies, 14*, 1–11.

Davie, G. (2007) *The Sociology of Religion*. London: Sage.

Davies, B. (1988a) Shared life space and sibling bereavement responses. *Cancer Nursing, 11*(6), 339–347.

Davies, B. (1988b) The family environment in bereaved families and its relationship to surviving sibling behaviour. *Children's Health Care, 17*(1), 22–31.

Davies, B. (1999) *Shadows in the Sun: Experiences of Sibling Bereavement in Childhood*. Philadelphia, PA: Brunner/Mazel.

Davis, C. G., Wortman, C. B., Lehman, D. R. & Silver, R. C. (2000) Searching for meaning in loss: Are clinical assumptions correct? *Death Studies, 24*, 497–540.

Dekel, S., Ein-Dor, T. & Solomon, Z. (2012) Posttraumatic growth and posttraumatic distress: A longitudinal study. *Psychological Trauma: Theory, Research, Practice & Policy, 4*, 94–101.

Dennis, M. R. (2011) Popular culture and the paradigm shifts in grief theory and therapy. *Death Studies*, in press.

Deutsch, H. (1937) Absence of grief. *Psychoanalytic Quarterly, 6*, 12–22.

Dickenson, D. & Johnson, M. (1993) (eds.) *Death, Dying & Bereavement*. London: Sage Publications and the Open University.

Doka, K. J. (1989a) *Disenfranchised Grief: Recognising Hidden Sorrow*. San Francisco, CA: Jossey-Bass.

Doka, K. J. (1989b) Grief. In R. Kastenbaum & B. Kastenbaum (eds.), *Encyclopaedia of Death*. Phoenix, AZ: Oryx Press.

Doka, K. J. (2002) *Disenfranchised Grief: New Directions, Challenges, and Strategies for Practice*. Champaign, IL: Research Press.

Doka, K. J. (2013) Historical and Contemporary Perspectives on Dying. In D. K. Meagher & D. E. Balk (eds.), *Handbook of Thanatology: The Essential Body of Knowledge for the Study of Death, Dying, and Bereavement* (2nd edition). New York: Routledge.

Doka, K.J. & Martin, T.L. (2010) *Grieving Beyond Gender: Understanding the Ways Men and Women Mourn* (revised edition). New York: Routledge.

Dunn, J. (2000) Siblings. *The Psychologist, 13*(5), 244-248.

Dyregov, K. & Dyregov, A. (2008) *Effective Grief and Bereavement Support.* London: Jessica Kinsley Publishers.

el-Guebaly, N., West, M., Maticka-Tyndale, E. & Pool, M. (1993) Attachment among adult children of alcoholics. *Addiction, 88*, 1405–1411.

Engel, G. (1961) Is grief a disease? *Psychosomatic Medicine, 23*, 18–22.

Erikson, E.H. (1963) *Childhood and Society* (2nd edition). New York: Norton.

Feeney, J.A. (2008) Adult romantic attachment: Developments in the study of couple relationships. In J. Cassidy & P.R. Shaver (eds.), *Handbook of Attachment* (2nd edition). New York: Guildford Press.

Feeney, J.A. & Monin, J.K. (2008) An attachment-theoretical perspective on divorce. In J. Cassidy & P.R. Shafer (eds.), *Handbook of Attachment: Theory, Research, and Clinical Applications.* New York: Guilford Press.

Feeney, J.A. & Noller, P. (1990) Attachment style as a predictor of romantic adult relationships. *Journal of Personality & Social Psychology, 58*, 281–291.

Fergusson, D.M., Horwood, L.J. & Ridder, E.M. (2006) Abortion in young women and subsequent mental health. *Journal of Child Psychology & Psychiatry, 47*(1), 16–24.

Field, N.P. (2006) Unresolved grief and continuing bonds: An attachment perspective. *Death Studies, 30*, 739–756.

Field, N.P. (2008) Whether to maintain or relinquish a bond with the deceased in adapting to bereavement. In M.S. Stroebe, R.O. Hansson, H. Schut & W. Stroebe (eds.), *Handbook of Bereavement Research and Practice: Advances in Theory and Intervention.* Washington, DC: American Psychological Association.

Field, N.P. (2010) Continuing bonds in coping with the loss of a husband. Unpublished raw data. (Cited in Carmack and Packman, 2011.)

Field, N.P. & Filanosky, C. (2010) Continuing bonds, risk factors for complicated grief, and grief outcome (bereavement-related adjustment). *Death Studies, 34*, 1–29.

Field, N.P. & Friedrichs, M. (2004) Continuing bonds in coping with the death of a husband. *Death Studies, 28*, 597–620.

Field, N.P., Gal-Oz, E. & Bonnano, G.A. (2003) Continuing bonds and adjustment at 5 years after the death of a spouse. *Journal of Consulting & Clinical Psychology, 71*, 110–117.

Field, N.P., Nichols, C., Holen, A. & Horowitz, M.J. (1999) The relation of continuing attachment to adjustment in conjugal bereavement. *Journal of Consulting & Clinical Psychology, 67*, 212–218.

Field, N.P., Orsini, L., Gavish, R. & Packman, W. (2009) Role of attachment in response to pet loss. *Death Studies, 33*(4), 332–355.

Field, N.P., Packman, W. & Carmack, B.J. (2007) Continuing bonds interview. Unpublished data. (Cited in Carmack and Packman, 2011.)

Field, N.P. & Sundin, E.C. (2001) Attachment style in adjustment to conjugal bereavement. *Journal of Social & Personal Relationships, 18*, 347–361.

Fletcher, G. (2002) *The New Science of Intimate Relationships.* Oxford: Blackwell.

Folkman, S. (2001) Revised coping theory and the process of bereavement. In M.S. Stroebe, R.O. Hansson, W. Stroebe & H. Schut (eds.) *Handbook of Bereavement Research: Consequences, Coping, and Care.* Washington, DC: American Psychological Association.

Fonagy, P., Steele, H. & Steele, M. (1991) Maternal representations of attachment during pregnancy predict the organisation of infant-mother attachment at one year of age. *Child Development, 62*, 891–905.

Fonagy, P., Steele, M. & Steele, H., Higgit, A. & Target, M. (1994) The Emmanuel Miller Memorial Lecture, 1992: The theory and practice of resilience. *Journal of Child Psychology & Psychiatry, 35*, 321–357.

Fontana, A. & Keene, J.R. (2009) *Death and Dying in America*. Cambridge: Polity Press.

Fraley, R.C. & Bonnano, G.A. (2004) Attachment and loss: A test of three competing models on the association between attachment-related avoidance and adaptation to bereavement. *Personality & Social Psychology Bulletin, 30*, 878–890.

Fraley, R.C. & Shaver, P.R. (1999) Loss and bereavement: Bowlby's theory and recent controversies concerning grief work and the nature of detachment. In J. Cassidy & P.R. Shaver (eds.), *Handbook of Attachment: Theory, Research, and Clinical Applications*. New York: Guilford Press.

Fraley, R.C. & Shaver, P.R. (2000) Adult romantic attachment: Theoretical developments, emerging controversies, and unanswered questions. *Review of General Psychology, 4*, 132–154.

Freud, S. (1912–1913/1961) *Totem and Taboo*. Standard Edition of the Complete Psychological Works of Sigmund Freud, Vol. 13. London: Hogarth Press.

Freud, S. (1913/1953) *Thoughts for the Times on War and Death*. Standard Edition of the Complete Psychological Works of Sigmund Freud, Vol. 4. London: Hogarth Press

Freud, S. (1917/1953) *Mourning and Melancholia*. Standard Edition of the Complete Psychological Works of Sigmund Freud, Vol. 14. London: Hogarth Press.

Fulton, R. (2003) Anticipatory mourning: A critique of the concept. *Mortality, 8*, 342–351.

Fulton, R. & Gottesman, D.J. (1980) Anticipatory grief: A psychosocial concept reconsidered. *British Journal of Psychiatry, 137*, 45–54.

Galvin, K.M., Bylund, C.L. & Brommel, B.J. (2004) *Family Communication, Cohesion, and Change* (6th edition). Boston, MA: Allyn & Bacon.

Gerber, I., Rusalem, R. & Hannan, N. (1975) Anticipatory grief and aged widows and widowers. *Journal of Gerontology, 30*, 225–229.

Gerwolls, M.K. & Labott, S.M. (1994) Adjustments to the death of a companion animal. *Anthrozoos, 7*(3), 172–187.

Gilbert, K.R. (1980) Interactive grief and coping in the marital dyad. *Death Studies, 13*, 605–626.

Gilbert, K.R. (1989) Interactive grief and coping in the marital dyad. *Death Studies, 13*, 605-626.

Gilbert, S.M. (2006) *Death's Door: Modern Dying and the Ways We Grieve*. New York: Norton.

Gill White, P. (2006) *Sibling Grief*. New York: Universe.

Glick, I., Parkes, C.M. & Weiss, R.S. (1974) *The First Year of Bereavement*. Chichester: Wiley Interscience.

Goffman, E. (1963) *Stigma: Notes on the Management of Spoiled Identity*. London: Penguin.

Goldberg, S. (2000) *Attachment and Development*. London: Arnold.

Golombok, S. (2010) Children in new family forms. In R. Gross, *Psychology: The Science of Mind and Behaviour* (6th edition). London: Hodder Education.

Golombok, S. & Fivush, R. (1994) *Gender Development*. Cambridge: Cambridge University Press.

Gordon, A. (1975) The Jewish view of death: Guidelnes for mourning. In E. Kübler-Ross (ed.), *Death: The Final Stage of Growth*. Englewood Cliffs, NJ: Prentice-Hall Inc.

Gorer, G. (1965) *Death, Grief, and Mourning in Contemporary Britain*. London: Cresset.

Graves, D. (2009) *Talking With Bereaved People: An Approach for Structured and Sensitive Communication*. Philadelphia, PA: Jessica Kingsley Publishers.

Green, J. (1991) *Death With Dignity*. Vol. I. London: Macmillan Magazines.

Green, J. (1993) *Death With Dignity*. Vol. II. London: Macmillan Magazines.

Griffin, D. W. & Bartholomew, K. (1994) The metaphysics of measurement: The case of adult attachment. In K. Bartholomew & D. Perlman (eds.), *Advances in Personal Relationships, Volume 5: Attachment Processes in Adulthood*. London: Jessica Kingsley Publishers.

Gross, R. (2012) *Being Human: Psychological and Philosophical Perspectives*. London: Routledge.

Gross, R. (2014a) *Themes, Issues and Debates in Psychology* (4th edition). London: Hodder Education.

Gross, R. (2014b) From attachment theory to terror management theory: Some thoughts on the 'true' nature of grief. *ATP Today*, October, 16–17.

Gross, R. (2015) *Psychology: The Science of Mind and Behaviour* (7th edition). London: Hodder Education.

Ha, J. (2008) Changes in support from confidantes, children, and friends following widowhood. *Journal of Marriage & Family, 70*, 306–318.

Haine, R. A., Wolchik, S. A., Sandler, I. N. et al. (2006) Positive parenting as a protective resource for parentally bereaved children. *Death Studies, 30*, 1–28.

Hansson, A. R. & Stroebe, M. (2007) *Bereavement in Later Life: Coping, Adaptation, and Developmental Influences*. Washington, DC: American Psychological Association.

Hansson, R. O., Berry, J. O. & Berry, M. E. (1999) The bereavement experience: Continuing commitment after the loss of a loved one. In J. M. Adams & W. H. Warren (eds.), *Handbook of Interpersonal Commitment and Relationship Stability*. Dordrecht, Netherlands: Kluwer Academic Publishers.

Harris, T., Brown, G. W. & Bifulco, A. (1986) Loss of parent in childhood and adult psychiatric disorder: The role of adequate parental care. *Psychological Medicine, 16*, 641–659.

Hazan, C. & Shaver, P. R. (1987) Romantic love conceptualised as an attachment process. *Journal of Personality & Social Psychology, 52*(3), 511–524.

Heard, D. & Lake, B. (1997) *The Challenge of Attachment for Caregivers*. London: Routledge.

Heelas, P. & Woodhead, L. (2005) *The Spiritual Revolution: Why Religion Is Giving Way to Spirituality*. Oxford: Blackwell.

Hertsgaard, L., Gunnar, M., Erickson, M. F. & Nacmias, M. (1995) Adrenocortical responses to the strange situation in infants with disorganised/disoriented attachment relationships. *Child Development. 66*, 1100–1106.

Hetherington, E. M. & Stanley-Hagan, M. (1999) The adjustment of children with divorced parents: A risk and resiliency perspective. *Journal of Child Psychology & Psychiatry, 40*(1), 129–140.

Hirsch, E. (2014) *Gabriel: A Poem*. New York: Knopf Publishing Group.

Hirst, M. & Corden, A. (2010) Change in living arrangements following death of a partner in England and Wales, 1971 to 2001. *Population Trends, 141*, 1–21.

Ho, S.M.Y., Chan, I.S.F., Ma, E.P.W. & Field, N.P. (2013) Continuing bonds, attachment style, and adjustment in the conjugal bereavement among Hong Kong Chinese. *Death Studies, 37*, 248–268.

Hobson, C.J. (1964) Widows of Blackton. *New Society*, 24 September, 13.

Holcomb, L.E., Neimeyer, R.A. & Moore, M.K. (1993) Personal meanings of death: A content analysis of free-response narratives. *Death Studies, 17*, 299–318.

Holland, J.M., Currier, J. & Neimeyer, R.A. (2006) Meaning reconstruction on the first two years of bereavement: The role of sense-making and benefit-finding. *Omega: Journal of Death and Dying, 53*, 173–191.

Holland, J.M., Neimeyer, R.A., Boelen, P.A. & Prigerson, H.G. (2009) The underlying structure of grief: A taxometric investigation of prolonged and normal reactions to loss. *Journal of Psychopathology & Behavioural Assessment, 31*, 190–201.

Holland, J.M. & Neimeyer, R.A. (2010) An examination of stage theory of grief among individuals bereaved by natural and violent causes: A meaning-oriented contribution. *Omega: Journal of Death & Dying, 61*, 105–122.

Holloway, M., Adamson, S., Argyrou, V., Draper, P. & Mariau, D. (2013) 'Funerals aren't nice but it couldn't have been nicer': The makings of a good funeral. *Mortality, 18*(1), 30–53.

Holloway, M., Adamson, S., Mc Sherry, W. & Swinton, J. (2011) *Spiritual care at the end of life: A systematic review of the literature.* Retrieved from http://www.dh.gov.uk/publications

Holloway, M. & Moss, B. (2010) *Spirituality and Social Work.* London: Palgrave Macmillan.

Horowitz, M.J. (1986) *Stress Response Syndromes.* Northvale, NJ: Aronson.

Horowitz, M.J. (1997) *Stress Response Syndromes* (3rd edition). Northvale, NJ: Aronson.

Horowitz, M.J., Krupnick, J., Kaltreidwer, N. et al. (1981) Initial psychological response to parental death. *Archives of General Psychiatry, 137*(10), 1157–1162.

Horowitz, M.J., Wilner, N. & Alvarez, W. (1979) Impact of event scale: A measure of subjective stress. *Psychosomatic Medicine, 41*, 209–218.

Hsu, M. (2008) *Continuing Bonds Expressions in Pet Bereavement.* Unpublished doctoral thesis. Pacific Graduate School of Psychology.

Hughes, M.E. & Waite, L.J. (2009) Marital biography and health at mid-life. *Journal of Health & Social Behaviour, 50*, 344–358.

Imber-Black, E. (2005) Creating meaningful rituals for new life cycle transitions. In B. Carter & M. McGoldrick (eds.), *The Expanded Family Life Cycle: Individual, Family, and Social Perspectives.* Boston, MA: Allyn & Bacon.

Jagger, C. & Sutton, C.J. (1991) Death after marital bereavement – is the risk increased? *Statistics in Medicine, 10*, 395–404.

Jones, D. (2008) Running to catch the sun. *Psychologist, 21*(7), 580–583.

Jordan, J.R. (2008) Bereavement after suicide. *Psychiatric Annals, 38*(10), 679-685.

Jordan, J.R. & McIntosh, J.L. (2011) Is suicide bereavement different? Perspectives from research and practice. In R.A. Neimeyer, D.L. Harris, H.R. Winokuer & G.F. Thornton (eds.), *Grief and Bereavement in Contemporary Society: Bridging Research and Practice.* New York: Routledge.

Joseph, S. (2012) What doesn't kill us . . . *Psychologist, 25*(11), 816–819.

Kastenbaum, R. (2000) *The Psychology of Death* (3rd edition). London: Free Association Books.

Katz, J. S. (1993) Jewish perspectives on death, dying, and bereavement. In D. Dickenson & M. Johnson (eds.), *Death, Dying & Bereavement*. London: Sage Publications and the Open University.

Keesee, N. J., Currier, J. M. & Neimeyer, R. A. (2008) Predictors of grief following the death of one's child: The contribution of finding meaning. *Journal of Clinical Psychology, 64*, 1145–1163.

Kelly, M. N. & Corriveau, D. P. (1995) The Corriveau-Kelly Death Anxiety Scale. *Omega: Journal of Death & Dying, 31*, 311–316.

King, B. J. (2013) When animals mourn. *Scientific American, 309*(1), 50–55.

Kissane, D. & Bloch, S. (2002) *Family Focused Grief Therapy: A Model of Family-Centred Care During Palliative Care and Bereavement*. Maidenhead: Open University Press.

Klass, D. (1986) Marriage and divorce among bereaved parents in a self-help group. *Omega: Journal of Death & Dying, 17*, 237–249.

Klass, D. (1999) Developing a cross-cultural model of grief: The state of the field. *Omega: Journal of Death & Dying, 39*, 153–176.

Klass, D. (2013) Religion and spirituality in loss, grief, and mourning. In D. K. Meagher & D. E. Balk (eds.), *Handbook of Thanatology: The Essential Body of Knowledge for the Study of Death, Dying, and Bereavement* (2nd edition). New York: Routledge.

Klass, D. & Chow, A.Y.M. (2011) Culture and ethnicity in experiencing policing, and handling grief. In R. A. Neimeyer, D. L. Harris, H. R. Winokuer & G. F. Thornton (eds.), *Grief and Bereavement in Contemporary Society: Bridging Research and Practice*. New York: Routledge.

Klass, D., Silverman, P.R. & Nickman, S. (eds.) *Continuing Bonds: New Understandings of Grief*. Washington, DC: Taylor & Francis.

Klein, M. (1940) Mourning and its relationship to manic depressive states. *International Journal of Psychoanalysis, 21*, 125–153.

Kleinman, A. and Kleinman, J. (1985) Somatisation: The interconnections in Chinese society among culture, depressive experiences, and the meanings of pain. In A. Kleinman & B. Good (eds.) *Culture and Depression: Studies in the Anthropology and Cross-Cultural Psychology of Affect and Disorder*. Berkeley, CA: University of California Press.

Kloep, M. & Hendry, L.B. (1999) Challenges, risks, and coping in adolescence. In D. Messer & S. Millar (eds.), *Exploring Developmental Psychology: From Infancy to Adolescence*. London: Arnold.

Kohner, N. & Henley, A. (2001) *When a Baby Dies: The Experience of Late Miscarriage, Stillbirth, and Neonatal Death*. London: Routledge.

Krebs, D. & Blackman, R. (1988) *Psychology: A First Encounter*. New York: Harcourt Brace Jovanovich.

Kübler-Ross, E. (1969) *On Death and Dying*. London: Tavistock/Routledge.

Kübler-Ross, E. & Kessler, D. (2005) *On Grief and Grieving: Finding the Meaning of Grief Through the Five Stages of Loss*. New York: Scribner.

Lalande, K. M. & Bonnano, G. A. (2006) Culture and continuing bonds: A prospective comparison of bereavement in the United States and the People's Republic of China. *Death Studies, 30*(4), 303–324.

Lamm, M. (1969) *The Jewish Way in Death and Mourning*. New York: David.

Larkin, P. (1993) 'Aubade.' In D. Dickenson & M. Johnson (eds.), *Death, Dying & Bereavement*. London: Sage Publications and the Open University. (From *Times Literary Supplement*, 29 November 1977.)

La Roche, M. (2012) *Cultural Psychotherapy: Theory, Methods, and Practice*. Thousand Oaks, CA: Sage Publications.

Latham, A. & Prigerson, H. (2004) Suicidality and bereavement: Complicated grief as psychiatric disorder presenting greatest risk for suicidality. *Suicide and Life-Threatening Behaviour, 34*, 350–362.

Lazarus, R. & Folkman, S. (1984) *Stress, Appraisal, and Coping*. New York: Springer.

Lewis, C. S. (1961) *A Grief Observed*. London: Faber & Faber.

Lichtenthal, W. G., Currier, J. M., Neimeyer, R. A. & Keesee, N. J. (2010) Sense and significance: A mixed methods examination of meaning-making following the loss of one's child. *Journal of Clinical Psychology, 66*, 791–812.

Lin, K., Sandler, I. W., Ayers, T., Wolchik, S. & Laucken, L. (2004) Resilience in parentally bereaved children and adolescents seeking preventive services. *Journal of Clinical Child & Adolescent Psychology, 33*, 673–683.

Lindemann, E. (1944) The symptomatology and management of acute grief. *American Journal of Psychiatry, 101*, 155–160.

Linley, P. A. (2000) Can traumatic experiences provide a positive pathway? *Traumatic Stress Points, 14*, 5.

Linley, P. A. & Joseph, S. (2003) Trauma and personal growth. *Psychologist, 16*(3), 135.

Linley, P. A. & Joseph, S. (2004) Positive change processes following trauma and adversity: A review of the empirical literature. *Journal of Traumatic Stress, 17*, 11–22.

Littlewood, J. (1992) *Aspects of Grief: Bereavement in Adult Life*. London: Routledge.

Lohan, J. A. & Murphy, S. A. (2006) Mental distress and family functioning among married parents bereaved by a child's sudden death. *Omega: Journal of Death & Dying, 52*(4), 295–305.

Lopata, H. Z. (1979) *Women as Widows: Support Systems*. New York: Elsevier.

Lopata, H. Z. (1996) *Current Widowhood: Myths and Realities*. London: Sage.

Lorenz, K. (1935) The companion in the bird's world. *Auk, 54*, 245–273.

Lorenz, K. (1963) *On Aggression*. London: Methuen.

Lovell, A. (1983) Some questions of identity: Late miscarriage, stillbirth, and neonatal loss. *Social Science & Medicine, 17*(11), 755–761.

Lund, D. A. (1989) Conclusions about bereavement in later life and implications for interventions and future research. In D. A. Lund (ed.), *Older Bereaved Spouses*. New York: Hemisphere.

Luoma, J. & Pearson, J. (2002) Suicide and marital status in the United States, 1991–1996: Is widowhood a risk factor? *American Journal of Public Health, 92*, 1518–1522.

Lyons-Ruth, K., Repacholi, B., McLeod, S. & Silva, E. (1991) Disorganised attachment behaviour in infancy: Short-term stability, maternal and infant correlates, and risk-related subtypes. *Developmental Psychopathology, 3*, 377–396.

Maciejewski, P. K., Zhang, B., Block, S. D. & Prigerson, H. G. (2007) An empirical investigation of the stage theory of grief. *Journal of the American Medical Association, 297*(7), 716–723.

Main, M. (1991) Matacognitive knowledge, metacognitive monitoring, and singular (coherent) versus multiple (incoherent) models of attachment: Findings and directions for future research. In C. M. Parkes, J. M. Stephenson-Hinde & P. Marris (eds.), *Attachment Across the Life Cycle*. London: Routledge.

Main, M. (1995) Recent studies in attachment. In S. Goldberg, R. Muir & J. Kerr (eds.), *Attachment Theory: Social, Developmental, and Clinical Perspectives*. Hillsdale, NJ: The Analytic Press.

Main, M. & Hesse, E. (1990) Parents' unresolved traumatic experiences are related to infant disorganised attachment status: Is frightened and/or frightening parental behaviour the linking mechanism? In M. T. Greenberg, D. Cicchetti & E. M. Cummings (eds.), *Attachment in the Preschool Years*. Chicago, IL: University of Chicago Press.

Main, M., Kaplan, N. & Cassidy, J. (1985) Security in infancy, childhood and adulthood: A move to the level of representation. In I. Bretherton & E. Waters (eds.), *Growing Points of Attachment Theory and Research*. Monographs of the Society for Research in Child Development, *50*(1–2, serial no. 209), 66–104.

Main, M. & Weston, D. R. (1981) The quality of the toddler's relationship to mother and to father: Related to conflict behaviour and the readiness to establish new relationships. *Child Development, 52*, 932–940.

Malinowski, B. (1925) *Magic, Science, and Religion*. Garden City, NY: Doubleday.

Malkinson, R. & Bar-Tur, L. (2001) The agony of grief: Parents' grieving of Israeli soldiers. *Journal of Personal & Interpersonal Loss, 5*, 247–261.

Malkinson, R., Rubin, S. & Witzum, F. (2006) Therapeutic issues and the relationship to the deceased: Working clinically with the two-track model of bereavement. *Death Studies, 30*, 797–815.

Mandelbaum, D. (1959) Social use of funeral rites. In H. Feifel (ed.) *The Meaning of Death*. New York: McGraw-Hill.

March, P. & Doherty, C. (1999) Dying and bereavement. In D. Messer & F. Jones (eds.), *Psychology and Social Care*. London: Jessica Kingsley Publishers.

Marris, P. (1958) *Widows and Their Families*. London: Routledge & Kegan Paul.

Marris, P. (1974) *Loss and Change*. London: RKP.

Marrone, M. (1998) *Attachment and Interaction*. London: Jessica Kingsley.

Marshall, B. & Davies, B. (2011) Bereavement in children and adults following the death of a sibling. In R. A. Neimeyer, D. L. Harris, H. R. Winokuer & G. F. Thornton (eds.), *Grief and Bereavement in Contemporary Society: Bridging Research and Practice*. New York: Routledge.

Martikainen, P. & Valkonen, T. (1996) Mortality after the death of a spouse: Rates and causes of death in a large Finnish cohort. *American Journal of Public Health, 86*, 1087–1093.

Martin-Matthews, A. (1991) The relationship between social support and morale: Comparisons of the widowed and never married in later life. *Canadian Journal of Community Mental Health, 10*(2), 47–63.

Martin, L. Neighbors, H. & Griffith, D. (2013) The experience of symptoms of depression in men vs. women. *JAMA Psychiatry, 70*(10), 1100–1106.

Martin, T. L. & Doka, K. J. (2011) The influence of gender and socialisation on grieving styles. In R. A. Neimeyer, D. L. Harris, H. R. Winokuer & G. F. Thornton (eds.) *Grief and Bereavement in Contemporary Society: Bridging Research and Practice*. New York: Routledge.

Mauksch, H. O. (1975) The organisational context of dying. In E. Kübler-Ross (ed.), *Death: The Final Stage of Growth*. Englewood Cliffs, NJ: Prentice-Hall.

May, R. (1969) *Love and Will*. New York: Norton.

McCreight, B. S. (2008) Perinatal loss: A qualitative study in Northern Ireland. *Omega: Journal of Death & Dying, 57*(1), 1–19.

McGoldrick, M. & Rohrbaugh, M. (1987) Researching ethnic family stereotypes. *Family Process, 26*, 89–99.

McGoldrick, M. & Walsh, F. (2005) Death and the family life cycle. In B. Carter & M. McGoldrick (eds.), *The Expanded Family Life Cycle: Individual, Family, and Social Perspectives* (3rd edition). Boston. MA: Allyn & Bacon.

Meagher, D. K. & Balk, D. E. (2013) (eds.) *Handbook of Thanatology: The Essential Body of Knowledge for the Study of Death, Dying, and Bereavement* (2nd edition). New York: Routledge.

Meins, E. (2003) Emotional development and early attachment relationships. In A. Slater & G. Bremner (eds.), *An Introduction to Developmental Psychology*. Oxford: Blackwell Publishing.

Meyer, B. & Pilkonis, P. A. (2002) Attachment style. In J. C. Norcross (ed.), *Psychotherapy Relationships That Work: Therapist Contributions and Responsiveness to Clients*. New York: Oxford University Press.

Mikulincer, M., Florian, V. & Weller, A. (1993) Attachment styles, coping strategies, and post-traumatic psychological distress: the impact of Gulf War in Israel. *Journal of Personality & Social Psychology, 64*, 817–826.

Mikulincer, M. & Shaver, P. (2007) *Attachment in Adulthood: Structure, Dynamics, and Change*. New York: Guilford Press.

Mikulincer, M. and Shaver, P. (2008) An attachment perspective on bereavement. In M.S. Stroebe, R.O. Hansson, H. Schut, & W. Stroebe (eds.) *Handbook of Bereavement Research and Practice: Advances in theory and intervention*, Washington, DC: American Psychological Association.

Mikulincer, M. & Shaver, P. (2013) Attachment insecurities and disordered patterns of grief. In M. Stroebe, H. Schut & J. van den Bout (eds.), *Complicated Grief: Scientific Foundations for Health Care Professionals*. London: Routledge.

Miles, M. S. (1985) Emotional symptoms and physical health in bereaved parents. *Nursing Research, 34*(2), 76–81.

Moitoza, E. (1982) Portuguese families. In M. McGoldrick, J. K. Pearce & J. Giordano (eds.), *Ethnicity and Family Therapy*. New York: Guilford.

Moss, M.S., Moss, S.Z. & Hansson, R. (2001) Bereavement and old age. In M.S. Stroebe, R.O. Hansson, W. Stroebe & H, Schut (eds.) *Handbook of Bereavement Research: Consequences, Coping and Care*. Washington, DC: American Psychological Assocation.

Moss, M. S., Moss, S. Z. & Hansson, R. O. (2008) Bereavement and old age. In M. S. Stroebe, R. O. Hansson, W. Stroebe & H. Schut (eds.), *Handbook of Bereavement Research: Consequences, Coping, and Care*. Washington, DC: American Psychological Association.

Munnichs, J.M.A. (1966) *Old Age and Finitude: A Contribution to Psychogerontology*. Basel: S. Karger.

Murphy, S. L. (2009) *Parenting the stillborn: Gender, identity, and bereavement*. Unpublished doctoral thesis, University of Surrey.

Murphy, S. L. (2012) Finding the positive in loss: Stillbirth and its potential for parental empowerment. *Bereavement Care*, 31(93), 98–103.

Nadeau, J. W. (2008) Meaning-making in bereaved families: Assessment, intervention, and future research. In M. S Stroebe, R. O. Hansson, H. Schut & W. Stroebe (eds.), *Handbook of Bereavement and Practice: Advances in Theory and Intervention*. Washington, DC: American Psychological Association.

Neimeyer, R. A. (2001) Meaning reconstruction and loss. In R. A. Neimeyer (ed.), *Meaning Reconstruction and the Experience of Loss*. Washington, DC: American Psychological Association.

Neimeyer, R. A. (2006) Complicated grief and the quest for meaning: A constructivist contribution. *Omega: Journal of Death and Dying, 52*, 37–52.

Neimeyer, R. A. (2009) *Constructivist Psychotherapy*. London: Routledge.

Neimeyer, R. A. (2011) Reconstructing meaning in bereavement. In W. Watson & D. Kissane (eds.), *Handbook of Psychotherapies in Cancer Care*. New York: Wiley.

Neimeyer, R. A., Baldwin, S. A. & Gillies, J. (2006) Continuing bonds and reconstructing meaning: Mitigating complications in bereavement. *Death Studies, 30*, 715–738.

Neimeyer, R. A., Burke, L., Mackay, M. & Stringer, J. (2010) Grief therapy and the reconstruction of meaning: From principles to practice. *Journal of Contemporary Psychotherapy, 40*, 73–84.

Neimeyer, R.A. & Burke, L. (2011) Complicated grief in the aftermath of homicide: Spiritual crisis and distress in an African American sample. *Religions, 2*, 145–164.

Neimeyer, R. A., Harris, D. L., Winokuer, H. R. & Thornton, G. F. (2011) (eds.) *Grief and Bereavement in Contemporary Society: Bridging Research and Practice*. New York: Routledge.

Neimeyer, R. A. & Jordan J. R. (2002) Disenfranchisement as empathic failure. In K. Doka (ed.), *Disenfranchised Grief*. Champaign, IL: Research Press.

Neimeyer, R. A. & Jordan J. R. (2013) Historical and contemporary perspectives on assessment and intervention. In D. K. Meagher & D. E. Balk (eds.), *Handbook of Thanatology: The Essential Body of Knowledge for the Study of Death, Dying, and Bereavement* (2nd edition). New York: Routledge.

Neimeyer, R. A. & Sands, D. C. (2011) Meaning reconstruction in bereavement: From principles to practice. In R. A. Neimeyer, D. L. Harris, H. R. Winokuer & G. F. Thornton (eds.), *Grief and Bereavement in Contemporary Society: Bridging Research and Practice*. New York: Routledge.

Nichols, R. & Nichols, J. (1975) Funerals: A time for grief and growth. In E. Kübler-Ross (ed.), *Death: The Final Stage of Growth*. Englewood Cliffs, NJ: Prentice-Hall.

Ogden, P., Minton, K. & Pain, C. (2006) *Trauma and the Body: A Sensorimotor Approach to Psychotherapy*. New York: Norton.

O'Hara, M. (2012) Deathly silence. *Guardian*, 4 January, 35.

Oliva, A., Jiminez, J. M. & Parra, A. (2009) Protective effect of supportive family relationships and the influence of stressful life events on adolescent adjustment. *Anxiety Stress Coping, 22*(2), 137–152.

Orbach, A. (1999) *Life, Psychotherapy, and Death: The End of our Exploring*. London: Jessica Kingsley Publishers.

Packman, W., Field, N. P., Carmack, B. J. & Ronen, R. (2011) Continuing bonds and psychosocial adjustment in pet loss. *Journal of Loss and Trauma: International Perspectives on Stress & Coping, 16*(4), 341–357.

Parkes, C. M. (1964) The effects of bereavement on physical and mental health: A study of the case records of widows. *British Medical Journal, 2*, 274–279.

Parkes, C. M. (1965a) Bereavement and mental illness: Part 1. A clinical study of the grief of bereaved psychiatric patients. *British Journal of Medical Psychology, 38*, 1–12.

Parkes, C. M. (1965b) Bereavement and mental illness: Part 1. A classification of bereavement reactions. *British Journal of Medical Psychology, 38*, 13–26.

Parkes, C. M. (1970) The first year of bereavement: A longitudinal study of the reaction of London widows to the death of their husbands. *Psychiatry, 33*, 444–467.

Parkes, C. M. (1971) Psychosocial transitions: A field for study. *Social Science and Medicine, 5*, 101–115.

Parkes, C.M. (1972) *Bereavement: Studies of Grief in Adult Life*. London: Tavistock Publications.

Parkes, C.M. (1975) *Bereavement*. Harmondsworth: Penguin.

Parkes, C.M. (1986) *Bereavement: Studies of Grief in Adult Life* (2nd edition). London: Penguin Books.

Parkes, C.M. (1990) Foreword. In T. Walter (ed.) *Funerals and How to Improve Them*. London: Hodder & Stoughton.

Parkes, C.M. (1993) Bereavement as a psychosocial transition: Processes of adaptation to change. In M.S. Stroebe, W. Stroebe & R.O. Hansson (eds.), *Handbook of Bereavement: Theory, Research and Intervention*. New York: Cambridge University Press.

Parkes, C.M. (1996) *Bereavement: Studies of Grief in Adult Life*. London: Routledge.

Parkes, C.M. (2006) *Love and Loss: The Roots of Grief and Its Complications*. London: Routledge.

Parkes, C.M. (2013) Elisabeth Kübler-Ross, *On Death and Dying*: a reappraisal. *Mortality: Promoting the Interdisciplinary Study of Death and Dying, 18*(1), 94–97.

Parkes, C.M., Benjamin, B. & Fitzgerald, R.G. (1969) Broken heart: A statistical study of increased mortality among widowers. *British Medical Journal, 1*, 740.

Parkes, C.M. & Prigerson, H.G. (2010) *Bereavement: Studies of Grief in Adult Life* (4th edition). London: Penguin Books.

Parkes, C.M. & Weiss, R.S. (1983) *Recovery from bereavement*. New York: Basic Books.

Parkinson, P. (1992) Coping with dying and bereavement. *Nursing Standard, 6*(17), 36–38.

Payne, S., Swami, V. & Stanistreet, D. (2008) The social construction of gender and its impact on suicidal behaviour. *Journal of Men's Health & Gender, 5*(1), 23–35.

Peppers, L.G. & Knapp, R.J. (1980) *Motherhood and Mourning: Perinatal Death*. New York: Praeger.

Ponzetti, J.J. (1992) Bereaved families: A comparison of parents' and grandparents' reactions to the death of a child. *Omega: Journal of Death & Dying, 25*, 63–71.

Preeman, D.L. & Bonnano, G.A. (2007) With whom do we grieve? Social and cultural determinants of grief processing in the United States and China. *Journal of Social & Personal Relationships, 24*(5), 729–746.

Prigerson, H.G., Frank, E., Kasl, S.V. et al. (1995a) Complicated grief and bereavement-related depression as distinct disorders: Preliminary empirical validation in elderly bereaved spouses. *American Journal of Psychiatry, 152*, 22–30.

Prigerson, H.G., Horowitz, M.J., Jacobs, S.C., et al. (2009) Prolonged Grief Disorder: Psychometric validation of criteria proposed for DSM-V and ICD-11. *PLoS Medicine, 6*(8), e1000121.

Prigerson, H.G. & Jacobs, S.C. (2001) Traumatic grief as a distinct disorder: A rationale, consensus criteria, and preliminary empirical test. In M.S. Stroebe, R.O. Hansson, W. Stroebe & H. Schut (eds.), *Handbook of Bereavement Research: Consequences, Coping, and Care*. Washington, DC: American Psychological Association.

Prigerson, H.G. & Maciejewski, P.K. (2006) A call for sound empirical testing and evaluation of criteria for complicated grief proposed by the DSM V. *Omega: Journal of Death & Dying, 52*, 9–19.

Prigerson, H.G. & Maciejewski, P.K. (2008) Grief and acceptance as opposite sides of the same coin: Setting a research agenda for studying peaceful acceptance of loss. *British Journal of Psychiatry, 193*, 435–437.

Prigerson, H.G., Maciejewski, P.K., Reynolds, C.F. et al. (1995b) Inventory of complicated grief: A scale to measure maladaptive symptoms of loss. *Psychiatry Research, 59*, 65–79.

Prigerson, H.G., Shear, M.K., Jacobs, S.C. et al. (1999) Consensus criteria for traumatic grief: A preliminary empirical test. *British Journal of Psychiatry, 174*, 67–73.

Prigerson, H.G., Vanderwerker, L.C. & Maciejewski, P.K. (2008) A case for inclusion of prolonged grief disorder in DSM-V. In M.S. Stroebe, R.O. Hansson, H. Schut & W. Stroebe (eds.), *Handbook of Bereavement Research and Practice: Advances in Theory and Intervention*. Washington, DC: American Psychological Association.

Prior, L. (1989) *The Social Organization of Death*. London: Macmillan.

Prior, L. (1993) The social distribution of sentiments. In D. Dickenson & M. Johnson (eds.), *Death, Dying & Bereavement*. London: Sage Publications and the Open University. (Abridged extract from *The Social Organisation of Death* (1989). London: Macmillan.)

Quackenbush, J.E. (1985) The death of a pet: How it can affect owners. *Veterinary Clinics of North America: Small Animal Practice, 15*, 395–402.

Radcliffe-Brown, A.R. (1922) *The Andaman Islanders*. Cambridge: Cambridge University Press.

Radke-Yarrow, M., McCann, K., de Mulder, E. et al. (1995) Attachment in the context of high-risk conditions. *Development and Psychopathology, 7*, 247–265.

Ramsay, R. & de Groot, W. (1977) A further look at bereavement. Paper presented at EATI conference, Uppsala. Cited in P.E. Hodgkinson (1980) Treating abnormal grief in the bereaved. *Nursing Times*, 17 January, 126–128.

Raphael, B. (1984) *The Anatomy of Bereavement: A Handbook for the Caring Professions*. London: Hutchinson.

Rando, T. (1993) *Treatment of Complicated Mourning*. Champaign, IL: Research Press.

Rando, T. (2013) On achieving clarity regarding complicated grief: Lessons from clinical practice. In M. Stroebe, H. Schut & J. van den Bout (eds.), *Complicated Grief: Scientific Foundations for Health Care Professionals*. London: Routledge.

Robertson, J. & Bowlby, J. (1952) Responses of young children to separation from their mothers. *Courier of the International Children's Centre*, Paris, *II*, 131–140.

Rodning, C., Beckwith, L. & Howard, J. (1991) Quality of attachment and home environments in children pre-natally exposed to PCP and cocaine. *Development and Psychopathology, 3*, 351–366.

Ronen, R., Packman, W., Field, N.P. et al. (2009) The relationship between grief adjustment and continuing bonds for parents who have lost a child. *Omega, 60*(1), 1–31.

Rose, S. (2000) Escaping evolutionary psychology. In H. Rose & S. Rose (eds.), *Alas, Poor Darwin: Arguments Against Evolutionary Psychology*. London: Jonathan Cape.

Rosenblatt, P.C. (1975) Uses of ethnography in understanding grief and mourning. In B. Schoenberg et al. (eds.), *Bereavement: Its Psychosocial Aspects*. New York: Columbia University Press.

Rosenblatt, P.C. (1983) *Bitter, Bitter Tears: Nineteenth Century Diarists and Twentieth Century Grief Theories*. Minneapolis: University of Minnesota Press.

Rosenblatt, P.C. (1993) Grief: The social context of private feelings. In M.S. Stroebe, W. Stroebe & R.O. Hansson (eds.), *Handbook of Bereavement: Theory, Research and Intervention*. New York: Cambridge University Press.

Rosenblatt, P.C. (2001) A social constructionist perspective on cultural differences in grief, In M.S. Stroebe, R.O. Hansson, W. Stroebe & H. Schut (eds.) *Handbook of Bereavement Research: Consequences, Coping and Care*. Washington, DC: American Psychological Association.

Rosenblatt, P.C. (2008a) Grief across cultures: A review and research agenda. In M. Stroebe, R.O. Hansson, W. Stroebe & H. Schut (eds.), *Handbook of Bereavement Research and Practice: Advances in Theory and Intervention.* Washington, DC: American Psychological Association.

Rosenblatt, P. C. (2008b) Recovery following bereavement: Metaphor, phenomenology, and culture. *Death Studies, 32*, 6–16.

Rosenblatt, P. C. (2013a) The concept of complicated grief: Lessons from other cultures. In M. Stroebe, H. Schut & J. van den Bout (eds.), *Complicated Grief: Scientific Foundations for Health Care Professionals.* London: Routledge.

Rosenblatt, P. C. (2013b) Culture and socialisation in death, grief, and mourning. In D. K. Meagher & D. E. Balk (eds.), *Handbook of Thanatology: The Essential Body of Knowledge for the Study of Death, Dying, and Bereavement* (2nd edition). New York: Routledge.

Rosenblatt, P. C. & Elde, C. (1990) Shared reminiscence about a deceased parent: Implication for grief education and grief counselling. *Family Relations, 39*, 206–210.

Rosenblatt, P. C., Walsh, R. P. & Jackson, D. A. (1976) *Grief and Mourning in Cross-Cultural Perspective.* New Haven, CT: Human Relations Area Files Press.

Rowe, D. (2007) *My Dearest Enemy, My Dangerous Friend: Making and Breaking Sibling Bonds.* Hove: Routledge.

Rubin, S. (1981) A two-track model of bereavement: Theory and application in research. *American Journal of Orthopsychiatry, 51*, 101–109.

Rubin, S. (1999) The two-track model of bereavement: Overview, retrospect and prospect. *Death Studies, 23*, 681–714.

Rubin, S., Malkinson, R. & Witztum, A. E. (2011) The two-track model of bereavement: The double helix of research and clinical practice. In R. A. Neimeyer, D. L. Harris, H. R. Winokuer & G. F. Thornton (eds.), *Grief and Bereavement in Contemporary Society: Bridging Research and Practice.* New York: Routledge.

Rubin, S., Malkinson, R. & Witztum, A. E. (2012) *Working with the Bereaved: Multiple Lenses on Loss and Mourning.* New York: Routledge.

Rutter, M. (1981) *Maternal Deprivation Reassessed* (2nd edition). Harmondsworth: Penguin.

Rutter, M., Kreppner, J. & Sonuga-Barke, E. (2009) Emmanuel Miller Lecture: Attachment insecurity, disinhibited attachment, and attachment disorders: Where do research findings leave the concepts? *Journal of Child Psychology & Psychiatry, 50*(5), 529–543.

Sanders, C. M. (1980–1981) Comparison of younger and older spouses in bereavement outcome. *Omega: Journal of Death & Dying, 10*, 303–322.

Sandler, I. N., Wolchik, S. A., Ayers, T. S. et al. (2008) Linking theory and intervention to promote resilience in parentally bereaved children. In M. S. Stroebe, R. O. Hansson, H. Schut & W. Stroebe (eds.), *Handbook of Bereavement Research and Practice: Advances in Theory and Intervention.* Washington, DC: American Psychological Association.

Sands (2012) *Preventing Babies' Deaths: What Needs to Be Done.* London: Sands.

Sands, D. C. (2008) A study of suicide grief: Meaning making and the griever's relational world. (Doctoral thesis, University of Technology, Sydney). Retrieved from http://handle.net/2100/777

Sands, D. C. (2009) A tripartite model of suicide grief: Meaning-making and the relationship with the deceased. *Grief Matters: The Australian Journal of Grief & Bereavement, 12*, 10–17.

Sands, D. C., Jordan, J. R. & Neimeyer, R. A. (2010) The meanings of suicide: A narrative approach to healing. In J. R. Jordan & J. L. McIntosh (eds.) *Grief After Suicide: Understanding the Consequences and Caring for the Survivors.* New York: Routledge.

Scannell-Desch, E. (2003) Women's adjustment to widowhood: Theory, research, and interventions. *Journal of Psychosocial Nursing & Mental Health Services, 41*, 28–36.

Schaffer, H. R. (2004) *Introducing Child Psychology*. Oxford: Blackwell Publishing.

Scheper-Hughes, N. (1992) *Death Without Weeping: The Violence of Everyday Life in Brazil*. Berkeley: University of California Press.

Schiffman, D. D. (2004) Coping with sudden infant death: An integrated approach to understanding family grief and recovery. Unpublished doctoral thesis, Alliant International University.

Schott, J., Henley, A. & Kohner, N. (2007) *Pregnancy Loss and the Death of a Baby: Guidelines for Health Professionals*. London: SANDS.

Schulz, R., Boerner, K. & Hebert, R. S. (2008) Caregiving and bereavement. In M. S. Stroebe, R. O. Hansson, H. Schut & W. Stroebe (eds.), *Handbook of Bereavement Research and Practice: Advances in Theory and Intervention*. Washington, DC: American Psychological Association.

Schut, H.A.W., Stroebe, M. S. & van den Bout, J. (1997) Intervention for the bereaved: Gender differences in the efficacy of two counselling programmes. *British Journal of Clinical Psychology, 36*, 63–72.

Schwartz-Borden, G. (1992) Metaphor: Visual aid in grief work. *Omega: Journal of Death & Dying, 25*(3), 239–248.

Seligman, M.E.P. (2011) *Flourish*. New York: Free Press.

Shanfield, S. B., Swain, B. J. & Benjamin, G.A.H. (1985) Parents' responses to the death of adult children from accidents and cancer: a comparison. *Omega, 17*(4), 289–298.

Shapiro, E. R. (1996) Family bereavement and cultural diversity: A social developmental perspective. *Family Process, 35*, 313–332.

Shapiro, E. R. (2013) Culture and socialization in assessment and intervention. In D. K. Meagher & D.E. Balk (eds.) *Handbook of Thanatology* (2nd edition). New York: Routledge.

Sharkin, B. S. & Knox, D. (2003) Pet loss: Implications for the psychologist. *Professional Psychology: Research and Practice, 34*, 414–421.

Shaver, P. R., Collins, N. & Clark, C. L. (1996) Attachment styles and internal working models of self and relationship patterns. In G.J.O. Fletcher & J. Fitness (eds.), *Knowledge Structures in Close Relationships: A Social Psychological Approach*. Mahwah, NJ: Lawrence Erlbaum Associates.

Shaver, P. R. & Fraley, C. (2008) Attachment, loss, and grief: Bowlby's views and current controversies. In J. Cassidy & P. R. Shaver (eds.), *Handbook of Attachment* (2nd edition). New York: Guildford Press.

Shaver, P. R. & Tancredy, C. M. (2001) Emotion, attachment, and bereavement: A conceptual commentary. In M. S. Stroebe, W. Stroebe, R. O. Hansson & H. Schut (eds.), *Handbook of Bereavement Research: Consequences, Coping, and Care*. Washington, DC: American Psychological Association.

Shear, M. K., Simon, N., Wall, M. et al. (2011) Complicated grief and related bereavement-issues for DSM-5. *Depression and Anxiety, 28*, 103–117.

Sherr, L. (1989) Death of a baby. In L. Sherr (ed.), *Death, Dying, and Bereavement*. Oxford: Blackwell Publishing.

Shih, M. (2004) Positive stigma: Examining resilience and empowerment in overcoming stigma. *Annals of the American Academy of Political and Social Science, 591*, 175–185.

Shuchter, S. R. & Zisook, S. (1993) The course of normal grief. In M. S. Stroebe, W. Stroebe & R. O. Hansson (eds.), *Handbook of Bereavement: Theory, Research and Intervention*. New York: Cambridge University Press.

Simpson, J. A. & Rholes, W. S. (1994) Stress and secure base relationships in adulthood. In K. Bartholomew & D. Perlman (eds.), *Advances in Personal Relationships, Volume 5: Attachment Processes in Adulthood*. London: Jessica Kingsley Publishers.

Simpson, J. A., Rholes, W. S. & Nelligan, J. S. (1992) Support-seeking and support-giving within couples in an anxiety-provoking situation: The integration of three behavioural systems. In R. J. Sternberg & M. Barnes (eds.), *The Psychology of Love*. New Haven, CT: Yale University Press.

Smith, K.R. (1990) *Risk of mortality following widowhood: Sex differences between sudden and expected bereavement*. Paper presented at 1990 annual meeting of the Society for Epidemiological Research, Birmingham, AL.

Smith, C., Tomassini, C., Smallwood, S. & Hawkins, M. (2005) The changing age structure of the UK population. In R. Chappell (ed.), *Focus on People and Migration*. London: UK National Statistics.

Smith, S.H. (2005) Anticipatory grief and psychological adjustment to grieving in middle-aged children. *American Journal of Hospice & Palliative Medicine, 22*, 283–286.

Solomon, S., Greenberg, J. & Pyszczynski, T. (2004) The cultural animal: Twenty years of terror management theory and research, In J. Greenberg, S. L. Koole & T. Pyszczynski (eds.), *Handbook of Experimental Existential Psychology*. New York: The Guilford Press.

Spangler, G. & Grossman, K. E. (1993) Biobehavioural organisation in securely and insecurely attached infants. *Child Development, 64*, 1439–1450.

Sroufe, L. A. & Waters, E. (1977) Attachment as an organisational construct. *Child Development, 48*, 1184–1199.

Steele, H., Steele, M. & Fonagy, P. (1995) Associations among attachment classifications of mothers, fathers, and their infants. *Child Development, 57*, 555–571.

Steele, H., Steele, M. & Fonagy, P. (1996) Associations among attachment classifications of mothers, fathers, and their infants. *Child Development, 67*, 541–555.

Stricherz, M. & Cunnington, L. (1981–1982) Death concerns of students, employed persons, and retired persons. *Omega: Journal of Death and Dying, 12*, 373–380.

Stroebe, M. (1992) Coping with bereavement: A review of the grief work hypothesis. *Omega, 26*, 19–42.

Stroebe, M. (1998) New directions in bereavement research: Exploration of gender differences. *Palliative Medicine, 12*, 5-12.

Stroebe, M., Boelen, P., van den Bout, M. et al. (2007) Ruminative coping as avoidance: A reinterpretation of its function in adjustment to bereavement. *European Archives of Psychiatry & Clinical Neuroscience, 257*, 462–472.

Stroebe, M., Folkman, S., Hansson, R. O. & Schut, H. (2006) The prediction of bereavement outcome. *Social Science & Medicine, 63*, 2440–2451.

Stroebe, M., Gergen, M. M., Gergen, K. J. & Stroebe, W. (1992) Broken hearts or broken bonds: Love and death in historical perspective. *American Psychologist, 47*(10), 1205–1212.

Stroebe, M. S., Hansson, R. O., Schut, H. & Stroebe, W. (2008) Bereavement research: Contemporary perspectives. In M. S. Stroebe, R. O. Hansson, H. Schut & W. Stroebe (eds.), *Handbook of Bereavement Research and Practice: Advances in Theory and Intervention*. Washington, DC: American Psychological Association.

Stroebe, M. & Schut, H. (1998) Culture and grief. *Bereavement Care, 17*, 7–10.

Stroebe, M. & Schut, H. (1999) The Dual Process Model of coping with bereavement: Rationale and description. *Death Studies, 23*, 197–224.

Stroebe, M. & Schut. H. (2001) Meaning making in the Dual Process Model. In R. Neimeyer (ed.) *Meaning reconstruction and the experience of loss.* Washington, DC: American Psychololgical Association.

Stroebe, M. and Schut, H. (2005) To continue or relinquish bonds: A review of consequences for the bereaved. *Death Studies, 29,* 477-494.

Stroebe, M. & Schut, H. (2008) The Dual Process Model of coping with bereavement: Overview and update. *Grief Matters: The Australian Journal of Grief and Bereavement, 11,* 1–4.

Stroebe, M. & Schut, H. (2010) The Dual Process Model of coping with bereavement: Rationale and description. *Omega, 61*(4), 273–289.

Stroebe, M., Schut, H. & Van den Bout, J. (2013) (eds.) *Complicated Grief: Scientific Foundations for Health Care Professionals.* London: Routledge.

Stroebe, M., Schut, H. & van den Bout, J. (2013) Introduction. In M. Stroebe, H. Schut & J. van den Bout (eds.), *Complicated Grief: Scientific Foundations for Health Care Professionals.* London: Routledge.

Stroebe, M. & Stroebe, W. (1987) *Bereavement and Health: The Psychological and Physical Consequences of Partner Loss.* Cambridge: Cambridge University Press.

Stroebe, M., Stroebe, W. & Hansson, R. O. (1993) (eds.) *Handbook of Bereavement: Theory, Research and Intervention.* New York: Cambridge University Press.

Stroebe, W., Schut, H. & Stroebe, M. (2005) Grief work, disclosure and counselling: Do they help the bereaved? *Clinical Psychology Review, 25,* 395–414.

Stroebe, M., Stroebe, W. & Schut, H. (2001) Gender differences in adjustment to bereavement: An empirical and theoretical review. *Review of General Psychology, 5,* 62–83.

Stroebe, M., van Vliet, T., Hewstone, M. & Willis, H. (2002) Homesickness among students of two cultures: Antecedents and consequences. *British Journal of Psychology, 93,* 147–168.

Swami, V., Stanistreet, D. & Payne, S. (2008) Masculinities and suicide. *Psychologist, 21*(4), 308–311.

Tafoya, N. & Del Vecchio, A. (2005) Back to the future: An examination of the Native American holocaust experience. In M. McGoldrick, J. Giordano & N. Garcia-Preto (eds.), *Ethnicity and Family Therapy* (3rd edition). New York: Guilford.

Taku, K., Cann, A., Calhoun, L. G. & Tedeschi, R. G. (2008) The factor structure of the posttraumatic growth inventory: A comparison of the five models using confirmatory factor analysis. *Journal of Traumatic Stress, 21,* 158–164.

Tedeschi, R. G. & Calhoun, L. G. (1995) *Trauma and Transformation: Growing in the Aftermath of Suffering.* Thousand Oaks, CA: Sage.

Tedeschi, R. G. & Calhoun, L. G. (1996) The posttraumatic growth inventory: Measuring the positive legacy of trauma. *Journal of Traumatic Stress, 9,* 455–471.

Tedeschi, R. G. & Calhoun, L. G. (2006) Time of change? The spiritual challenges of bereavement and loss. *Omega: Journal of Death & Dying, 53,* 105–116.

Tedeschi, R. G. & Calhoun, L. G. (2012) Pathways to personal transformation: Theoretical and empirical developments. In P. T. Wong (ed.), *The Human Quest for Meaning: Theories, Research, and Applications.* New York: Routledge.

Templer, D. I. & Ruff, C. F. (1971) Death anxiety scale means, standard deviations, and embeddings. *Psychological Reports, 29,* 173–174.

Teno, J. M., Clarridge, B. R., Casey, V. et al. (2004) Family perspectives on end-of-life care at the last place of care. *Journal of the American Medical Association, 291,* 88–93.

Thorson, J. A. & Powell, F. C. (1994) A revised death anxiety scale. In R. A. Neimeyer (ed.), *Death Anxiety Handbook*. Washington, DC: Taylor & Francis.

Toray, T. (2004) The human-animal bond and loss: Providing support for grieving clients. *Journal of Mental Health Counselling, 26*, 244–259.

Torrie, M. (1970) *Begin Again: A Book for Women Alone*. London: Dent.

Traylor, E. S., Hayslip, B., Kaminski, P. L. & York, C. (2003) Relationship between grief and family system characteristics: A cross lagged longitudinal analysis. *Death Studies, 27*, 575–601.

Triandis, H. (1995) *Individualism and Collectivism*. Boulder, CO: Westview.

Umberson, D., Wortman, C. B. & Kessler, R. C. (1992) Widowhood and depression: Explaining long-term gender differences in vulnerability. *Journal of Health & Social Behaviour, 33*, 10–24.

Umphrey, L. R. & Cacciatore, J. (2014) Love and death: Relational metaphors following the death of a child. *Journal of Relationships Research, 5*, e4, 1–8.

Utz, R. L. (2006) Economic and practical adjustments to late life spousal loss. In D. Carr, R. M. Nesse & C. B. Wortman (eds.), *Spousal Bereavement in Late Life*. New York: Springer Publishing.

Valentine, C. (2006) Academic constructions of bereavement. *Mortality, 11*, 57-78.

Valsiner, J. (2102) *Handbook of Cultural Psychology*. New York: University of Oxford Press.

van Doorn, C., Kasl, S. V., Beery, L. C. et al. (1998) The influence of marital quality and attachment styles on traumatic grief and depressive symptoms. *Journal of Nervous & Mental Disease, 186*, 566–573.

Van Ijzendoorn, M. H. & Bakjermans-Kranenburg, M. J. (1996) Attachment representations in mothers, fathers, adolescents and clinical groups: A meta-analytic search for normative data. *Journal of Consulting & Clinical Psychology, 64*, 8–21.

Van Ijzendoorn, M. H. & Schuengel, C. (1999) The development of attachment relationships: Infancy and beyond. In D. Messer & S. Millar (eds.), *Exploring Developmental Psychology: From Infancy to Adolescence*. London: Arnold.

Van Ijzendoorn, M. H. & De Wolff, M. S. (1997) In search of the absent father: Meta analyses of infant-father attachment: A rejoinder to our discussants. *Child Development, 68*, 604–609.

Vaughn, B. E., Gove, F. L. & Egeland, B. R. (1980) The relationship between out-of-home care and the quality of infant-mother attachment in an economically disadvantaged population. *Child Development, 51*, 1203–1214.

Vess, J. S., Moreland, J. R. & Schwebel, A. I. (1985) A follow-up study of role functioning and the psychological environment of families of cancer patients. *Journal of Psychosocial Oncology, 3*(2), 1–14.

Wakefield, J. C. (2013) Is complicated/prolonged grief a disorder? Why the proposal to add a category of complicated grief disorder to the DSM-5 is conceptually and empirically unsound. In M. Stroebe, H. Schut & J. van den Bout (eds.), *Complicated Grief: Scientific Foundations for Health Care Professionals*. London: Routledge.

Walsh, F. & McGoldrick, M. (2004) *Living Beyond Loss: Death in the Family* (2nd edition). New York: W.W. Norton & Co.

Walter, T. (1993) Modern death: Taboo or not taboo? In D. Dickenson & M. Johnson (eds.), *Death, Dying & Bereavement*. London: Sage Publications and the Open University. (Abridged from *Sociology, 25*(2), 293–310.)

Walter, T. (1994) *The Revival of Death*. London: Routledge.

Walter, T. (1997) Letting go and keeping hold: A reply to Stroebe. *Mortality, 2*, 263–266.

Walter, T. (1999) *On bereavement: The culture of grief.* Buckingham: Open University Press.

Waskowic, T.D. & Chartier, B.M. (2003) Attachment and the experience of grief following the loss of a spouse. *Omega, 47,* 77–91.

Waters, E. (1978) The reliability and stability of individual differences in infant-mother attachments. *Child Development, 49,* 483–494.

Wayment, H.A. & Vierthaler, J. (2002) Attachment style and bereavement reactions. *Journal of Loss & Trauma, 7,* 129–149.

Weinberg, N. (1994) Self-blame, other blame, and the desire for revenge: Factors in recovery from bereavement. *Death Studies, 18*(6), 583–593.

Westendorp, R.G.J. & Kirkwood, T.B.L. (2007) The biology of ageing. In J. Bond, S. Peace, E. Dittman-Kohli & G. Westerhof (eds.), *Ageing in Society* (3rd edition). London: Sage Publications.

Westly, E. (2012) Different shades of blue. *Scientific American Mind, 21*(2), 34–41

Widgery, D. (1993) Not going gently. In D. Dickenson & M. Johnson (eds.), *Death, Dying & Bereavement.* London: Sage Publications and the Open University. (Abridged extract from *Some Lives!* (1991) London: Sinclair-Stevenson.)

Wierzbicka, A. (2003) Emotion and culture: Arguing with Martha Nussbaum. *Ethos, 31,* 577–600.

Wijngaards, U., Stroebe, M.S., Stroebe, W. et al. (2008) Parents grieving the loss of their child: Interdependence in coping. *British Journal of Clinical Psychology, 47,* 31–42.

Wikan, U. (1988) Bereavement and loss in two Muslim communities: Egypt and Bali compared. *Social Science & Medicine, 27,* 451–460.

Wikan, U. (1990) *Managing Turbulent Hearts: A Balinese Formula for Living.* Chicago, IL: University of Chicago Press.

Wilcox, S., Evenson, K.R., Aragaki, A. et al. (2003) The effects of widowhood on physical and mental health, health behaviours, and health outcomes: The women's health initiative. *Health Psychology, 22,* 513–522.

Williams, K. & Umberson, D. (2004) Marital status, marital transitions, and health: A gendered life course perspective. *Journal of Health & Social Behaviour, 45,* 81–98.

Wilson, G. (1939) Nyakyusa conventions of burial. *Bantu Studies, 13,* 1–31.

Wilson, M. (1957) *Rituals of Kinshio Among the Nyakyusa.* London: Oxford University Press.

World Health Organisation (2011) *Suicide Rates per 100,000 by Country, Year and Sex.* Geneva: WHO.

Worden, J.W. (1982) *Grief Counselling and Grief Therapy: A Handbook for the Mental Health Practitioner.* New York: Springer.

Worden, J.W. (1983) *Grief Counselling and Grief Therapy.* London: Tavistock Publications.

Worden, J.W. (1991) *Grief Counselling and Grief Therapy: A Handbook for the Mental Health Practitioner* (2nd edition). New York: Springer.

Worden, J.W. (2002) *Grief Counselling and Grief Therapy: A Handbook for the Mental Health Practitioner* (3rd edition). New York: Springer.

Worden, J.W. (2009) *Grief Counselling and Grief Therapy: A Handbook for the Mental Health Practitioner* (4th edition). New York: Springer.

Wortman, C.B. & Boerner, K. (2011) Beyond the myths of coping with loss: Prevailing assumptions versus scientific evidence. In H.S. Friedman (ed.), *Oxford Handbook of Health Psychology.* New York: Oxford University Press.

Wortman, C.B. & Silver, R.C. (1987) Coping with irrevocable loss. In G.R. Vanden Bos & B.K. Bryant (eds.) *Cataclysms, Crises, and Catastrophes: Psychology in Action*. Washington, DC: American Psychological Association.

Wortman, C.B. & Silver, R.C. (1989) The myths of coping with loss. *Journal of Consulting & Clinical Psychology, 57*, 349–357.

Wortman, C.B. & Silver, R.C. (1992) Reconsidering assumptions about coping with loss: An overview of current research. In L. Montada, S-H. Filipp, &. M.J. Lerner (eds.) *Life Crises and experiences of loss in adulthood*. Hillsdale, NJ: Erlbaum.

Wray, T.J. (2003) *Surviving the Death of a Sibling: Living Through Grief When an Adult Brother or Sister Dies*. New York: Three Rivers Press.

Yalom, I.D. (1980) *Existential Psychotherapy*. New York: Basic Books.

Yamamoto, T., Okonogi, K., Iwasaki, T. & Yoshimura, S. (1969) Mourning in Japan. *American Journal of Psychiatry, 125*, 1661–1673.

Yo, S.M.Y., Chan, I.S.F., Ma, E.P.W. & Field, N.P. (2013) Continuing Bonds, Attachment Style, and Adjustment in the Conjugal Bereavement among Hong Kong Chinese. *Death Studies, 37*, 248-268.

Zampitella, C. (2006) Using nature-based rituals as an intervention for adult sibling survivors. *Forum, 32*(1), 9–15.

Zech, E. & Arnold, C. (2011) Attachment and coping with bereavement: Implications for therapeutic interventions with the insecurely attached. In R.A. Neimeyer, D.L. Harris, H.R. Winokuer & G.F. Thornton (eds.), *Grief and Bereavement in Contemporary Society: Bridging Research and Practice*. New York: Routledge.

Zeifman, D. & Hazan, C. (2000) A process model of adult attachment formation. In W. Ickes & S. Duck (eds.), *The Social Psychology of Personal Relationships*. Chichester: John Wiley & Sons.

Zisook, S., Schuchter, S.R., Sledge, P.A., Paulus, M. & Judd, L.L. (1994) The spectrum of depressive phenomena after spousal bereavement. *Journal of Clinical Psychiatry, 55*(4) (Suppl.), 29–36.

Index